LIM KIM SAN

LIM KIM SAN

A BUILDER OF SINGAPORE

Asad-ul Iqbal Latif

ISEAS

INSTITUTE OF SOUTHEAST ASIAN STUDIES

Singapore

First published in Singapore in 2009 by ISEAS Publishing
Institute of Southeast Asian Studies
30 Heng Mui Keng Terrace
Pasir Panjang
Singapore 119614

E-mail: publish@iseas.edu.sg
Website: <http://bookshop.iseas.edu.sg>

*The responsibility for facts and opinions in this publication rests exclusively with the
author and his interpretations do not necessarily reflect the views or the policy of the
publisher or its supporters.*

All net proceeds from the sale of this book will go to the YMCA-Lim Kim San
Volunteers Programme as the YMCA was one of Mr Lim's favourite causes.

ISEAS Library Cataloguing-in-Publication Data

Latif, Asad-ul Iqbal.
　　Lim Kim San : a builder of Singapore.
　　1. Lim, Kim San, 1916–2006.
　　2. Cabinet officers—Singapore—Biography.
　　3. Singapore—Politics and government—1963–1965.
　　4. Singapore—Politics and government—1965–1990.
　　DS610.63 L73L35　　　　　　　　　2009

ISBN 978-981-230-927-3 (soft cover)
ISBN 978-981-230-928-0 (hard cover)
ISBN 978-981-230-929-7 (PDF)

Cover Photo: Singapore Ministry of Culture, obtained from the Lim Family.
Typeset by Superskill Graphics Pte Ltd
Printed in Singapore by Utopia Press Pte Ltd

Contents

Foreword

Lim Kim San was a man of great determination. He lived a full life and also made great contributions to Singapore. Singaporeans now own their HDB homes. They owe this to him for setting a system that made this result possible.

Of all my old guard colleagues, he was the most active after he retired as minister in 1980. He became Senior Adviser to Singapore Press Holdings where he helped until illness overcame him in the last nine months of his life just before his death at the age of nearly ninety.

He suffered during the Japanese Occupation. The dreaded Kempeitai (Japanese Military Police) tortured him, accusing him of being pro-communist and pro-British. He was flogged, beaten, kicked and physically abused. He was confined in a filthy over-crowded room of thirty persons, sitting on his haunches all day and slept on a hard surface without a blanket at night which caused aches and pains. Released after a week, he was re-arrested a second time. Again more blows, kicks and lashes. In the cell with thirty other persons, there was only one squatting toilet, the water from which was used for defecating, washing and drinking.

In 1959 when I first assumed office, I made him a member of the Public Service Commission and later Deputy Chairman. In 1960, I made him Chairman of the HDB (Housing and Development Board).

The HDB was under the Minister for National Development, one Ong Eng Guan who was wildly popular for his theatrical populist gestures, posturing as an anti-colonialist by sacking and humiliating expatriates in his Ministry. To show the other expatriates still in our service that we wanted them to stay, that they were not at the mercy of the capricious Ministers, I had the expatriate Permanent Secretary, one Val Meadows, transferred to my office as the Permanent Secretary, Special Duties.

As Minister for National Development, Ong Eng Guan told Lim Kim San to hire workers direct and not use contractors in building the flats. Kim San sought me out to ask whether I wanted him to build flats or to become a labour contractor. I overruled his Minister and told Kim San to do things the way he knew best. With his keen business sense, he built the homes we needed speedily and economically with the labour skills and technology of that era.

He built two blocks of flats comprising 324 units along Cantonment Road in my Tanjong Pagar constituency. At the election time in September 1963, it was half completed. Huge crowds of leftist students from the Chinese middle schools and Nanyang University worked the ground, visiting nearly every household in Tanjong Pagar. They wanted to unseat me. These two uncompleted blocks of flats reminded the people that I could complete the building of the few hundred homes, not these leftists. I was re-elected.

I persuaded Kim San to stand for elections in September 1963. I needed men of integrity, courage and ability, who could get things done. He fought in Cairnhill and won. I made him Minister for National Development.

He had told me he could not make speeches, and that he was unsuited for politics. I replied that if he spoke his mind and did not worry whether his speeches had oratorical flourish, he would carry the people with him. He spoke with sincerity and people could sense it. He also carried out what he promised. He won their confidence.

He has an intuitive sense to feel people's characters, motivation and capabilities. Once he described to me how, after he shook hands with a thug, a Chinese Singaporean who had become an important good friend of Tengku Abdul Rahman, the Prime Minister of Malaysia, he felt repulsed and wanted to wash his hands. He was dead right about that evil man. I had him join me to interview candidates for jobs for high office and even candidates for elections and MPs, to help select the right candidates.

After he retired in September 1988, he became Chairman of Singapore Press Holdings (SPH). He trimmed costs, and cut waste in staff and materials and increased profits in SPH. Convinced that advertising would increasingly come from the electronic media, he took SPH into the digital fields and made SPH one of the most profitable newspaper groups.

Ever the shrewd businessman, he arranged an SPH dinner on 16 September 1998 on my seventy-fifth birthday to launch the first volume of my memoirs that he had urged me to write for SPH/ Times.

He remained active until the last few months before he died just before reaching ninety. Whenever I needed someone with integrity and judgement to carry out a mission, I called upon Kim San. He became Chairman of the Council of Presidential Advisers and a Chancellor of Singapore Management University.

He enjoyed life. He was a gourmet. He dressed smartly and with good taste.

He refused to allow physical infirmities to disable him. He had had several operations for his neck and spine over the last forty years of his life. A surgeon fused his neck vertebra but with no great improvement. Then an excruciating back pain led to another operation. Again, the operation was not fully successful. He forced himself to walk daily despite the pain. Finally, he got his muscles to loosen up and the pain bearable for him to golf again. He made his life worth living by his indomitable spirit. He was a valued colleague and a great friend.

Lee Kuan Yew
Minister Mentor of Singapore
April 2009

Acknowledgements

I wish to thank Ambassador K. Kesavapany, Director of the Institute of Southeast Asian Studies, for trusting me with this work. Mr Lim Kim San's family, particularly Mr Lim Kiat Seng, was a wonderful source of help, not least in helping me select the photographs that appear in this book. I am also grateful to Ms Mylene Ng, Personal Assistant to Mr Lim at Singapore Press Holdings, for her help during the initial stages of writing it. I thank Mrs Gretchen Liu for her help in identifying people in the photographs. This book would not have been possible without the excellent Oral History Interview conducted by Mrs Lily Tan of the National Archives. Ms Fatanah Sarmani, production editor in the Publications Unit of ISEAS, was a source of unfailing support.

The YMCA-Lim Kim San Volunteers Programme

The YMCA of Singapore is a community organization, based on Christian values and affiliated worldwide, that engages a critical mass of volunteers to serve others regardless of race, language or religion.

The late Mr Lim Kim San was an Honorary Life Member and an active supporter of the YMCA.

To honour this distinguished son of Singapore, recognize his life in the service of others, and to hold him out as an inspirational challenge to our volunteers, the YMCA Volunteers Service Programme has been named after him.

The Programme aims to:

a) Promote volunteerism amongst Singaporeans, in particular in YMCA local community and international service programmes,

b) Attract and retain volunteers to undertake sustained service in specific service programmes, as well as recognise their service,

c) Enhance the capability of volunteers to better serve and understand the beneficiaries under their care,

d) Identify and develop leaders amongst our volunteers, and

e) Encourage and facilitate corporate volunteerism.

Family Tree

LIM KIM SAN
30 November 1916 – 20 July 2006

Parents: Lim Choon Huat and Wee Geok Khuan

Siblings: Lim Yan Siew, Lim Yan Lian, Lim Cheng Siong, Lim Yan Swee, and Lim Yan Leng.

Wife: Pang Gek Kim

Children: Lim Eng Tin (m. Lee Weng Yan), Lim Eng Hong (m. Ee Kean Leong), Lim Kiat Seng (m. Pauline Lim Mee Goh), Lim Siu Tin (m. Jimmy Beng Kian Siew), Lim Kiat Beng (m. Linda Lee), and Lim Siu Horng (m. Tay Puan Siong).

Grandchildren: Lee Yu Chuan (m. Amy Ng Ka Yin), Lee Yu Ching (m. Wee Seng Hong), Ee Kuo-Ren (m. Natalie Ho Chin Yee), Ee Yuen-Ling, Lim Ee Ming, Beng Teck Liang (m. Connie Yang), Beng Li-Siier (m. Shashi Kumar), Beng Li-Hsien, Jonathan Lim (m. Cony Ee), Anthony Ee-Li Lim (m. Jean Chang), and Adrian Tay (m. Leslie Tay).

Great-Grandchildren: Samuel Wee Rui Chang, Matthew Wee Rui Jie, Bradley Beng, Brandon Beng, Annalisa Wei-Ling Lim, Isabella Hui-Ling Lim, Alexander Jie-Hao Lim, and Joshua Zu-Hui Lim.

1

The Man with the Blanket

Soon after being appointed Chairman of Singapore's Housing and Development Board (HDB) in 1960, Lim Kim San went around the slum area in Chinatown. He came across a labourer in a bunk who had a blanket pulled right up to his neck. Lim asked the man whether he was sick. The labourer replied: "No. I've got no pants on." Lim asked him why. He replied: "My other brother has just taken my pants out. I'm wearing briefs." Lim's thoughts on the man's reply: "No, I don't think he was in briefs. There was no such thing as briefs at that time. You see how poor they were! They had to share [clothes]."[1] The dead were not exempt from sharing, either. "In those days, there were shops which pulled clothing and shoes off the dead to sell them. 'My God,' I thought to myself, 'I really must help these people.' "[2]

It was a moment of transformation for Lim, then in his forties. Scion of a well-to-do business family, a product of the prestigious Anglo Chinese School and the elite Raffles College, he was a talented and successful businessman. The gourmet and racecourse enthusiast had access to what the good life could offer in Singapore. He had often driven past Upper Nanking Street, but had never been inside the shophouses where Singapore's poor huddled — lured from China and elsewhere, ironically by the island's prosperity.

Prosperity during colonial times had been a mixed blessing. Singapore had prospered since Stamford Raffles had established an entrepôt on the island in 1819 to service the East India Company's China trade. As East-West trade grew during the nineteenth century, the British colony became the clearing-house for the region's produce and the distribution centre for the European goods traded in return. Indeed, the city became the trading, banking and insurance headquarters for the whole of Southeast Asia. However, the population grew as well. From a mere 52,900 in 1850, it rose to 229,900 by 1901, shot up to 940,700 by 1947, and almost doubled in the following decade. People crowded into the shop houses at the centre of the city area.

> Originally built to accommodate a shop on the ground floor and house the people who worked there, these buildings themselves began to grow. Extra stories were tacked on, bringing them usually up to four, and extensions were added at the back. As more and more immigrants came, first the houses and then individual rooms were divided and subdivided into a dark warren of tiny cubicles — airless holes with room in them for little more than a bed. Thus buildings originally designed for one family were made to house 10 families or more, without privacy or sunlight, with a single tap, a single latrine, a single cooking space. For lack of any other place the street became dining room, meeting place and children's playground.[3]

Yet the population continued to expand, driving some families from the city and forcing them to build shelters illegally wherever they could. Up came squatter settlements that "developed in a girdle of squalor and misery around the central city".[4] Unemployment, crime, gangsterism, extortion and prostitution flourished, and racial tensions simmered, in the vast underbelly of the city even as the island, and its ablest inhabitants, prospered in the seas of global commerce.

The gulf between the two kinds of life in Singapore hurt Lim, although he lived in a far better part of the city. Under his leadership, as many housing units were built during the three years from 1960 as had been built during the preceding three decades. He would go on to become a minister holding crucial portfolios such as National

Development, Education, Finance, and Interior and Defence. He would chair the Council of Presidential Advisers. He would come to play a gatekeeper's role in the screening process through which Singapore's ruling People's Action Party (PAP) put prospective members of parliament and ministers. He would helm the Economic Development Board, critical to Singapore's success; chair the Port of Singapore Authority, also crucial to a port-city; would serve in the Monetary Authority of Singapore and the Public Utilities Board; and he would head the profitable Singapore Press Holdings. While these contributions were substantial, it is as "Mr HDB" — the architect of Singapore's early, ambitious and phenomenally successful public housing programme — that he is best remembered.

Lim Kim San died on 20 July 2006.

The following chapters will trace "Mr HDB's" development from being a successful businessman keen on building a fortune for himself, to being a successful nation-builder literally. But first, it is necessary to sketch the context in which that transformation occurred. A process that began with self-government for Singapore and the PAP's rise to power in 1959, and continued through Singapore's difficult years in Malaysia from 1963 to 1965, culminated when the island was ejected from its geographical hinterland and set about becoming a global city.

A PLAN FOR SINGAPORE

Raffles had a vision of Singapore becoming "the emporium of the East, on the route between India and China" "on the basis of free competition". Given its origins, the independent city-state did not mind importing capital, managers, engineers and others. It did not share the fears of many newly-independent countries, which regarded multinational corporations (MNCs) as exploiters of cheap Third World labour and raw materials that would "suck a country dry". Singapore had no raw materials for anyone to exploit, and nobody else "wanted to exploit the labour". So it welcomed MNCs that, instead of exploiting Singapore, taught its people to do jobs that they otherwise would not have learned to do.[5] By tuning into the global economy, Singapore was able to overcome its drawbacks, such as the fact that it had little by way of natural resources except for its harbour. What the country brought to the table were values such as hard work, discipline, thrift, ruggedness and openness to change.

The test came soon after independence. When the British decided in 1968 to withdraw from their bases, they caused what could have turned into a major economic crisis for Singapore. However, the threat was converted into an opportunity. The military facilities and the technicians working for them were released for productive civilian industries, Lee Kuan Yew, Singapore's founding prime minister, recalled. "We developed an economy in which the enterprise of American, European, and Japanese MNCs transformed British military bases into industrial facilities for manufacturing, and for servicing of ships, oil rigs, aircraft, telecommunications, banking and insurance."[6]

The economy grew by leaps and bounds, providing the resources necessary for the country's defence. The introduction of National Service in 1967 created a citizens' army and obviated the need for Singapore to invest in a large and costly standing army.

On the political front, the need for stability loomed large. Political stability, the PAP Government believed, was necessary to make Singapore a worthwhile and safe investment destination for foreign and local capital.

Stability required good leadership. Leaders would have to be honest, capable, clear in their thinking, and committed to Singapore's long-term good. Bureaucrats, too, would have to share these qualities and goals and emerge from a process of stringent selection. Together, political leaders and competent bureaucrats formed the governing elite.

Under Lee Kuan Yew's dynamic and charismatic leadership, the PAP functioned as a broad church open to a variety of thinkers and doers. It attracted a range of minds, from the philosophical Sinnathamby Rajaratnam and the cerebral Goh Keng Swee to the intellectual C.V. Devan Nair and the earthy Lim Kim San. Each member of the Old Guard complemented the others in ensuring the survival and success of Singapore.

Singapore was a racially diverse society descended largely from immigrants. If the new Singapore were to succeed, this society would have to be given a stake in the land. This is where public housing, and Lim Kim San, came in.

LIM KIM SAN: TECHNOCRAT OR POLITICIAN?

Lim was initially reluctant to join politics. He made few political speeches as a member of parliament and as a minister. He had a reputation as a nuts-and-bolts person who got things done. These aspects of his life have created the notion that he was a technocrat and not really a politician.

That myth was present in the headline of an article that appeared on him after his death: "The most unpolitical of men".[7] In the same article, however, appeared a paragraph that was much closer to the truth. Lim, Chua Mui Hoong wrote, "was among the legendary core of Old Guard ministers known for their 'political entrepreneurship', bold to experiment with new ways of doing things".

In short, he was a politician.

The headline was not wrong: Lim was indeed the most apolitical of men. However, that was before he joined politics. What he became once he had entered public life was far more than a technocrat: He evolved into a politician who acted in the full knowledge that he was taking decisions that would affect the lives of thousands down the decades.

It is true that the breezily apolitical Lim, the businessman, is evident in his Oral History Interview. That phase of his life covered two epochal events: The Great Depression of the 1930s in the long aftermath of World War I, and the Japanese invasion and occupation of Singapore — which the British had touted as their impregnable fortress — in the 1940s during World War II.

Although his family suffered financially during the Depression and he suffered physically at Japanese hands, the first catastrophe did not lead him to ponder deeply the connections between economics and war. Even during and after the second calamity, he remained apolitical in the sense that he did not set about driving the British — who had lost their colony to Japan in a war that had cost innocent Singaporeans dearly — out of Singapore when they returned to it victorious after the war.

All this is true. However, what transformed Lim into one of Singapore's founding fathers was the social impact of the PAP's arrival on the political stage. He saw a party that matched its anti-colonial rhetoric with a pragmatic blueprint for action. Lim understood that it was natural that, when political life resumed in Singapore after the war, there would be a "sort of flux", "with things going this way, that way". But what was required was that, out of the flux, a party would emerge with "a cohesive plan for Singapore". He was looking for something concrete. "And that I think was what the PAP did. And not only that. I was attracted to the PAP not only because I believe in their platform, but also because I trust… I know the people who run it and I have great faith in them."[8] He joined the PAP in 1959.

Appointed HDB chairman, he realized quickly what his job entailed. At the physical level, it meant having to deal with a terrible housing shortage. At the political level, however, this meant providing houses not merely for the sake of housing, but to give the people of an independent Singapore a tangible stake in their new society.

Lim is commended rightly as "Mr HDB" for his hands-on approach to providing public housing. His businessman's instinct for keeping costs down, his unerring eye for detail, his frenzied pace of work, and his integrity all came together to create the masterpiece that is Singapore's public housing.

However, that is not all there is to the story. The HDB was nothing if it was not political; it was proof that good and effective governance could change mental as well as physical landscapes among a largely immigrant people. The HDB was an act of faith to make immigrants believe that a place of sojourn could become a home, that a place to buy and sell could become a nation to inhabit and to defend.

It was that sense of political possibility that galvanized the hitherto apolitical Lim. Asked why low-cost housing had failed in so many other countries, he answered: "Well it is a question of political will, isn't it? The political will to do whatever is required to achieve the goal."[9]

Indeed, by his own account, it might actually be misleading to think of him as a technocrat. A technocrat is someone who brings specialized skills to a job. In his own assessment, he was anything but a specialist. He spoke of his philosophy, whether as a minister or in managing a statutory board or in running a company:

> My policy is roughly this: I am not a specialist at anything. Neither am I a professional. But I listen to the specialist and the professional... I use my common sense to ask questions like 'How about this or that?' If they cannot agree, then I must myself decide.... But the whole thing is this: *listen to people.*[10]

The ability to listen to experts, use one's common sense, take decisions oneself and then take responsibility for those decisions is a political trait by any standard.

But is there a case for making a distinction between politicians and technocrats at all? If so, what role did a "technocrat" like Lim play in strengthening the government in what was, after all, a very politicized era? Or was it precisely "technocrats" like him who made an important difference to Singapore?

Minister Mentor Lee Kuan Yew argued in an extensive interview, given not long before Lim died, that such distinctions are artificial.

> Categorizing people as technocrats and politicians is an oversimplification. Nobody is completely a technocrat or completely a politician. It is a continuum of where your interests and special skills lie. He may not have been politicized in the sense that he was not thinking of self-government, getting rid of the British and taking over the running of the system and changing the social order. Yes, he was basically a businessman. But he had a social conscience and had gone through personal privation during the Japanese Occupation.[11]

It was that background of having known privation that made Lim empathize with Singapore's poor.

> Working in HDB, you begin to see how poor people are living, how miserable their conditions were, and you begin to feel this is something worth doing. You are giving them a home; the CPF [Central Provident Fund] will enable them to buy their homes; and will create a better society. So, in the end, he became a politician nearly as much as anyone else in Cabinet. He may not be well-versed in the idiom of politics — he never went to the LSE [London School of Economics] and listened to Harold Laski or whoever, but in real-life situations, whether you want to create a fairer society, you feel and respond as a human being. In today's terms, the media and the general public like to say that "O, he's a technocrat, he's not a real politician". That's utter rubbish. You may start off as a technocrat.[12]

In that context, Lee recalled the career of former Finance Minister Hon Sui Sen.

> Hon Sui Sen was a civil servant but he faced enormous problems, first with Malayanization and then he had to find jobs when the British withdrew. I fielded him as an MP, and he wasn't very happy because it was new to him and he wasn't a man who could make speeches. I said: "Never mind. You do it, you get in, you'll solve, the jobs have to be done." So, finally, he got the EDB [Economic Development Board] going, he became the Finance Minister, he

got the Development Bank going. He's as good a politician as anybody.[13]

Lee talked about his own career as well.

To say that of Lim Kim San [that he was a technocrat] is an oversimplification in categorizing people. People see me as a politician, but I am not a politician alone. Yes, I concentrated on the overthrow of the system and on getting a new system in place and creating a different social order. I started life wanting to make a good living as a lawyer. Later I decided that the law would lead me nowhere. I made money fighting other people's battles with each other or with the state, but to what purpose? To my purpose, for money. I am not to be concerned whether the man is right or wrong; my job is get him off or to win his case. That was not the life that I wanted.[14]

Asked how he would characterize himself, Lee replied: "As someone who was thrown into politics; it started with the Japanese beating me up during Japanese Occupation."[15] The same thing happened to Lim, but he did not take to politics as Lee did. Was that not the difference?

No, he reacted in a different way. He didn't go to England. I had not only that experience with the Japanese here but I saw the British come back, new military officers in uniform trying to run this country with no experience whatsoever. Then I saw how they were running their own country. Yes, it was a different system from ours, but I concluded that there's nothing they can do for Singapore which I cannot do as well if not better, because I would represent the people. They were representing the British people, and their job was to extract out of Singapore as much economic benefits as they could from Singapore and Malaya to get the dollars which they required to support the British pound and pay for their imports. So it was a combination of these two that made me what I am. I decided that their system was flawed, that they were not capable of governing me better than my friends and I who had grown up under the system, and suffered, knew what it was all about and could be as competent. We went through that process; Lim Kim San did not.[16]

Lee returned to the theme of the educational experiences of the first-generation leaders, particularly their exposure to education in Britain.

> He did not go to England, he did not go through that same sequence of experiences. Goh Keng Swee did and so did Toh Chin Chye. A few of us who went to England decided that, no, they were not more capable than us. Definitely they did not send their best people here. The best people they kept for their home civil service, the next best the Indian Civil Service and then next the colonial civil service. We knew their ranking. We knew what the graduates in Oxbridge chose to do, would join the Foreign Service, the Home Service, the professions, the Indian Civil Service (that came to an end after India's independence in 1947), and only then the colonial service But that came to an end in the 1960s. So we knew the quality of the people who came to rule over us. I saw my contemporaries come out here to earn a living. How could they run the place better than I? It's a different experience that we went through.[17]

Yet, at the end of the day, Lim had a social conscience that made his transition to a political career natural.

The man with the blanket would have understood that sentiment fully.

Lim's role in the unfolding of the Singapore story provides a fascinating glimpse into how, faced with the task of making an improbability work, a businessman came together on a platform with people of very dissimilar backgrounds and outlooks to produce a nation where the dead would not have to share their clothes with the living.

Notes

1. Lim Kim San, Oral History Interview, by Lily Tan, Oral History Centre, Accession Number 000526/21, Project: Economic Growth of Singapore, 1955–79, Date transcribed: 25 February 1985, pp. 134–35. Hereafter OHI.
2. Lim Kim San, Interview, in *Leaders of Singapore*, by Melanie Chew (Singapore: Resource Press, 1996), p. 163.
3. "Biography of Lim Kim San", in *The 1965 Ramon Magsaysay Award for Community Leadership*, <www.rmaf.org.ph/Awardees/Biography/BiographyLimKimSan.htm>.

4. Ibid.
5. Lee Kuan Yew, Speech at the 26th World Congress of the International Chamber of Commerce, 5 October 1978, cited in *Lee Kuan Yew: The Man and His Ideas*, by Han Fook Kwang, Warren Fernandez, and Sumiko Tan (Singapore: Times Editions and The Straits Times Press, 1998), pp. 109–11.
6. Ibid., p. 111.
7. *Straits Times*, Singapore, 21 July 2006.
8. OHI, p. 103.
9. Chew, *Leaders of Singapore*, op. cit., p. 165.
10. Ibid., p. 168.
11. Interview with Minister Mentor Lee Kuan Yew, the Istana, 16 June 2006.
12. Ibid.
13. Ibid.
14. Ibid.
15. Ibid.
16. Ibid.
17. Ibid.

2

Early Life

Lim Kim San was born into a conservative Peranakan Chinese family in Singapore on 30 November 1916, the eldest son among six children of Lim Choon Huat and Wee Geok Khuan. His ancestry was interesting. When the British colonized Malaya and Singapore, the Peranakan Chinese — local-born and permanently-settled Chinese who spoke Malay or a local language at home and who were culturally more assimilated into Southeast Asian society than the fresh arrivals from China — came to be known as the Straits Chinese. This name reflected the fact of their residence in the Straits Settlements that were formed when Penang, Singapore and Malacca were placed under a single administration in 1826.[1] Not all Straits-born Chinese were Peranakan, but the Peranakan Chinese were born locally.[2] Defined, and defining themselves, as Straits Chinese, the elite of Chinese society possessed certain characteristics: Their families had been living in the region in general, and in the Straits Settlements in particular, for generations; they had become British subjects within the empire; they had generally retained their clan and dialect-group links, but tended to speak English and send their children for an English education to one of the prestigious local private schools; and they ran a network of business organizations that were influential in the settlements.[3]

Lim's family had been out of China for three to four generations. His mother's family came from Bengkalis; her father, uncles and one of her brothers were *Kapitan China* in Bengkalis.[4] The title of *Kapitan China* (or *Cina*) is believed to have originated in the Portuguese who ruled Malacca after the defeat of the Malacca Sultanate. They continued the sultanate's system of administering foreign traders in Malacca — Indian, Arab, Javanese or Chinese — through a headman that the community chose and who was then confirmed by the ruler. *Kapitan Cina*, who enjoyed the powers of a typical Malay chief, had to keep the peace, administer civil and criminal law, and collect tax occasionally.[5]

Lim, whose parents came from Sumatra, grew up in an extended family living in a Straits Chinese-style bungalow[6] in River Valley Road. Surrounded by durian trees and rubber estates, it had servants' quarters and a stable. His father, who had been educated at Raffles Institution, spoke perfect Malay, wrote Jawi and wrote English very well. His mother, probably schooled in Singapore, read English and Malay in the Roman script. "And I remember very early she used to read all these Chinese stories, you know, these ancient stories like See Jin Quee and the Monkey God, all that, in Romanized Malay."[7]

His father wore a coat and tie, his mother, a *sarong kebaya* (Malay-influenced fusion attire) "all the time", although she would don a Western gown for a photograph at a function. The family spoke Malay, a bit of Hokkien, and English, and ate *Baba* (Peranakan) food. It practised Confucianism, with his mother visiting the temple regularly. There was also a Malay woman who looked after him. "And then when I am sick, she says all sorts of mumbo jumbo, chews betel nut and spits into your face, that kind of thing. Quite superstitious. The family was quite superstitious. My father doesn't subscribe to it."[8]

The Lim family business was in shipping and commodities. As early as at four, his father would bring him to the store and offices in Market Street. "And I can still remember the very strong smell of rubber, sago. And also, the first and last time I ever saw [a] great amount of salt, looks like [a] snowy mountain, was in a storehouse in Tanjong Rhu."[9] His parents "never resented" British rule because they enjoyed a good standard of living.[10] Indeed, the family owned one of the first cars in Singapore, "a Rover, with hand-brakes outside the car", and a Studebaker.

However, even when he was seven or eight, the child was struck by the arrogance of Dutch officials who confiscated a bottle of mouthwash (because it was supposed to contain alcohol) during a family visit to Sumatra. The Dutch attitude was one of "complete contempt" of the natives and the Chinese. By contrast, he noticed "the politeness of the Indonesians".[11]

Later, he experienced British racism when, during his school days, a bishop denounced some of the boys who had put rouge on their faces and powdered themselves up. The bishop noted acidly that boys in England had natural rosy cheeks, which the Asians were trying to imitate. "That annoyed me a lot. Because you may have rosy cheeks, but if we are in China, in the cold climate, we also have rosy cheeks."[12] He encountered imperious behaviour again when working at Straits Steamship, where "I know that chap who was supervising me has got less brains than I have." "So all this adds up to your resentment against 'orang puteh'."[13]

At home, the young Lim cried a lot, was not very strong and was a difficult boy to look after, but he was a "spoilt brat",[14] being the only boy in a large household with lots of women. He caught malaria and did not go to school till he was seven or eight. The family had moved to Somerset Road by then, and he attended a private school run by a Eurasian woman. This proved to a doubly daunting experience, for while discipline meant getting hit on the knuckles, reality meant getting bullied by the older girls in his mixed class. Overaged for other schools, he then went to Oldham Hall, a school located where Plaza Singapura would be built. "It was a very rickety building, three or four storeys high. And when you climb up the steps, you can feel the whole place shaking, or when the schoolchildren come rushing out."[15] Discipline there, too, was strict, but a Chinese teacher helped him in mathematics, of which he knew nothing, and he made the grade.

He joined the Anglo Chinese Continuation School and, after his results improved, Anglo Chinese School (ACS). His account of his primary school years unearthed the memory of Mrs Yap Pheng Geck and her son, Eugene. "I don't know what they were teaching. But the moment you are out of order, my God, they really pinch you. You know, they come behind you and pinch here. They pinch you — blue black! Scared of them. I was scared of them."[16] Spelling mistakes meant holding out a hand and getting whacked.

But there were also games to be played, seasonal joys like kite flying and tops, catching fish in the drain behind in Somerset Road, rearing fish, geese, ducks, chickens and fighting cocks. He also had six or seven pelicans that he thought he had tamed and took out, but the lot flew away. "I was quite close to nature, doing all these things."[17] At secondary school in ACS, Latin was a "waste of time".[18] His favourite subject was by now mathematics, and he left school at sixteen with Honours. He wanted to go to Britain to study law.

THE GREAT DEPRESSION

The year that Lim wanted to travel to Britain to study was 1933. It was not a propitious time to seek educational advancement. The Great Depression of 1929–33 had shaken the world. On Black Tuesday, 29 October 1929, the American stock market crashed, triggering the longest and most severe economic collapse in the history of the modern industrial world. The slump spread from the United States to the rest of the world, and the protectionist imposition or raising of tariffs in response curtailed trade further, exacerbating the gloom.

The Depression caused havoc in a Singapore dependent on international trade, particularly the export of Malayan tin and rubber to the American market. Quotas imposed on Chinese immigrants saw their numbers drop from 242,000 in 1930 to less than 28,000 in 1933. Large numbers of Chinese and Indians were expatriated at public expense and, in 1931, emigrants outnumbered immigrants for the first time in Singapore's history. In 1932, the government cut salaries, dismissed many officials, reduced public works and health services, and increased taxation.[19] The slump disrupted the almost continuous growth that had been associated with the imperial era.

The elder Lim declared that he could not afford to send his son abroad. The young man did not want to attend Raffles College to obtain a general Arts degree. So he went out to work, joining Straits Steamship as a clerk and later helped his father run five petrol pumps, which closed down one after the other. A trading firm on his maternal side also closed down. "I remember my mother having to pawn her belt to pay for light and water."[20]

Notwithstanding Lim's experience of privation during the Great Depression, he remained apolitical. There is no recorded evidence that he thought deeply about the problems of war and peace, of how Nazism had arisen in Germany and militarism had grown in Japan in the midst of economic turmoil. In spite of the downturn in his family's fortunes, Singapore still provided an economic comfort zone in which an ambitious young man could think about making a good living instead of pondering where the world was headed.

RAFFLES COLLEGE AND BEYOND

Lim Kim San joined Raffles College when it started a Department of Economics, graduating with a diploma in 1939. He chose to read economics because he thought that it was related to doing business.

It was difficult for him to adjust to academic life after a break, and he managed to get a zero — any marks below 32 meriting that grade — for English in the first-term examination. But by the end of the year he beat "the smart guys".[21]

He remembered an economics lecturer in the first term, Professor Arakia, who returned to Singapore for the second term after a holiday in Shanghai. He hanged himself in the ship's cabin when he arrived in Singapore, the story being that he had been overcome by the poverty that he had witnessed in China. Another lecturer, "very fluent", was one Joseph who said that he knew nothing about economics, "so I'm going to read to you". The students' timeless response: "Well, then we took turns cutting classes."[22] Lim Kim San acquired knowledge by visiting the library, and always at the last minute.

One horrible experience was finding out that he had failed the first-year examination in history. What had happened was that there was a third-year student by the name of Lee Kim San, and so when the history professor, "a pompous little fellow called Dyre", came across a paper by Lim Kim San, "he just chucked it away". Luckily, all the papers were thrown into a corner of his room. The paper was re-marked, Lim Kim San got through, and he received a bursarship that enabled him to live in the hostel.[23]

Extra-curricular activities were not much to speak of. There was an annual dance, but not much of a social life. "The girls kept to themselves. Scared like hell. The boys kept to themselves." That version is contradicted, however, by others who remembered him as a handsome young man who attracted girls. One student remembered him as being "the Robert Taylor of the campus. He was often seen with some girl or other, one of whom they considered the Vivien Leigh of the campus".[24]

Intellectually, in his own words, he was close to fellow-students Tan Heng Jin, Lee Thiam Choy and Goh Keng Swee. It was his friendship with Goh that would lead him into politics one day. Their economics teacher, Professor Thomas Silcock, commented later: "Of the group which graduated in 1939 two are of outstanding importance…. They are probably the most important graduates of the Economics Department from the point of view of Singapore's history and its influence in the world outside. These two are Goh Keng Swee and Lim Kim San."[25] Silcock saw that "the young Goh already had the mark of a leader while the young Lim had the temperament to be a generalist of distinction."[26]

Lim recalled the professor as having labelled him as the "least politically-minded of the lot" as a student.[27] Asked about political activities at Raffles College, Lim said:

> I must say that we were not politically conscious as it were. The only one then was probably Eu Chooi Yip, you see. And then we were studying economics at that time. You were thinking about having a very fair world. And we would sit down and discuss — Dr Goh, myself and a few others — the kind of world that we want to have, where everything is being equal, everybody has a job and all that. It's a very idealistic thing. Then in the process of talking, somehow or other I always call Eu Chooi Yip a Communist, and he resented that. But I must confess that at that time it was not very clear in my mind what Communism, you know, the means and the.... Well, government is a form of social order. It didn't strike me as being a wicked government and that kind of thing. So we were looking at it more from an academic point of view rather than from a practical point of view — whether it's good for us or not. We thought, well, look, you know, a social order where everybody is given equal chance. We didn't go deeply into it. Of course it's the dictatorship of the.... Some people are more equal than others. But we thought, yes, there's no unemployment, it's also good when looking forward to those things. And we were not encouraged to talk about politics or think about politics in one way or other. And the things we read in the papers were all about Municipal Council and local issues. The broader issues never.... Foreign affairs and all that never struck us of course. In studying history, you study the history of political thought purely as an academic exercise. It was only towards the end when we were about to graduate (or we have graduated) that a few, I believe, people from the CID met us and told us about the dangers of Communism. Or even later than that, I think just before the Japanese invasion. But that was too late. Try to awake us to the dangers of Communism. Apart from that, I don't think we ever ever took a serious interest in... At least I. The others may, in politics. At least I. I don't.[28]

Their main concern was on getting through college. Did discussions touch on the anti-colonial struggle and overthrowing the British?

> No, no, never on those lines. I don't remember that at all now. Not on any militant lines or any revolutionary lines. We knew that there was this discrimination but at least, as far as I am concerned, I never said and thought how the hell do we change that. That all came later on when we suffered under the Japanese. And then we were thinking: why should our fortune be decided upon by other people? And then when the Japanese just walked in, then we knew how we had been bluffed.[29]

How to deal with the consequences of the bluff would come later. After graduation, he worked at his father's petrol station for about a year, doing some insurance on the sidelines.

It was after his marriage to Pang Gek Kim in 1940 that his business interests broadened. He became a partner in his father-in-law's sago factory, running it while managing his father's business at the same time.

Soon Hin Sago Factory in Geylang was quite a large one, employing about 200 workers among whom Lim improved his Hokkien and learnt Teochew. The raw sago came from Sumatra, was refined into sago flour and sago pearl, and exported all over the world. Interestingly, the realities of business sharpened his anti-colonial sentiments when, by the late 1940s, farina — a flour made from sweet potatoes and produced mainly in South America — cut into sago exports.

> And it's only doing this business that I felt that as a colony, our fortune is decided by the ruling country. Because overnight when UK signed an agreement with South America (they were short of food then) to purchase their meat, in turn, South America says, "You must buy our farina flour." As a result of that, the demand for sago flour in Singapore dropped. And overnight, the prices... I can't remember, but it's a terrific drop and I lost a lot of money. And they sent a commission out here to find out why and all that. And it was just a bluff. We tell them the fact. It was just a bluff, just

to cover what they have done. And we suffered. This is one of the instances where I felt that you are at their mercy. Your fate is not of your own making.[30]

But the experience of working in the sago business also enabled him to make his first million when he invented machines to manufacture sago pearl. The mechanization, which allowed him to lower costs and increase output, took place when prices went up.

He went into the diamonds and jewellery business as well of his father-in-law, who also had a sawmill in Singapore, and banking and pawnshop interests up-country. "That's how I got initiated into banking because when he died, I just took over his directorship. The son was not interested."[31]

This happened after the outbreak of World War II.

Notes

1. Leo Suryadinata, "Peranakan Chinese Identities in Singapore and Malaysia: A Re-Examination", in *Ethnic Chinese in Singapore and Malaysia: A Dialogue between Tradition and Modernity*, edited by Leo Suryadinata (Singapore: Times Academic Press, 2002), p. 72.
2. Ibid.
3. Clive J. Christie, *A Modern History of Southeast Asia: Decolonization, Nationalism and Separatism* (London and New York: I.B. Tauris, and Singapore: Institute of Southeast Asian Studies, 1996), p. 30.
4. Lim Kim San, Interview, in *Leaders of Singapore*, by Melanie Chew (Singapore: Resource Press, 1996), p. 160.
5. <yapahloy.tripod.com/the_title_of_kapitan_cina.htm>.
6. Chew, *Leaders of Singapore*, op. cit.
7. Lim Kim San, Oral History Interview, by Lily Tan, Oral History Centre, Accession Number 000526/21, Project: Economic Growth of Singapore, 1955–79, Date transcribed: 25 February 1985, p. 5. Hereafter OHI.
8. OHI, p. 15.
9. Ibid., p. 4.
10. Ibid., p. 41.
11. Ibid., p. 3.
12. Ibid., p. 23.
13. Ibid., p. 27.

14. Ibid., p. 8.
15. Ibid., p. 14.
16. Ibid., p. 18.
17. Ibid., p. 20.
18. Ibid., p. 24.
19. C.M. Turnbull, *A History of Singapore: 1819–1988* (Singapore: Oxford University Press, 1989), Second Edition, pp. 133–35.
20. OHI, p. 30.
21. Ibid., p. 28.
22. Ibid., p. 29.
23. Ibid., p. 34.
24. Joan Hon, *Relatively Speaking* (Singapore: Times Books International, 1984) cited in Lam Peng Er, "The Organisational Utility Men: Toh Chin Chye & Lim Kim San", in *Lee's Lieutenants: Singapore's Old Guard*, edited by Lam Peng Er and Kevin Y.L. Tan (St. Leonards: Allen & Unwin, 1999), p. 17.
25. Thomas Silcock, *A History of Economics Teaching and Graduates: Raffles College and the University of Malaya in Singapore 1934–1960* (Singapore: NUS, 1985), cited in ibid., p. 16.
26. Lam Peng Er, "The Organisational Utility Men", op. cit., p. 16.
27. Ibid., p. 16.
28. OHI, pp. 39–40.
29. Ibid., p. 40.
30. Ibid., p. 46.
31. Ibid., p. 49.

3

The Japanese Years

Young people like Lim Kim San might not have been very interested in the times, but the times were extremely interested in them. Even as the colonial police were warning him and his fellow-Rafflesians about the insidious threat of Communism, another disaster was in the making: Japan's invasion of Southeast Asia.

World War I had proved to be a windfall for Japan. As Western colonial powers diverted resources away from their possessions in the East, Japan gained political ground by acting as Britain's ally in the regional "power vacuum". When British warships left Singapore in 1914 to reinforce the European front, the colony's defence fell to the Japanese navy, which played a crucial role in putting down the Indian Mutiny of 1915 in Singapore.

Japan's economic penetration of the region continued as well. Cheap Japanese goods flooded a market starved of European merchandise; retailers, wholesalers, entrepreneurs and speculators entered the fray. In 1922, Eifuku Tora successfully brought modern fishing methods to the colony, and he and others from Kagoshima and Okinawa prefectures ushered in an era of Japanese domination over the local fisheries. Then the aggressively expanding Ishihara Sangyo, which had major mining concerns on the Malay peninsula, opened a Singapore office in 1925.[1]

The closing of American markets during the Great Depression led Japanese manufacturers to look at emerging markets to their south even as the Slump provided economic impetus for an aggressive nationalism. "Japan needed an easily plundered store of raw materials and already had a client kingdom in the Manchukuo, the former Chinese province of Manchuria. But now Nationalist China itself was stirring under the leadership of the mercurial Chiang Kai Shek and began to re-assert its sovereignty in the north."[2]

Japan's Southeast Asian push continued and fuelled the region's modern economic dynamism. Japanese goods formed the core of the consumer boom in Malaya in the later 1930s. Seeking to corner the market in goods from matchboxes to condensed milk, Japanese firms imported more than half of Malaya's everyday goods, while in Singapore, about 100 motorized fishing boats and 1,500 fishermen supplied the larger proportion of the colony's needs. Japanese photographic studios, chemists and taxidermists existed in every small town in Malaya; Japanese hotels flourished.[3]

Indeed, right till December 1941, Japanese barbers were cutting the hair of British and Australian troops while, ironically, "the small army of Asian clerks depended on Japanese stores such as Echigoya for the cheap white shirts and ties they were required to wear in European offices."[4] "There was underway no less than a creeping Japanese colonization of Southeast Asia. It is striking in the years before 1941 how much of the region's trade had fallen, almost by stealth, to the Japanese."[5]

The inter-war years revealed a gap between Britain, with which Japan had allied in World War I, and Chinese feelings in Singapore and Malaya. These feelings had been provoked, as mainland Chinese opinion had been, by the transfer of former German concessions in Shandong to Japan at the post-war Versailles Peace Conference. The May 4 Movement of 1919 by Beijing students focused on this capitulation; after more than a month of strikes and boycotts of Japanese goods, the Chinese government acceded to popular demands and refused to sign the peace treaty with Germany.

Repercussions of Northeast Asian events were felt in Southeast Asia. Friction between Japanese and the local Chinese went back to at least 1908, when the Chinese arrest of the Japanese vessel, the Daini Tatsumaru, off Macao led to a diplomatic row between them and sparked an anti-Japanese boycott in China and in overseas Chinese communities in Southeast Asia. Worsening Sino-Japanese relations caused clashes between Japanese and Chinese in Singapore from 1919, when Chinese attacks on Japanese homes forced the latter to take refuge in the Japanese Trade Exhibition Centre, to 1931, when Chinese actions caused the Japanese Primary School to close temporarily.[6]

The Japanese government and firms kept an eye on Southeast Asia, where the Nationalist government had wealthy supporters. As Sino-Japanese relations deteriorated sharply in the 1930s, so did the views of the Chinese in Singapore about Japan. When Japan attacked China in 1937, launching a brutal programme of occupation and suppression, Chinese in Singapore responded by contributing generously to the China Relief Fund.

By the turn of the decade, Japan's war on China had broadened into conflict with Western empires in Southeast Asia. Tokyo wanted to break out of what it called the "ABCD encirclement" — America, Britain, China and the Dutch East Indies — and build its own, bigger Asian empire by defeating the Nationalist Chinese, seizing the oil of the Dutch East Indies, and the mineral resources and rubber of French Indochina and British Malaya. "It would create a Greater East Asian Co-Prosperity Sphere in which grateful Asian nations would live under the tutelage of Japan and contribute in turn to its material needs."[7]

The Greater Co-Prosperity Sphere, codified in an official statement of the Japanese government on 1 August 1940, was a comprehensive notion based on a total mobilization of society. It envisaged "a state structure for national defence, capable of bringing into full play the total strength of the nation". At the heart of the concept lay the creation of a national defence economy, of which the keynote was "the autonomous development of the economy of Japan, Manchoukuo and China with Japan as the centre". This foundation would entail establishing "a sphere of co-operative economies, with the Japan-Manchoukuo-China group as one of the units".[8]

The purpose of the co-prosperity sphere was to create the economic foundations for attacking Western imperialism. Meanwhile, Tokyo went about undermining the West where it was weakest: In Asian colonies where nationalists were desperate to be rid of European domination.

Japan had demonstrated the credentials for undertaking this enterprise. In 1904–05, it had decimated attacking Russian armies and sunk the Russian imperial navy, becoming the first Asian nation to defeat a European power for more than a century.[9] As anti-colonial movements spread in India and Southeast Asia, radical nationalists made political pilgrimages to Tokyo and Asian students joined new Japanese universities. Japanese tourists arrived in India, Nepal and Southeast Asia. Among them were intelligence agents relying on contacts made by Asian radicals. By the time that British, French and Dutch colonial intelligence services found out what exactly was going on, it was too late.[10]

That Japan had the support of Asian nationalists, or that it intended to liberate Asians from the colonial yoke, is not in doubt. What was left unspoken, and became clear soon enough, was the second aspect of the Japanese endeavour: To colonize in all but name those whom they had liberated. Japanese imperialism was of a piece with British imperialism, but in claiming to reverse it, Japan's invasion and occupation of Singapore and Malaya far exceeded in atrocity the worst ravages that British rule had been capable of.

The leading scholar of China and Southeast Asia, Wang Gungwu, who witnessed the brutality of Japanese liberation as a child in Malaya, speaks of a "classic imperialist war" in which the Japanese were "the last of the Great Powers and the first modern empire".

The tragedy for Malayan Chinese was that they became a part of the war whether they liked it or not. There were among them those who saw Japanese imperialism in Southeast Asia as an extension of the brutal logic of the invasion of China, responded accordingly, and faced the expected consequences. But even those Chinese who saw the war in China as someone else's war, faced Japanese wrath purely because they were of Chinese origin. "The Japanese did not distinguish, when they shot and arrested the Chinese, whether they were born in China or were local-born third, fourth or fifth generation of Chinese descent." Indeed, if someone of Chinese descent spoke Malay and identified himself with Malaya, he was "suspected of being pro-British and equally an enemy of the Japanese empire".[11]

The indiscriminate victimization of the Chinese displayed during the Japanese Occupation, combined with its sheer brutality, strengthened Chinese consciousness in Malaya and Singapore, driving Straits Chinese and recent immigrants closer. Malayan Communist Party (MCP) members made common cause, for a while, with Kuomintang supporters in the Malayan People's Anti-Japanese Army, as did MCP members with colonials in the loyalist Force 136.

But if Chinese resistance to the Occupation took the shape of guerrilla warfare, large numbers of people — Chinese, Malays, Indians and Eurasians — tried to stay alive as best as they could. Some were collaborators: Most were survivors.

LIM KIM SAN AND THE JAPANESE

Lim Kim San was one of the survivors. His family was not anti-Japanese; in fact, his father, who was selling Japanese tyres, received a letter with a bullet in it saying that if he kept selling them, he would get into trouble. At the same time, asked whether he had been approached to donate money to help the Chinese resist the Japanese in China, Lim remembered: "I think I must have. The managers must have given. I gave a certain amount of discretion to my managers. They don't consult me on everything."[12]

When the war broke out, Lim and Goh Keng Swee went to join the Local Defence Corps. Goh, being a government servant, was taken into the Volunteers. But Lim was rejected because he would serve the country better by continuing with his manufacturing. "And as far as business is concerned, we were all taken in by the propaganda that Singapore is impregnable."[13] He was really worried when the Japanese sank the British battleships — the Repulse and the Prince of Wales. But the horrors of the invasion did not sink in till the Japanese had captured and detained him. "Then you feel how oppressive the Japanese were. I came to the conclusion that whatever culture they had was a very thin veneer. Beneath the veneer is the beast."[14]

He joined the Ambulance Corps. He did not witness any fighting on his rounds but there were shells screaming over his head. "You know, guns firing, you hear the shells exploding, and then the return fire when there is a whistling sound. And then the crash of artillery from your side. So you are in the middle of it. And you see fires everywhere."[15]

He first saw a dead body in Bukit Timah. "That fellow was squatting and had his top cleaned off. So I was looking at it and an English Major came along and looked at me. He says, 'This is your first dead body?' I said, 'Yes.' He says, 'You look like him. You're just as white as him.' "[16]

It never occurred to Lim or to members of his family "to really go away to India or anywhere. We thought this was our home."[17] A week before the Japanese reached Singapore, the family moved to Sumatra in a junk to avoid some of the horror of the bombing. He returned to Singapore after a week because "it's still your home" and "you just come back" the moment "you see there's no more fighting".[18]

He arrived at Clifford Pier, dressed in black shorts and barefoot and trying to pass himself off as a labourer. But his feet were too small for his size and "my hands were too fine for that kind of a thing."[19] He was detained the whole day till the Japanese in charge arrived in the evening. The man probably had had a few drinks and was jolly. He asked him how many wives and children he had. When he replied that he had two children but only one wife, the Japanese roared with laughter and said "Watku or something like that". The Chinese interpreter present there said: "Run you bloody fool…." So he ran.[20]

Now, facing the Japanese, occurred something that had eluded Lim Kim San, something that no event, no mishap, no sudden shock of conviction in his untroubled, apolitical youth had foretold. At a time when people were frightened to even talk, "I was listening to the radio" and "like a bloody fool, typing all the news and distributing it around".[21] What made him not only listen to forbidden broadcasts but disseminate the news?

> Well, you were wishing the worst for the Japanese. So any news like that, you will like to spread it round and raise hopes among your friends — that this thing will end soon, you see. Not because of any heroic motive. I don't think it ever entered into your head that you are doing something. Only just through hatred of the system and then you just say, "Well, look, anything that is bad for them is good news, so we will just spread it around."[22]

Not only was he distributing news at danger to himself, he refused to become a "two-star" — a collaborator who was responsible for rounding up young people for labour. He was detained thrice for that transgression and also because a Communist, to whom he had refused to give money, had implicated him falsely as a contributor after his own arrest.

Taken to the torture chambers of the Kempeitai on Oxley Rise, he was confined for forty days or so in a room with forty other men and women, sitting on his haunches "until you had two humps like a monkey" and drinking from a single "damned toilet" where "you do everything on the toilet".[23]

> Life was hardly monotonous, however, for there was the dreaded torture. Oh, they just judoed and kicked you, and then they used a rope and hammered you. But you watched out the other torture — the water torture, the beatings and all that, beating people to death. Water torture, everything. You see that right in front of you….[24]

And there was an Indian with a broken leg. He was tortured every day. He was beaten until his leg was broken. Then a Kunpo will come, throw a stick and make him crawl to take it and bring it back again. And every step was a torture to him."[25]

Witnessing the torture first-hand had a strange effect on him. He grew as defiant in life-threatening danger as he had been uncommitted in peace and prosperity.

Especially galling was the sight of *Kunpo*, "local chaps" who tortured other "local chaps". Educated, indeed, English-speaking, they were collaborators in the Japanese enterprise. He told them off, asking them why they did such a despicable thing. They apologized, saying that they had answered advertisements for clerks but had found themselves becoming *Kunpo*. The Japanese were different. "So I told those chaps, 'You want to win our hearts? You'll never win our hearts. You'll never win.' " The consequences of providing that unsolicited piece of advice? "Fly through the windows and all sorts of things."[26]

Released, he saw that life outside was not marked by the same degree of terror, but his family's houses were confiscated and its business was as good as gone. The Japanese acquired Soon Hin Sago Factory, and Lim found himself reporting at a *Kumiai*, run by a Japanese firm, with the head in an officer's uniform.

> They called them up by trades, you see. So sago factory people were asked to go up one day. And they just said they are taking over and you'll be paid your rents, that's all.... We went down somewhere in Raffles Place, to a Japanese firm. And you find an officer with a sword, putting his sword down, he says, "Well, look, you know, this is it." That's all.[27]

The family crowded into a small shophouse and he indulged in a little bit of black marketing, in gold and diamonds.

> And then, well, I had no more sago factory. My father's petrol stations all were taken over. No job. My mother will be selling some cakes at home, doing nonya cakes. And then I'll be at the jewellery shop learning about jewellery and diamonds and gold.... So you

buy all these jewellery stuff and then you dismantle them, sell the diamonds or re-do the diamonds, and then melt the gold. And then there was some trading in gold bars.[28]

His father-in-law's sawmill was closed down, although his United Chinese Bank opened later with other banks.

> But I never believed that the Japanese currency would be good. So from time to time, I have changed Japanese currency into British currency, and I have hidden them underground in biscuit tins… I didn't operate an account with the United Chinese Bank. I didn't operate one of my accounts. I just left it dormant. And then when the British came back, it was good. I had every cent. So I restarted my business with that.[29]

Lim remembers meeting Lim Boon Keng, a "very gentle, nice, old man" and a "very sad man", who knew his father-in-law and dropped in occasionally. "You talk about the Japanese Occupation, what is happening, who and who join them and make money…. But I think he must have been a very disappointed sad old man at that stage of his life to be forced to play a role like that."[30]

This was a reference to the Japanese decision to exact $50 million from the Chinese in Singapore, Penang, Malacca and the Malay States as a token of atonement for having supported the Kuomintang with money to fight the Japanese, and for their hostility to Japan in the past. Many Chinese were forced to sell their property and others had to give up their savings to meet the demand. Lim Boon Keng, as chairman of the Overseas Chinese Association, handed over the cheque to Lieutenant-General Yamashita at Fullerton Building.[31] Lim Kim San, then just emerging on the business scene, was spared, but his father-in-law, a member of the Chinese Chamber of Commerce and a prominent member of the community who had given money for the anti-Japanese fund, had to contribute. "They had to sell the jewellery to contribute."[32]

The Japanese Surrender in September 1945 saw Lim on the roof of the Cricket Club. The first Commonwealth soldier that he saw, along Balmoral Road, was an Indian. "I was so happy I shook him by the hand. And he had oil all over. I thought I almost could kiss him. And I could smell the oil on him, you know."[33] But he and his friends had a premature celebration before the official surrender. As "Happy Days Are Here Again" was being played on the piano, in walked a Japanese with his sword. "Happy eh? You happy eh?" The rest bolted, but Lim plied the armed visitor with drinks. When the Japanese fell asleep, he carried him out and deposited him on a field.[34]

When the official Japanese announcement of surrender arrived, Lim went looking for those who had collaborated with them, particularly two men whom he believed were responsible for his detention. He did not find them. But retribution arrived for other collaborators. Some were hanged; a detective who had bullied residents around North Bridge Road was "skewered alive".[35]

The Japanese Occupation left a deep imprint on Lim. The Japanese were "bastards.... Very thin veneer [of] civilization. Beneath it is the beast."[36] The British hoax about Singapore being an impregnable fortress rankled, and "I really got mad over white people" after the Japanese Occupation when, doing business, "you come across young punks who know nothing, coming here and trying to boss it over you."[37] But the British played by certain rules, were not that brutal, and "don't squeeze everything out of you".[38]

Lim's feelings about rapacious Japanese remained long after the war was over. Disagreeing with the policy of letting Japanese firms into Singapore's retail trade, he argued that it enabled the Japanese to simply take over what locals were doing.

> So he opens up, you give him the best concession in Jurong and he sets up a retail trade to compete with your local chaps. And he buys from all over where he has got an advantage. And you call that free competition. You are weighted. You know, your local entrepreneur, the moment he starts, he's weighted against. There is already a handicap. So in the end what will you become? You become drawers of water and hewers of wood for the international companies.[39]

Letting the Japanese in as manufacturers was fine, but the retail and agency business "should be ours".[40]

Such strong words from one of the key figures in Singapore's economic success after its independence bear the scars left by Lim's Japanese years, when everything from business to the lottery of life and death depended on Tokyo's imperial whims.

In an interview, Lim summed up his life during the war years, during which he lost an uncle, a cousin and several other members of his family, as the "wasted years".[41] The Occupation had disrupted Lim's comfortable existence. But he had kept in touch with his friend, Goh Keng Swee, through whom he met Lee Kuan Yew.[42] A new chapter in Lim Kim San's life was about to begin.

Notes

1. Tsu Yun Hui, "Japanese in Singapore and Japan's Southward Expansionism, 1860–1945: Historical Notes for Under Another Sun", National University of Singapore, <aems.uiuc.edu/HTML/UAS/Tsu.html>.
2. Christopher Bayly and Tim Harper, *Forgotten Armies: The Fall of British Asia 1941–1945* (London: Allen Lane, 2004), p. 2.
3. Ibid., pp. 5–6.
4. Ibid., p. 6.
5. Ibid., p. 5.
6. Tsu , "Japanese in Singapore and Japan's Southward Expansionism", op. cit.
7. Bayly and Harper, *Forgotten Armies*, op. cit., p. 3.
8. For the full text, see <www.worldfuturefund.org/wffmaster/Reading/Japan/Japan-1940.htm>.
9. Bayly and Harper, *Forgotten Armies*, op. cit., p. 4.
10. Ibid., p. 5.
11. Wang Gungwu, "Memories of War: World War II in Asia", in *War and Memory in Malaysia and Singapore*, edited by P. Lim Pui Huen and Diana Wong (Singapore: Institute of Southeast Asian Studies, 2000), p. 17.
12. Lim Kim San, Oral History Interview, by Lily Tan, Oral History Centre, Accession Number 000526/21, Project: Economic Growth of Singapore, 1955–79, Date transcribed: 25 February 1985, p. 50. Hereafter OHI.
13. OHI, p. 51.
14. Ibid.
15. Ibid., p. 55.

16. Ibid., p. 54.
17. Ibid., p. 51.
18. Ibid., p. 57.
19. Ibid., p. 58.
20. Ibid., p. 53.
21. Ibid., p. 55.
22. Ibid., pp. 71–72.
23. Ibid., p. 56.
24. Ibid., p. 58.
25. Ibid., p. 75.
26. Ibid., p. 56.
27. Ibid., p. 61.
28. Ibid., p. 62.
29. Ibid., p. 63. The Japanese "banana" currency became all but useless when the British returned after the war.
30. Ibid., p. 65.
31. <www.streetdirectory.com/travel_guide/singapore/world_war_2_military_site/180/civilian_war_memorial_war_memorial_park.php>.
32. OHI, p. 64.
33. Ibid., p. 80.
34. Ibid., p. 81.
35. Ibid., p. 83.
36. Ibid., p. 78.
37. Ibid.
38. Ibid.
39. Ibid., p. 79
40. Ibid.
41. Melanie Chew, *Leaders of Singapore* (Singapore: Resource Press, 1996), p. 161.
42. Lam Peng Er, "The Organisational Utility Men: Toh Chin Chye & Lim Kim San", in *Lee's Lieutenants: Singapore's Old Guard*, edited by Lam Peng Er and Kevin Y.L. Tan (St. Leonards: Allen & Unwin, 1999), p. 17.

4

Choosing Sides

When the British returned to Singapore after the end of World War II in 1945, food and medical supplies were scarce, electricity and other services were in disarray, and the death rate was twice what it had been before the war.[1] Gambling and prostitution were growth industries, with opium and alcohol serving as religion to the most dispossessed among the masses. In September 1945, Singapore became the headquarters of the British Military Administration (BMA). The BMA, cynically renamed the "Black Market Administration", was rife with incompetence, arbitrary rule and corruption. Profiteers and former collaborators thrived as the returning British depended on the "professional survivors" who had served the Japanese with the same effortless chicanery that they had displayed previously towards the British.

However, by April 1946, when military rule came to an end, the BMA had restored gas, water, and electric services to levels that were above their pre-war capacity. The port returned to civilian control; several companies received priority in importing sorely-needed supplies and materials; Japanese prisoners were made to repair docks and airfields; and schools were reopened. By late 1947, the economy began to recover because of growing demand around the world for tin and rubber. The following year, Singapore's rubber production reached an all-time high, and abundant harvests in neighbouring rice-producing countries ended the most serious food shortages. By

1949, trade, productivity, and social services were restored to their pre-war levels. By 1951, demand for tin and rubber for the Korean War brought an economic boom to Singapore.

After the war, Lim's family went about rehabilitating its business interests. His father restarted his petrol stations, and his father-in-law reactivated his gold, jewellery and pawnshops business. The establishment in 1946 of the Malayan Union and the exclusion from it of Singapore, which became a separate Crown Colony, did not affect his father-in-law's business interests in Malaya because there were no policies then that favoured indigenous *bumiputra* (native Malays). Lim liquidated the pawnshops in Malaya because the high rates of interest that they charged hurt poor people, and because inflation ate into the trade. He reorganized the Batu Pahat bank into the Pacific Bank, increased its capital to $2 million, and sold his share and that of major holders to OCBC bank. The Communist insurgency that had provoked the Malayan Emergency was especially strong in rural areas, and so did not affect his father-in-law's business, which was town-based. The Lim family's business life was humming again.[2]

Politically, however, Asia was in ferment. Indonesia had proclaimed independence in 1945 and gained it in 1949, within which period India had become independent in 1947; and although China had never been colonized formally, it went farthest along the revolutionary path by becoming Asia's first Communist country in 1949. Popular movements took centre stage across the continent.

Lim was not immune to the mood of the times. After the Japanese Occupation, Lim recalled, "we were all feeling a bit sore, having been let down by the British and having no say in our future. We felt rather anti-colonial and anti-white." He was "an interested observer" watching different parties perform and was "quite impressed by anyone who comes up and pronounces very anti-white policies".[3]

That attitude attracted him to the Malayan Democratic Union (MDU), Singapore's first indigenous political party. As Singapore looked set to becoming a separate Crown Colony with the onset of the Malayan Union, opposition to the colony's separation from Malaya led to the MDU's formation in December 1945. Several prominent Communists, who figured among its founders, considered the Malayan Union to be a threat to their vision of a Communist, united Malayan republic and hung on to a desire to see Singapore included eventually in an independent Malaya.

Two years into its inception, the Malayan Union failed because of opposition from Malay Nationalists. It was disbanded and replaced by the Federation of Malaya in 1948. Again, Singapore remained a separate Crown Colony. The MDU was by then a Communist front organization.

Lim dropped in for meetings with MDU leaders such as Lim Kean Chye and Philip Hoalim, but only for friendly chats and not to discuss politics. He was not "politically-minded at that time".[4] He did not meet Wu Tian Wang, one of the Communist founders of the MDU, but he did meet John Eber, another leading left-wing figure. He was drawn somewhat to Hoalim, "a very anti-white person, very independent in his thoughts".[5] He did not think that the MDU had Communist connections, but he was so "naïve politically" then that, apparently, he did not probe Eu Chooi Yip, a Communist leader then, when Eu warned him about Lim Kean Chye having Communist links.

The Communist challenge was growing in both Singapore and Malaya. The Malayan Communist Party (MCP) had been set up in Singapore in 1930. The MCP was committed to the violent overthrow of British rule. Its attraction to its followers, overwhelmingly Chinese, lay in the legacy of the war, when it had been associated with the resistance against Japan, particularly the Malayan People's Anti-Japanese Army (although the MPAJA had included many non-Communists). The MPAJA was disbanded in January 1946 at a ceremony during which the British supremo Louis Mountbatten presented medals to the guerrilla commander, Chin Peng, and the other leaders. However, the MCP retained secretly large stocks of weapons that the guerrillas had received in airdrops from the British during the war or which they had taken from the Japanese.[6]

When the Federation of Malaya came into being, Singapore's Communists crossed over to the peninsula, where they reactivated the MPAJA and launched an uprising. The violence led to a declaration of the Malayan Emergency, which lasted from 1948 to 1960. The colonial authorities in Singapore proscribed the MCP; the MDU dissolved itself.[7] But the MCP continued to influence the aspirations of younger-generation Chinese, particularly in the vernacular middle schools and the labour unions, who drew from the Chinese revolutionary model their hope of ejecting British colonialism from Singapore and Malaya through guerrilla war.

On the business front, the Communists were "giving trouble" to Lim.[8] On one occasion, several of his workers, who were provided with two meals a day, marched into his office and complained about the quality of the rice. So he took it and said: "Yes, I'll eat the rice. I don't eat such good rice at home. This is Thai No. 1 I'm giving you." It was "just a pretext to give trouble".[9] Eu Chooi Yip, whom Lim knew and who considered him a friend, once advised him to give in to the workers or else he might be hurt physically.[10] Indeed, there were threats to his life. The road to his sago factory was so bad that he had to park his car and walk a quarter-mile (0.4 kilometres) to the factory. He began to carry a tin of cigarettes, "pretend that it's a revolver or something", and walk on. One of his partners was a former detective, who provided a "sort of protection".[11]

In those trying times, Lim continued to meet political leaders from other parts of the political spectrum. They included leaders of the Singapore Progressive Party. Formed in 1947 and led by English-educated members of the elite, it was a conservative party that advocated gradual progress towards self-government and concentrated on making electoral gains in the legislative and city councils in the short term.[12] It leaders had been seen as the "Queen's Chinese" for their pro-colonial positions and conservative economic policies.[13]

Lim "might have met" the Progressive leader John Laycock, but the Progressives "didn't impress me", except for A.P. Rajah, "who was strongly anti-British when he stood up".

There was also the Chinese-leaning Democratic Party, led by upper-class businessmen. Lim was suspicious because "if the businessmen are there to back it, they are going to get something out of it". Also, the party appealed to the Chinese, and "you must distinguish between the English-educated like me and the Chinese-educated. So we don't speak the same language…. You don't tell them what you think and they don't take you into [their] confidence."[14]

Then, there was the Labour Front, set up in 1954 by two former members of the Singapore Labour Party, Lim Yew Hock and Francis Thomas, and the prominent lawyer David Marshall. The Singapore Labour Party — formed in 1948 by mostly British-educated leaders who had adopted moderate political positions — had all but disintegrated by 1952.

Marshall, Singapore's first Chief Minister, was "flamboyant", "impressive", and took on the white man. But when he struck up one of his flamboyant postures, "you begin to think that he's more suited to be an actor than a politician". He had no concept of economics and how to run Singapore; all he wanted was freedom from the British. Race — Marshall was a Jew — had "something to do" with the fact that the Marshall regime was short, and he struck people as being "unstable". His handling of the Hock Lee Bus riots and the student demonstrations showed that he was "naïve" and that he gave "the benefit of the doubt" to people who came to him with a story. "And that is his downfall. He's not a politician … I think he was lost amongst the Chinese and the trade unionists."[15]

By contrast, Lim Yew Hock, Singapore's second Chief Minister, was decisive in dealing with the industrial and student unrest. He was a trade unionist, received valuable feedback, and depended on advice from the British. He was "courageous" but also had his drawbacks, which made him go too far against popular sentiments.

He had been "thrust on the stage and without the education or background for politics". There was a lesson in his downfall. "So, well, you're native, you're being used, and where the British can make use of you, they make use of you as far as possible until your time runs out."[16] Lim Yew Hock had asked him to join politics, but he declined. Why? Did not Lim Yew Hock have a plan for Singapore? "If he had, I was not aware."[17]

Ironically, Lim Kim San's association with the MDU, however apolitical, might have paved the way for his joining the PAP. He met John Eber for the first time at the Stamford Club, a gathering of former graduates of Raffles College. A prime mover behind the club was Toh Chin Chye, who would become one of the founders of the PAP. Members hoped that their discussions could lead to the setting up of a political club to educate people, thus carrying forward the work of the Malayan Forum in London, where former Rafflesians such as Lee Kuan Yew, Goh Keng Swee and Toh Chin Chye had sought to spread political consciousness in their quest for an independent Malaya that would include Singapore. Lim attended the Stamford Club meetings.

> Toh Chin Chye, Keng Swee and PM [Lee Kuan Yew] probably had an idea of forming the PAP already. So this is the forerun where they can spot for people who are interested in politics, people who are interested in political life. So I think this was the forerunner.[18]

The People's Action Party (PAP), formed in 1954, occupied a unique place on the political spectrum. It was a non-communal party, distinct from other parties that operated in Singapore: The Singapore Malay Union; the United Malays National Organization (UMNO), the dominant racial party in Malaya; the Singapore Indian Regional Congress, modelled on the Malayan Indian Congress across the Causeway; and the Singapore branch of the Malayan Chinese Association (MCA).

The appeal of the Malay and Indian parties was limited by the fact that these communities were minorities in Singapore. The Chinese-leaning parties, led by commercial figures and other notables, could not appeal to younger members of the Chinese community whose future did not lie in becoming trading or commercial successes but in the prospects of the working class and the middle class. The young Chinese-educated were carried away by the propaganda of rapid industrialization under communism in China.

Like the conservatives and unlike the Communists, the PAP abjured revolution and chose the parliamentary path instead. However, unlike the conservatives and like the Communists, the PAP was radical because its demand for self-government was not limited to elite jousting with the British but required it to build up mass support for an anti-colonial movement. Like the conservative parties, the PAP was led by English-educated members of the intelligentsia and was non-communal, but unlike them, it did not equate multiracialism with the economic interests of the cosmopolitan upper class. Instead, it joined hands with pro-Communists to advance an inclusive vision of democratic socialism that promised the bulk of citizens a vastly improved material and social future.

The PAP drew on the support of Chinese-educated Singaporeans because they believed that the PAP was going to follow something akin to China's development policy. These Singaporeans also were proud of their ethnic heritage but they were unwilling to lend their weight to chauvinism.

In the fascinating and complex interplay of race and class produced by the introduction of electoral reforms after the war, the PAP emerged as the only party following the parliamentary path to combine organization and mass support at the close of 1955.[19] It took power in 1959.

It was also the party that Lim Kim San joined.

As a businessman, was he not worried at the prospects of the left-wing PAP coming to power?

I was not worried because I know the leaders of the PAP. I know
them well. And, you know, as a student you have got a very idealistic
view of the world. Equal opportunities sound very reasonable, that
they will want to solve the unemployment problem, give education
and housing. So that doesn't worry me.[20]

The English-educated business community was worried over the
PAP coming to power because the newspapers were against the party
and were "giving a very false picture and a very gloomy picture of
what the future will be".[21] The civil servants, too, were hostile towards
the party. But the PAP's rallies in Finlayson Green and Fullerton
Square drew good crowds. He attended every one of them.

In fact, Goh Keng Swee, Toh Chin Chye and Lee Kuan Yew
approached Lim Kim San to contest the 1959 elections. He declined
because of his business commitments, but he drew on his overdraft to
finance the PAP's campaign. He and some friends also placed bets on
the party's chances of victory. He made some money. "In fact, on
individual seats too, I had some bets. Some people never paid me."[22]

As a new era began in Singapore's politics, "to be in politics was
the last thing I expected".[23] Yet, that is exactly what happened, for Lim
had chosen sides finally.

Did parts of Singapore's business community shun him because
he was teaming up with what many saw as the "Communist" PAP?

Lee disagreed.

No, the Chinese business community in Singapore saw us as extreme
radicals and we had associated ourselves with pro-Communist
elements in the trade unions and in the students' unions. They
were extremely anxious and fearful that we were really not in
command. They didn't think that we were communists but that
we'd be swallowed up by the communists, that the communists
were using us as a moderate front to capture power, and then
everybody would be in trouble. We knew the risks, and we decided
that we'll risk it, that we could contain the danger. In fact, I now
believe we were over-confident. If you ask me now, I'll be most
apprehensive about repeating that exercise, [getting the communists
in a close alliance], and risking a total capture by them.[24]

Was Lim's inclusion into the party's highest ranks in the years to come an indication that the PAP would co-opt and not shun business in its pursuit of democratic socialism through pragmatic means? Lee agreed.

> Yes, we were not doctrinaire, never were. If anyone was an ideologue, it was probably Toh Chin Chye. He once told me that he wasn't happy with Medisave and co-payment. He said that in China, where he had just been, Mao Zedong and the Chinese peasant had the same medical treatment in similar hospitals. He was then Minister for Health — I said: "Chin Chye, do you believe that Mao Zedong has the same doctors or the same medicine or the same operating theatre as the Chinese peasant?" But he believed it. They showed him the Beijing Hospital and shot him the line that it was the same and free for everybody. He believed it. I did not. I never went to Beijing Hospital (but) I knew that this could physically not be. You cannot treat the country's top leaders the same as you treat your farmers. Not everybody is a top surgeon; not everybody is a top doctor. There must be priorities. In a capitalist system, that priority is resolved by who can pay; in a communist system, by who you are, your standing. So we decided that we would do it in a practical way. We are not born equal; we cannot be equal in our earning capacity; we cannot get equal medical services; but we'll do our best to make sure that everybody gets basic medical services. It is a pragmatic approach to socialism. The British tried the National Health Service, and they can't get out of it. Because it is free and equal for everybody, they have enormous troubles. The people with money are going abroad for their treatment to France and elsewhere and to private clinics which are not allowed to expand to become real hospitals.[25]

Lim, with his pragmatic bent of mind, had found his true home in the PAP.

Notes

1. This account of the immediate aftermath of the war is drawn from *Singapore: A Country Study*, edited by Barbara Leitch Lepoer, Federal Research Division, US Library of Congress, Research Completed in December 1989, <http://lcweb2.loc.gov/cgi-bin/query/r?frd/cstdy:@field(DOCID+sg0029)>.

2. Lim Kim San, Oral History Interview, by Lily Tan, Oral History Centre, Accession Number 000526/21, Project: Economic Growth of Singapore, 1955–79, Date transcribed: 25 February 1985, pp. 84–95. Hereafter OHI.
3. OHI, pp. 100–101.
4. Ibid., pp. 96–97.
5. Ibid, pp. 99–100.
6. *Singapore: A Country Study*, op. cit.
7. Ibid.
8. OHI, p. 85.
9. Ibid., p. 85.
10. Ibid., p. 86.
11. Ibid., p. 88.
12. Yeo Kim Wah, *Political Development in Singapore 1945–55* (Singapore: Singapore University Press, 1973), pp. 130–31.
13. *Singapore: A Country Study*, op. cit.
14. OHI, pp. 108–109.
15. Ibid., pp. 102–104.
16. Ibid., p. 105.
17. Ibid., p. 107.
18. Ibid., p. 100.
19. Yeo, *Political Development in Singapore*, op. cit., p. 131.
20. OHI, p. 111.
21. Ibid.
22. Ibid., p. 114.
23. Ibid.
24. LKY interview.
25. Ibid.

5

Judging People:
The Public Service Commission

Singapore's Public Service Commission (PSC) was set up in 1951 to advise the British governor on the recruitment, employment, promotion and terms of service of colonial civil servants. Its functions were extended later to cover the dismissal and disciplinary control of civil servants. In its early years, it did its work against the backdrop of demands for self-government in Malaya. These demands included moves towards the Malayanization, or localization, of the Civil Service, in which the PSC "was called to walk a fine line in balancing the need to find and promote more local men of talent and ability while also ensuring that the hallmarks of integrity and independence were maintained".[1]

This goal was codified in Government Command Paper 65 of 1956 called "Statement of Policy — Malayanisation", which declared:

> One of the fundamental rights and privileges of a self-governing country is that it must have control of its public service. No outside authority must be in a position to determine, even in the last instance, what appointments, promotions and disciplinary actions are taken in respect of the civil service. The establishment of a Public Service Commission with responsibility for these matters is the most effective way of achieving this objective and at the same time of securing freedom from interference in service matters by politicians and political parties. We must aim at a civil service that

will loyally discharge its duties irrespective of the political complexion of the government...."[2]

The Malayanization process was pushed ahead by the agitation of the Council of Joint Action which, led by top civil servants Goh Keng Swee and K.M. Byrne, protested against expatriate officers enjoying bigger allowances than their local counterparts. The opposition to these allowances symbolized "a general dissatisfaction with the status quo".[3]

Lim Kim San declined to get involved in active politics in 1959 because of his business preoccupations, but he told Goh, Toh Chin Chye and probably Byrne, that if the PAP won and there was anything that he could do for them, he would not mind doing so. The party won, and he was appointed to the PSC that very year, and served as member or deputy chairman till 1963, when he took part in elections.

Lim recalled that because the PSC had come under the control of local people for the first time, it was essential to ensure that there was impartiality in public service appointments and that sound discipline was maintained. The "whole system would break down" if it was shown that there was "hanky panky" in appointments.[4] But another crucial issue was at stake. He and his colleagues wanted to change the system so that bureaucrats would serve the public instead of the public having to obey "its beck and call". "All these gave us a very sour Civil Service."[5]

Another reason for the sourness was perhaps that, even as public servants found themselves coming to terms with the PAP's results-oriented governing style, they were affected by a move to freeze appointments and reduce the variable allowances of local civil servants from 1 July 1960. About 6,000 of the 14,000 officers serving then were affected, with some losing as much as a third of their allowances. The cuts were an important part of an economy drive meant to reduce a glaring budget deficit of $14 million. The reduction was necessary to prevent the new government from going into the red in its very first year in office.[6] Lee Kuan Yew wrote in his memoirs:

> There was great unhappiness, especially among the senior officers. The English-educated believed we had set out to punish them for having voted against us. That was not our motive. We wanted to show everyone in Singapore, especially the Chinese-educated majority, that for the public good, the English-educated were prepared to make sacrifices, led by the ministers. I thought it not unreasonable that they make this sacrifice to help us get the message across that, in this new era, we would all share hardships and joys equally.[7]

Government servants were "very demoralized" by the pay cut, Lim said, but "they did pull up their socks later on when they realised that the PAP knew what they wanted."[8] However, there was no political interference in appointments that the PSC made.

At the PSC, Lim's problem was to get officers who would have sufficient strength of character to report fairly on their juniors and also have the ability to say no. "Because the weakness here is the inability of our own officers to say no to our own men and also for the subordinates to be disciplined by the local people. They would take a reprimand from an expatriate but they would not take a reprimand from a local one." The challenge in the post-colonial era was to get civil servants to accept the notion that they had to listen to what their senior officers had to say whether they were white or brown.[9] "And what is most unsatisfactory is the report from [the] Head of that department. I have never come across an adverse report. Which is nonsense! No adverse report! Satisfactory, satisfactory. So you know when it's put 'satisfactory', it's most unsatisfactory."[10]

Heads of department were so unwilling to put in an adverse report against any man, and assessments varied so much, that Lim had to assess staff himself by asking other people, watching the officers at work, looking at what they produced, forming judgements, and enquiring among other PSC members whether they had personal knowledge of those bureaucrats. It was possible to know within a few minutes who was an outstanding bureaucrat. The problem arose when judging between average candidates for promotion.[11]

Lim had harsh words for those who found their responsibilities too hard to bear.[12]

> Quite a number of occasions where I see people breaking down under a load that is too heavy for that person. It's not the work itself, it's the sense of responsibility. So in many instances, you'll find that a good Number Two does not necessarily make a good Number One. Because if the Number Two is [a] damn good worker, good adviser, but when he shoulders the responsibility, he can break down.[13]

Two members whom Lim found lacking in other respects were a "good man but already getting rather old", and "a poet who will dream while we are interviewing". "So I remember doing most of the talking and most of the selection and most of the decision at that time, which I think was a good thing; helped me decide on things very fast."[14]

But more than his interactions with those colleagues, Lim remembered the Meadows episode from those years. Minister for National Development Ong Eng Guan had taken it upon himself to torment expatriate officers. One of his prime targets was a deputy secretary called Val Meadows, whom Lee Kuan Yew in his memoirs called "a most capable officer, stout-hearted, with a distinguished war record". Ong bore Meadows a grudge, and so "physically banished" him to the southern islands to improve conditions there. He did his work quickly. "But instead of being complimented, he was evicted from his office in the ministry in his absence." His office simply vanished, and he was asked to work from the communal work office. Ong walked in to "savour his discomfiture", but Meadows did not overreact, preferring to resign soon after. The head of the establishment office asked him to stay on because a rescue operation was in progress. "That was my taking the portfolio away from Ong and instructing Val Meadows to discharge his duties from my office," Lee wrote. He made Meadows his deputy secretary and gave him several duties. "I wanted to signal to expat officers and civil servants generally that I did not approve of what had happened and that I was not afraid of being dubbed their puppet."[15] To Lim, Ong had disgraced Meadows on the pretext of not wanting expatriate officers. "I never took a liking to that guy," Lim said,[16] highlighting a relationship with Ong that would come into even sharper focus later.

On hindsight, Lim remembered his PSC years for having sharpened his ability to assess people because "you see quite a lot of people and you've got to make your judgement."[17] The talent for judging people would serve him throughout life, including the time when he would play the role of gatekeeper at interviews at which the PAP assessed candidates for political office.

Complimenting Lim on his ability to see through people, Lee said at his colleague's eightieth birthday celebrations in 1996: "He has an intuitive sense for judging people, their character, their motivation and their capabilities...". Looking back at those years, Lee remembered that

> he would tell me of Khaw Kai Boh, who was the Special Branch Director in Singapore and became a minister in the Tunku's government: "That man I would not touch. When I shake his hand, I am repulsed. He is no good." But the Tunku said "I like that man." Lim can give me a rundown of each Malaysian minister he met — Tan Siew Sin, Sambanthan — that was useful. Some views coincided with mine; some are little variations of my feelings, but I took note of what he said.[18]

At the birthday celebrations, Lee added: "I used this uncanny ability to good purpose when I wanted candidates to be interviewed for jobs, especially for prospective MPs, to gauge their potential." Former Member of Parliament Chor Yeok Eng, who had worked as a senior parliamentary secretary under Lim when he had been the environment minister, said: "After talking to the candidates, listening to their responses and observing their attitude, he was able to tell you if a person was dependable or not, whether or not he could be trusted. And his judgements were usually very accurate."[19] Indeed, in one version of the PAP's interview system, the party would use a psychiatrist and a psychologist to run tests on candidates. The media reported: "It had been found that the assessments by the selection panel headed by [the] former Cabinet Minister, Mr Lim Kim San, have matched those of the two men, using their scientific method."[20] The PAP attempted to "pick and parachute worthy candidates" from outside its ranks. A "rigorous selection process and a gatekeeper like Lim were especially important to identify and vet new blood".[21]

Much as the PAP valued Lim's abilities as a political headhunter, "not everyone appreciated it, especially the candidates". It could be an unnerving experience.

> One contender recalls going before the assessment panel and Lim immediately barking at him: "So what makes you think you're good enough to be a PAP candidate, eh?" Taken aback, the candidate made as if to leave, saying that there were plenty of scholars waiting outside to take his place. Lim then softened and told him to stay. "It was just a test to see what they would do under stress," he says. That candidate is now a three-term MP.[22]

Senior Minister Goh Chok Tong recalled his own involvement with the selection process and Lim's role in it:

> He was very shrewd in judging people. I have sat in a few candidates selection interviews with him. He would ask a few harmless questions to get to know a candidate. He would make up his mind quickly from the way a candidate answered the questions and from the latter's eye contact and body language. Basically, he was assessing whether the candidate was an honest and sincere man, as well as his character and interest in society rather than the content of his answers. From the people selected, I would say his instinct was right. We did not track those who were rejected, so I cannot say whether he had made mistakes in rejecting some of those.[23]

On his part, Lim was adamant that there should not be any suspicion of nepotism in his role. Thus, he abstained from the selection process when the PAP chose a nephew of his to run as its candidate against

Workers' Party leader Joshua Benjamin Jeyaretnam in a by-election in Anson constituency in 1981. His nephew lost.[24]

In the larger scheme of things, it is not a small irony that the man whom many considered a technocrat among politicians should have ensured that the PAP continued to inject into its parliamentary and ministerial ranks the political talent with which it has ruled Singapore since 1959.

Notes

1. Warren Fernandez, *Without Fear or Favour: 50 Years of Singapore's Public Service Commission* (Singapore: Times Media Private Limited for the Public Service Commission, 2001), p. 12.
2. Cited in ibid., pp. 12–13.
3. Ibid., p. 25.
4. Lim Kim San, Oral History Interview, by Lily Tan, Oral History Centre, Accession Number 000526/21, Project: Economic Growth of Singapore, 1955–79, Date transcribed: 25 February 1985, p. 115. Hereafter OHI.
5. OHI, p. 121.
6. Fernandez, *Without Fear or Favour*, op. cit., p. 33.
7. Lee Kuan Yew, *The Singapore Story: Memoirs of Lee Kuan Yew* (Singapore: Times Editions Pte Ltd and Singapore Press Holdings, 1998), p. 318.
8. OHI, p. 121.
9. Ibid., p. 120.
10. Ibid., p. 119.
11. Ibid., p. 118.
12. Ibid., p. 116.
13. Ibid., p. 117.
14. Ibid.
15. Lee, *The Singapore Story*, op. cit., pp. 335–37.
16. OHI, p. 122.
17. Ibid., p. 120.
18. Interview.
19. Ken Kwek, "The Trusted Political Headhunter", *Straits Times*, 21 July 2006.
20. Cited in Joan Hon, *Relatively Speaking* (Singapore: Times Books International, 1984) cited in Lam Peng Er, "The Organisational Utility Men: Toh Chin Chye & Lim Kim San", in *Lee's Lieutenants: Singapore's Old Guard*, edited by Lam Peng Er and Kevin Y.L. Tan (St. Leonards: Allen & Unwin, 1999), pp. 21–22.

21. Ibid., p. 21.
22. Roger Mitton, "Singapore's Other Founding Father", *Asiaweek*, 5 December 2000, <www.pathfinder.com/asiaweek/foc/2000/12/05/>.
23. Interview with Senior Minister Goh Chok Tong, the Istana, 11 July 2006.
24. Lam Peng Er, "The Organisational Utility Men", op. cit., p. 22.

6

Housing a Nation: The Housing and Development Board

Housing had been a persistent problem for Singapore since the early years of the twentieth century. Reports produced by visiting health and sanitary authorities in 1907 spoke of overcrowding and insanitary conditions in heavily populated parts of the island's city area. A Housing Commission report in 1918 noted that poorer residents could not afford to pay rent for individual flats for each family, causing a "general subdivision of housing space into cubicles thus further aggravating the overcrowding conditions and leading to a high percentage of sickness and a high rate of mortality".[1] It recommended the creation of an Improvement Commission, which in turn resulted in the setting up of the Singapore Improvement Trust (SIT) in 1927.

SINGAPORE IMPROVEMENT TRUST

Writing two decades later, SIT Chairman L. Rayman noted that its mission was "to rehouse the people and to abolish the fearful slums of the town with their terrible overcrowding and their attendant evils of crime and disease".[2] How far the SIT lay from achieving its goal is manifest in its own publication, *The Work of the Singapore Improvement Trust 1927–1947*, which blames its "limited means" and "circumscribed powers" for its woes.[3] For example, the colonial government earmarked, and placed at the SIT's disposal, $10 million in 1926 for the clearance of slums, but the fund's nature and purpose were never defined clearly, and at the end of 1947, it had decreased to a miserly half-a-million dollars.[4] Then, the government's General Improvement Plan for Singapore was not intended to be a complete plan for the entire island. "It is merely a record of existing development together with layouts and subdivisions which have reached the stage of statutory approval. It has been built up in piecemeal fashion in circumstances over which the Trust has had no control."[5] Consequently, the SIT undertook practically no improvement schemes in the decade from 1937 because its energies were directed to working on back lanes and ordinary planning duties.

Back lane work was important, no doubt: It brought light, ventilation, kitchen and bathroom accommodation and sewerage to about ninety blocks of congested and overcrowded property in slum areas which were in insanitary condition. However, the programme was held up by high costs and "reluctance in present conditions to take any action however desirable which decreases the amount of living accommodation".[6] Also, renewing the rear portions of old and dilapidated buildings merely gave "a new lease of life to property which is obsolete and overdue for demolition and rebuilding" — quite apart from the fact that reconstructing the rear portion of a house for back lane purposes cut down the living accommodation by about a half in many cases, "and thus creates rehousing problems and aggravates overcrowding".[7]

It was clear to SIT officials that they had to focus on housing to address the source of all these problems, but their hands were tied. The situation was ironical because the Housing Commission of 1918 had laid the trust's foundation, "and one would have thought that specific provision would have been made in the Singapore Improvement Ordinance for Housing".[8] However, it was only in 1932 that the Trust's power to build was clarified in the ordinance, and even then, there was a refusal to concentrate on housing to deal with the fundamental source of the problems that caused overcrowding, misery and crime. "The Trustees were for many years reluctant that the Trust should undertake any housing on a large scale as such was apparently not the original intention when the Trust was created. The Singapore Improvement Ordinance lays no obligation on the Trust to provide housing except for persons dishoused by reason of Improvement or Insanitary Schemes."[9]

The housing shortage grew acute as the population increased and Singapore port expanded. Private enterprise was reluctant to provide accommodation. The SIT's role gained prominence. In 1936, it was required to act as agents of the government in providing low-cost housing. The first public housing scheme began the same year with the erection of a single block of flats on a modified shophouse plan in Tiong Bahru. These were advertised for sale, but it was a failure because the reserve price was not reached at the auction. Nevertheless, the SIT continued to build flats in the Tiong Bahru area and to develop a large estate of single-storey artisan quarters in the Balestier area. Some blocks of tenement buildings were also put up in the few places where land became available in the congested parts of the city.[10]

In 1938, about 100 acres (40.5 hectares) of old and derelict property in the valuable city area reverted to the Crown, providing the government an opportunity to set up a committee to recommend measures to alleviate the housing shortage. The Weisberg Committee noted that the housing shortage was becoming acute and that it was not financially attractive to provide housing for the poor unless gross overcrowding and the creation of slum conditions were accepted. It recommended that a public housing authority be set up to provide housing for the poor at little profit or even a loss. The SIT was the only organization that came close to being such an authority. It was recommended that a housing programme be drawn up for the years 1939 to 1942.[11]

The outbreak of the Pacific War in 1941, the Japanese invasion of Singapore in 1942, and the Japanese Occupation till 1945 put paid to the Weisberg Committee's plans. The housing problem, already crucial, became critical as thousands of houses were destroyed in the war and a free-for-all during the Occupation saw people constructing unauthorized homes. Widespread destruction was accompanied not by new building construction, but by the deterioration of existing property owing to a lack of maintenance. "By the end of the War tens of thousands of people were living in huts made of attap, old wooden boxes, rusty corrugated iron sheets and other such salvage material. They lived in congested squatter settlements with no sanitation, water or any of the elementary health facilities."[12]

The British Military Administration that followed the Japanese Occupation depleted the strength and efficiency of the surveying and other staff on whom the SIT depended.[13] As a consequence of Japanese rule, many houses and flats were occupied by people other than those who should have been there, according to records. Huts were erected illegally and with "astonishing rapidity" on trust lands; once in existence, they were difficult to demolish. "Regard had to be paid to the hardship which would result from wholesale demolition of insanitary huts even if this could have been effected."[14] Eviction faced political hurdles as well. "Furthermore some of the buildings in the centre of the City which had been occupied by the Japanese had within a day or two of the liberation been occupied by various clubs and political societies the latter usually of extreme political views."[15]

By 1947, the housing shortage had reached "famine proportions".[16] A Housing Committee report in 1947 showed that many blocks in the city area contained populations of more than 1,000 persons to the acre. As the population increased by 40,000 a year, the squatter problem grew, and land got scarcer and more expensive.[17] The Housing and Development Board's *Annual Report 1960* places the situation in historical perspective. It notes that a housing shortage existed even as early as in 1907, when the town population was less than 250,000 and there were more than 20,000 buildings, representing 9.7 persons to a building. By 1931, conditions were worse. The population increased to 567,000, and there were about 37,000 buildings, representing 15 persons per building. In 1947, when the population stood at 938,000, the scarcity assumed epidemic proportions: Congestion in the city area amounted to 18 persons per building. Compounding the housing problem were demographic factors that were changing the population's character from a migratory to a settled one — and thereby increasing the demand for housing. In 1931, the sex ratio was 357 males to 209 females; by 1957, the ratio was reduced to 1,000 males to 876 females.

The Housing Committee report of 1947 acknowledged the scale of the problem. It declared:

> The disease from which Singapore is suffering is Gigantism. A chaotic and unwieldy megalopolis has been created, as in other countries, by haphazard and unplanned growth. The symptoms are obvious. Shops, residences, and factories are huddled together with patches of undeveloped land where the owners are waiting for unearned incremental values. No provision is made for road improvements, open spaces or public buildings or amenities, the land for which has to be purchased by the public later at enormous cost, while in the meantime a generation has lived and grown under conditions which are detrimental to health and morals.[18]

Translated into numbers, this is how the situation appeared:

> A quarter of a million people already require housing. The population is increasing at a rate of between 25,000 to 30,000 a year. This will mean a further quarter of a million in ten years. A programme covering ten years should therefore provide for housing half a million people. If the population of the Municipal area is limited to, say, 800,000 (or 40 persons per acre), then 400,000 people must be housed outside Municipal limits within the next ten years.[19]

The report called for, among other things, the creation of a Master Plan that would provide for satellite towns, industrial estates and land acquisition. It also thought that the SIT should continue to be the planning and housing authority.

While the Housing Committee was admirably accurate in its reading of the problem, its recommendations of immediate measures fell short of the effort required to meet the housing crisis. It proposed that sufficient units be built to house, in three to four years, 35,700 people — "what the increase of population demanded in one year".[20] Private enterprise would not step in to make up the shortfall for the lower-income groups although they formed the vast majority of those in need of housing. These facts pointed again to the need for the SIT to play a vigorous role, but political and bureaucratic inertia scuttled the prospects of meaningful change. In 1951, the SIT was tasked with preparing a Diagnostic Survey and Master Plan for Singapore. A team to draw up the plan was formed in early 1952, and the Master Plan was submitted in November 1955, but it did not receive government approval until August 1958. All this while, the SIT's housing programme provided on average 1,720 houses a year, when the need was almost ten times this number. The trust built 3,841 units in 1958, the highest number that it would attain in its thirty-two years of existence.

The situation was not sustainable. By the end of 1958, recommendations were made for the SIT's dissolution, and for provisions for the formation of a new housing and development authority and a separate planning authority to carry out the trust's functions. The Housing and Development Board (HDB) was constituted and the Planning Department was set up within the central government machinery in 1960.[21]

There were several reasons for the SIT's failure to tackle the housing crisis. As noted earlier, it was less a housing authority than a municipal body. Housing had not been a part of its original mandate, and even when it turned its attention to the dismal state of affairs, there was little political and administrative will to empower it to do what was needed. The SIT did not fare well in the management of finances, either: Although it was fortunate to enjoy revenues from several sources, its accounts were in the red in 1959. "Inadequate attention was paid to balancing the budget or to the practice of economy."[22] Rents were decided on an ad hoc basis, some being calculated on the basis of construction costs, "others on political expediency and still other[s] on no apparent basis at all".[23] At one point, there were more than 100 categories of rents, with similar units in the same locality often costing very different sums.[24] Expatriate officers working for the SIT believed that the maximum capacity of the building industry in Singapore was 5,000–6,000 units. Building beyond this level, they argued, would increase prices seriously and make low-cost housing uneconomical. Yet their own building costs averaged $7,000 a unit, which was "way above" the figure at which the HDB would build units.[25]

The SIT departed from the Singapore scene as a new political era took shape. The fully-elected government that came into power in June 1959 caused "great anxiety" to the SIT's expatriate officers, most of whom elected to leave the service while collecting Provident Fund benefits on a higher scale. The mass resignation demoralized the remaining staff; with the SIT's demise looming, almost no work was done on the construction of low-cost housing in the second half of 1959.[26]

What was required was a new housing authority, different from the SIT in both purpose and style. The new organization would have to be a proper building authority, not a municipal body. It would have to implement the new government's commitment to tackling the housing crisis as part of its vision for Singapore. It would have to be structured differently from the SIT — which was characterized by a maze of committees and subcommittees — so that the chain of command was clear, decisions could be taken quickly and work could be carried out efficiently. It would have to be led by someone capable of ensuring that the new body, and its staff, lived up to its mandate.

Here was a job crying out for a mover and shaker.

HOUSING AND DEVELOPMENT BOARD (HDB)

Within weeks of coming into power in 1959, the PAP Government began to complete the draft legislation to dissolve the SIT and set up an organization that that would have the funds and the legal powers to deal with public housing construction and management, urban renewal, and related issues. The HDB was established on 1 February 1960.[27]

By 1960, Singapore's population had reached 1.6 million and was expanding at about 4.6 per cent a year. It was estimated that 250,000 people living in ramshackle shophouses in the city centre, and another 200,000 to 250,000 in squatter settlements around the edge of the city, needed rehousing.[28] Experts averred that the construction industry in Singapore could not build more than 6,000 units a year — against the required 15,000 — without prices being pushed very high. At an average of five persons to a unit of housing, the figures meant that 12,000 new units a year would be required to tackle just the increase in population alone. And if some of the deteriorating housing were to be replaced as well, another 3,000 units would be needed — or a total of 15,000 units a year. The private sector, catering to middle and higher income groups, could build about 3,000 units a year. Hence, the public sector would need to build at least 10,000 units per year, or a total of 50,000 over the following five years.

Breaking boldly with the SIT's incrementalist approach to meeting the housing shortage, the new board decided on an immediate programme to build as many low-cost housing units as possible to meet the needs of people in the lower-income groups whose requirements private enterprise had never catered to. This measure would form part of a short-term plan to relieve acute congestion in the city's central areas by creating "new centres of population in the form of properly planned housing estates which would be within easy means of communication to the city".[29] The HDB also embarked on a long-term plan to provide for the city's eventual redevelopment based on a more detailed study and the support of a team of urban renewal experts. There was a practical problem with even the short-term plan. Studies had confirmed that the majority of people most in need of public housing depended entirely on central area activities for their livelihood; thus, they would be unwilling to move into public housing estates away from their places of work if transport costs were to deter them. Unfortunately, public transport was very expensive compared to the earnings of these groups of people. It was unlikely, therefore, that the poor could be attracted to living in housing more than five miles from the city centre unless the maximum fares charged could be brought down to twenty-five cents or less, irrespective of the distance travelled. Since there was little likelihood of such low fares being available in the foreseeable future, the HDB decided to concentrate its building activities in housing estates that were within a radius of five miles (eight kilometres) from the city centre. These estates were in Tiong Bahru, Alexandra and Queenstown in the West, St. Michael's Estate, Toa Payoh and MacPherson Estate in the North, and Kallang Estate in the East.[30]

An essential question was how much rent the lower-income groups could afford to pay to live in this new housing, and whether a government subsidy would be required. The government made its calculations based on an average income of S$100 a month; figuring rent at 20 per cent of income, it decided that the most that the really poor could pay was S$20. Hence, rents were fixed at S$20 for a one-room unit, S$40 for a two-room unit, and S$60 for a three-room unit. The subsidy required: S$15 for one room, S$35 for two rooms, and none for three rooms. These calculations were projected into the board's first Five-Year Building Programme (1960–64), a forecast of capital expenditure, revenue expected, annual recurrent expenditure, and subsidy from the government, and were incorporated into Singapore's Government Development Plan for 1961–64.[31]

Lim Kim San was appointed chairman of the HDB in 1960. Under his leadership, as many housing units were built during the next three years as had been built during the preceding three decades altogether. The largest project completed during the first five years was Queenstown, a satellite town of more than 17,500 flats housing almost 150,000 people. Development at Queenstown had begun under the SIT in 1953. However, by 1960, when the HDB took over, only a miserly 3,000 units had been completed. While the board approved the original plan of five residential neighbourhoods, each with its own communal amenities grouped around a town centre, the low population density envisaged was no longer acceptable to the authorities. Given the population's rate of expansion, more intensive use of the land was essential. This meant embarking on high-rise housing. Actual construction on the Queenstown site began in 1961. By the end of 1964, more than 17,000 units had been constructed and the residential areas were almost finished. The town centre was completed in 1965. Other estates built around the city during these same five years included Alexandra Hill, 2,222 flats and a number of shops, completed in 1962; St. Michael's, 2,296 flats completed in 1962; MacPherson Road (South) completed in two phases, 1962 and 1964, for a total of 8,300 units housing around 70,000 people; Kallang, 1,500 flats plus a market completed during 1962; Tanjong Rhu/ Mountbatten Road, 1,144 flats completed in 1963; and Fort Road, 3,800 flats completed by 1964.[32] Singapore's housing shortage was being tackled. Lim Kim San was at the heart of that epic effort.

Lee Kuan Yew remembered well why he had chosen Lim as HDB chairman.

> When we took office, we had to look for people whom we knew had good judgement and understood what we were trying to do, to appoint them to various bodies like PSC and HDB. Goh Keng Swee was his good friend. They were in the same year at Raffles College although LKS was a few years older. Keng Swee who knew him well said: "Take him." I also knew him though not as well. So, I spoke to him. The important job was not PSC because there he was one of several members; he wasn't the chairman. The important job was HDB, where he would be in charge. We knew that we had a maverick,

unstable minister in the National Development Ministry who was out to make a name for himself at all costs and was unstable and reckless. He had wanted to use the Istana into public housing to make a name for himself. He goes for populist gestures, like 'take away the Mace' (of the Mayor) and that sort of posturing. So we needed a strong man whom we knew we could depend on and would stand up to the minister (Ong Eng Guan), and we would back him. So he took on the job knowing that there would be a clash with the minister, which subsequently took place and eventually led to the removal of the minister.[33]

In his Oral History Interview, Lim recalled vividly his clashes with then National Development Minister Ong Eng Guan.

I knew there were some sort of disagreement between Ong Eng Guan and the party because of... I, from the very beginning, have been watching the antics of Ong Eng Guan with great distaste and I have made my feelings known to leaders of the party — Toh Chin Chye, Byrne and Goh Keng Swee... And a few days later, Prime Minister rang me up in my office (that petrol station in Finlayson Green) and asked me whether I had been to the Housing Board. I told him, "No. I have not been there.

I have received no letter of appointment nor have I heard from the Minister."[34] Lee promised to put matters right, and the next thing that Lim knew, Ong Eng Guan rang him up and asked him to meet him.

It was not a pleasant meeting. Lim asked Ong whether he had a parking place for him, and was assured that he had. But when he arrived there, there was no parking place for him. Worse was to come. Ong, who knew that Lim liked good food, invited him to lunch but ordered merely rice and egg with something on top of them. They ate. Then in a gratuitous act of showmanship, the minister touched his toes with his hands to show how fit he was. So Lim, too, touched the floor with his hand, just to show him that what he could do, he could do better. After wishing Ong goodbye, Lim went to his office, met the secretary, and asked where his promised parking was. He was not being arrogant, but wanted to make his position in the HDB clear. He went down, looked for a parking place himself, found it, and had it reserved for him.

Lim could take on Ong because he was not a paid chairman. Had he accepted payment, he would have had to obey the minister. For example, Ong's advice to him was never to put anything on paper, a directive that Lim considered wrong because once a decision had been taken, it would have to be clear whose decision it was, and the fact must be put on record. Otherwise, if a mistake were made, who would be responsible?[35] Lim would have found it difficult to disagree with Ong had he been paid. But as an unpaid chairman, Lim reminisced, if Ong did not like what he was doing, he could just walk out.

What Lim found when he first walked into HDB and saw the departments was how broken the staff were. They reminded him of the Japanese Occupation, when a Japanese would walk into any place and the rest would have their heads down. Indeed, in another throwback to the days of the Occupation, he was told that there were spies around him to report to the minister what he was doing. He could not care less because he was interested only in doing the work, and Ong would not find anything else.

Morale was low. All the expatriates were out except two, one of them being a civil engineer named J.R. Stevens. To Lim, Ong did not want anyone who could report to the prime minister to be near him. "And the pretext of not wanting orang putehs [white men]... disgracing Meadows was just a.... Well, it serves his purpose then."[36] Another victim was P.C. Marcus who, although he was a PAP supporter, was made a scapegoat.

Yet, even as competent expatriates were treated meanly, many of the local staff appeared to enjoy Ong's extraordinary benevolence. Lim enquired whether the staff were qualified officers, and was shocked to discover that forty or fifty of them were not qualified to be in the HDB. "They were Ong Eng Guan's gang, you see."[37] So he decided to throw them out, and served notice around. He received a call from

Lee, who asked what he was doing. He replied that he could not work with people who were not competent. He knew that they were party boys, and that Ong would fight for them, but where he was concerned, he was sacking them. Lee heard him out and then said that a mass rally would be held on the Padang. "Ask them to come. He'll have to explain why they should not be sacked. You stand up and explain why they should be sacked." "I said, 'Okay.'" Lee warned him that he was up against political opponents. As it turned out, the sacked staff did not turn up at the Padang. However, there was a big row in the office, with the sacked workers demanding a month's notice. Lim ordered that they be paid straight away and told to go home. "That was how I started the Housing Board."[38]

Straightening Things Out

The Housing and Development Act set up a board comprising the chairman, deputy chairman, and not less than three but not more than five members, all of whom were appointed by the Minister for Law and National Development. Below the board was the chief executive officer, who served as the main link between the board and its departments. The original seven departments were the Secretariat, Finance Department, Statistics and Research Department, Building Department, Estates Department, Urban Renewal Department, and the Resettlement Department.[39] In his work at the HDB, Lim enjoyed Lee's assurance that he could choose anybody whom he liked from the Civil Service to assist him. He had known Howe Yoon Chong for a short time in the Public Service Commission, and thought that he would be a good man. So he picked him as the Chief Executive Officer. Howe, being a civil servant, would be able to get to know the lower members of the staff and have greater rapport with them than would Lim, who had just come in, was unknown, and had been put on top. Between them, they identified other officers, including Teh Cheang Wan, whom they made Chief Architect. Stevens, too, was of great help to them. Then, Lim began interviewing heads of departments one by one and assessed their capability. He told them that they had a job to do and that they had better get going and do it well.

What really helped Lim was that he did not have to worry about money. Goh Keng Swee, then-Finance Minister, had promised him that money would not be a problem, and he was given a free hand in spending it. Also, since the HDB had been freed from observing the Building Ordinance, Lim and his team drew up and passed plans and went to work on them straightaway. So long as they kept within certain legal limits, such as the height of the ceiling and fire escape, they did not have to consult the various authorities.

The new leadership cut a lot of red tape. Under the SIT, there had been many committees. Lim abolished all of them, but set up a committee for allocations consisting of MPs so that there would be fair play. He did away with the SIT system, adopted by HDB, of allocating points to applicants for housing. It was replaced by the principles of first-come, first-served, and the number of families. Lim made it clear to members of the allocation committee for flats that they should not take advantage of their position on it. In the process of making such changes, there were some altercations. Then-PAP stalwart Lee Siew Choh came in one day and threw in front of Lim a piece of paper with a list of the names of his constituents who had applied for jobs. He wanted houses to be allocated to them. Lim asked his staff, and was told that those people had just applied for flats. So he told Lee Siew Choh that he had to decline his request. "So he says, 'Then what are you here for, if not to give priority to party supporters?' I said, 'I am here exactly to prevent misuse of position.' "[40]

Looking back on the HDB's teething years, several issues stood out in Lim's mind. The first was the scarcity of skilled staff that it had to face. The HDB needed architects, along with engineers, supervisors and technicians. The standing order at that time was that no one who had less than ten years' experience as a practising architect would be allowed to design and build flats. But the situation was so desperate that anyone with a diploma or qualification was called in, and those who would do a good job were identified. The HDB recruited a small nucleus of former civil servants, but most of the recruits were young, with at most a year's experience in engineering, architecture, finance or administration. Although almost everyone who had graduated in these fields was taken in the beginning, it was on condition that they would not be part of the Civil Service. Lim said: "We will try them out for two, three months. If they are no good, out they go. And it speaks well for the young people that during the first year… I had occasion only to dismiss two of them."[41] There was also an acute shortage of technicians to supervise the contractors. Singapore Polytechnic offered a three-year diploma in building course, but

> we couldn't wait for three years so we ran a course ourselves. Each year 60 students who had passed the Senior Cambridge were taken in as apprentices. They were trained on the job by senior workers, in the evening they had classes. At the end of six months, they received a junior certificate.[42]

The second issue was the need for the HDB to do the earthwork itself because at that time, there were only two earthwork contractors in Singapore, and "before you can get them to do any work, it takes at least six months".[43] Also, given the scope of the housing programme, there were fears of a possible shortage of building materials — granite, sand and cement — and a resulting escalation in prices.

> If there is a shortage of materials, those people who have bid will… lose money and the housing programme is going to be let down.… So we set up one office to watch prices.… Sure enough, certain operators who supplied sand and gravel began to form a cartel among themselves. I called them up and told them this is against community interest, and if you really form a cartel and bring up the prices, then we will do something drastic.[44]

When operators paid no attention to his warning, he carried out his threat:

We started exploring what granite quarries can we open, what sand quarries can we open. So we were ready for them. The moment they boom up the prices, we open up these quarries to stabilize the market. So similarly with all other commodities. We were ready to make our own bricks if the brick factories formed a cartel, but after one or two examples in the granite and sand quarries, they came to us and said, "Look, how much do you require for your housing? We will supply that to you at the same rate. The balance, if you don't mind, if private developers want it, we sell at another price." Fair enough, we say. You can make your money.[45]

The HDB also looked into ways of mass production or the prefabrications of housing units, its objective being to ensure the continuous production of housing units even after the building industry in Singapore was working at full capacity. The Board examined methods used by British, French, Danish and Swedish firms. Although they were mainly labour- and time-saving processes that were invariably more expensive than the methods used traditionally in Singapore, the HDB was prepared to invest if necessary in capital equipment in any suitable economic assembly line method of producing prefabricated components for housing units that could be found. However, after more than half a year of investigations, it found no satisfactory method and continued with the traditional methods. Fortunately, the costs of construction were not affected very much in the first year of the HDB's existence. The average cost — excluding piling and land — worked out to S$8 per square foot of living area with water, electricity and modern sanitation included, as well as public roads, drains, car parks, and open spaces. This cost compared favourably with the HK$25 per square foot that the Hong Kong Housing Authority spent on a similar type of housing, in spite of the fact that in Hong Kong, labour was paid less than half the wages earned by construction workers in Singapore.[46] Keeping costs down became a cardinal principle at the HDB.

The third, related issue in the HDB's early years had to do with selecting contractors. Lim broke up the ring of contractors who were known as registered contractors. There were only four contractors on the SIT's register, and

> the businessman will tell you that if only four chaps have got the power to tender, they will very soon form a ring and see that the prices go high. We broke that and said "nothing doing". We will allow everyone who thinks that he can build for us to tender. But at the same time we were very careful to make sure that those who tendered bids had some experience and also the financial ability to carry the thing through.[47]

Among the new contractors selected on the basis of competitive bids were former foremen. To ensure that they carried out their work properly, the Board's architects and administrators supervised them. "And the next thing was we made clear to the contractors that we are going to build on a massive scale and they would be allowed to make money — reasonable amount of profit — but they are not allowed to profiteer."[48]

Fourthly, Lim made sure that the contractors were paid on time and that there was no corruption. Indeed, he made it known that if, by the first and the fifteenth of every month, they were not paid, they could have access to him and he would find out why the delay was occurring. These measures put a stop to the "little corruption and delaying tactics" that some officers employed, and created confidence among the contractors.[49] They knew how to adjust their cash flow so that they did not have to add to their bills a large sum for interest incurred.

Probity
Probity was the hallmark of Lim's stewardship of the HDB. His experience as a businessman helped him to take decisions and understand the important role that finance played among contractors and the private sector that supplied materials. They needed to be paid promptly so that they would offer the best prices available. Lim himself did not deal with the contractors or the suppliers because

the relationship might get too personal and they would ask for favours from him indirectly. He kept away from them, leaving it to officials to deal with them, but he ensured that they were dealt with fairly and that no favouritism was shown towards any of them. "You know, you may be a good friend, but if you don't do your job properly, you've had it."[50] Lim put his personal stamp on ensuring that there was no case of corruption or bribery during the years that he spent at the HDB.

Not that businessmen did not try, however.

> During Christmas time, I remember the first Christmas, I went one morning and found, before Christmas, my whole room filled with Christmas presents. So I got all the contractors together and tell them, "Stop doing this. But since you have sent these presents here, they are going to the charitable organisations." And once they understand it's not appreciated, they stopped.[51]

It did not bother him that the businessmen could get offended.

> Well, I have got to offend them otherwise I'll be fending off all the time all sorts of presents. Once you accepted that, they know you accept that, everytime there's an occasion, my place will be filled with all sorts of presents. And after that, they will probably come to the house. And after that, they will probably come quietly and try and get favours. So you may as well do away with it.[52]

Lim recalled how a very good personal friend sent him a valuable Peking carpet when he moved into his new house. He had to call him and ask him to take it back. The friend was terribly annoyed, but Lim told him that if he wanted to give him a present, he could just give him a sheep's skin, which cost about S$5 or S$10 at that time, in place of the carpet, which had cost a few hundred dollars. Although he had no business connection with the friend, he explained to him that an expensive gift could be misunderstood.

Honesty was a trait that Lim had learned from his father. When, during the Japanese Occupation, Lim had wanted to make money on the black market for his father, the elder Lim had advised him sternly

not to do so. Lim senior was a very honest man, and was quite
fatalistic as well, believing that it was not his way of life or his luck to
make money that way and would lose any money made dishonestly.
Looking back at those years made Lim reflect on business culture,
social perceptions of businessmen, and his own record in business.

> You see, this is where I think in a way our government servants and
> government are a bit unfair. They think all businessmen are crooks
> and they get up the crooked way. Well, maybe quite a lot of them
> are. But buying cheap and selling high.... The main thing is to do
> business. And of course there are certain principles to observe.
> Quite a lot of them observe these principles. A lot of them don't. So
> there are honest businessmen and dishonest businessmen. Well, I
> consider myself an honest businessmen though at that time when
> there was black marketing, I was doing black marketing. Because
> that was the thing to do.... Without black marketing, there is no
> business. Then you don't do business, you see. But profiteering,
> that's another thing. You should not profiteer by it. So that's why
> sometimes I wonder how I reconciled my public posture with my
> private thing. So I rationalise it. It's that way because you want to
> do business that time. Yes. But later on, when things are much
> better, then you don't have to do those unprincipled things. But
> you don't profiteer. Some people profiteer. And you don't cheat,
> you see that?[53]

Pressed by the oral history interviewer, Lim made a distinction between
English-speaking and Chinese-speaking businessmen. According to
him, English-educated businessmen were honest and straightforward,
and not devious at all, but that was so partly because there were so
few of them, and because they had lost their provincial characteristics.
By contrast, a spirit of camaraderie marked Chinese-speaking
businessmen, such as those from the Hokkien or Teochew community.
The English-educated might bring a bottle of whisky along during
Christmas, and that was that. Among others, the Japanese, for example,
"everytime they come here, they give you something."[54] Lim
remembered his first trip to Japan in 1964. The Singapore officials
had said expressly that they would not accept gifts. Yet, he received a

record player and other expensive electronic goods. He must have annoyed the Japanese by refusing to accept the presents and sending them back. All said, however, the penchant for giving gifts in order to shore up business relationships was not a peculiar Asian trait. The West was not beyond it. "You know, the French, the Americans... Americans, their banking community... here... quite bad."[55]

Lim's insistence on honesty in his and in the HDB's dealings with contractors and suppliers did not go unchallenged. In one famous incident, he had heard about contractors being crooked and so thought that it would be a good idea for him to go round and look at some of the buildings under construction. The first structure that he saw was along Margaret Drive. The block appeared crooked to him. He went back and told Howe Yoon Chong: "Either my eyesight is bad or there is something wrong with that block of flats there. So please get the technicians to look at it properly."[56] True enough, it was crooked. The HDB made the contractor rebuild the whole thing. That provided a blunt indication to contractors that the HDB would not tolerate any fooling around. On another occasion, when he went to another block of flats under construction, he happened to look at some of the wiring. Although he had no experience, he thought that the wires were much thinner than the electrical wiring that he had in his own house. So he pulled out the wiring and asked the architect who was following him why it was so thin. The architect said that it did not meet specifications. Lim pulled out the whole wiring out and ordered that it be replaced.

> So we went from place and place. And gradually it became known that, you know, contractors can get their payment on time. There is no fooling around, no corruption, and that what we specify we want to get.... And once the contractor understood what we wanted, where they stood and how we treat them, then we have no more further problems with them. Standard of work improved.[57]

The private sector played a role in the HDB's success because building construction workers were not unionized. There were many skilled subcontractors who worked on their own and contributed to high productivity and low costs. There was very strong competition among subcontractors, but they were highly motivated because they kept the money that they made.[58]

As a result of the steps that Lim took, things got moving at the HDB. He remembered calling his officers together and saying to them:

> Look, each of you has got certain function to do. And if you do your function well, perform your duties without any vested interest, and though your decision is wrong, I'll stand by you. But if you made more wrong decisions than right decisions, then I have to move you. But if I find that in making the decision you have a vested interest involved, then I go for you. Apart from that, I say "carry on".[59]

His approach worked.

> And I think young people like to have a certain sense of responsibility. And if they discharge it well or if they make a mistake, they like to be protected, told but not to be just dismissed straightaway. They must be given a chance. And I think I was right in giving them a chance.[60]

The effect of this outlook on the staff was infectious. "They were told what to do.... And then when they see things were moving, they get enthusiastic. This is what the young people want, you know — things done."[61]

> In the end we got a very enthusiastic staff because they saw things were getting along. And there was no such things as having to wait for a committee to decide on anything which has got to be done. They will come up to me and I will just say yes or no. And I meet them almost every day the first year or so. Almost every day [I] met heads of departments, discussed the problems, made decisions there and then, cutting off all red tape. And things were done quickly rather than having things on paper and having a formal meeting. We will just sit around and discuss right up to 9[p.m.], and we will adjourn and have dinner — steak, you know, Chinatown.[62]

Indeed, the enthusiasm went so far that "after some time it was more my duty to stop ideas, stop carrying out ideas rather than to have to resort to encouraging them to put forth new ideas."[63]

What also helped Lim was that the work of the HDB, unlike that of other official departments, was highly visible to the public. Talented young people wanted to be associated with an organization that others could see producing results. To entrench the spirit of pride, an emblem was designed and placed on each HDB project. Soon, Singaporeans came to realize that an HDB emblem meant that a really big project was underway. "Then, the housing workers could say to their friends, 'Look, I am a member of the Housing Board,' and that gave them pride."[64]

In the midst of this fervour, Lim's business took a back seat.

> But I must say that administrative chore in the Housing Board as Chairman is tremendous. Oh, you are tied in more with details and daily routine than in any of the ministries that I have been. In the ministries you deal with policies. But in the statutory bodies like [the] Housing Board and PUB, you really go into it.[65]

However, the results were felicitous.

> I've worked very hard a few stages of my life. But this one I really worked hard. But I must say it's [been] thoroughly enjoyable. It's something completely new and well, the story of it is… I've stayed… I've never gone to office that early. I go down about over 9 o'clock and I stayed till late at night. Come back exhausted.[66]

But he enjoyed working full-time on what was supposed to be a part-time job.

> I can tell you that we were so immersed in work, I was so immersed in work, that it took your full time. I was not able to attend much attention to my business. The main idea was to get things going. And I didn't even know within six months that we had quite a massive block of flats in Queenstown, until one day I was driving with the Prime Minister going round at dusk I think, then he says, "My gosh, that is quite a lot already up and you should announce

it." We were so immersed in work that we didn't regard it as any achievement, until someone who has been knowing it or who is from outside, look at it and say, "Well, my God, this is a tremendous amount of work that has been put in." And we have made good progress.[67]

The HDB was off to a good start. Lim had won the accolade that would stick to him: Breaking the back of the housing problem in Singapore. However, much more would need to be done to transform the country's housing landscape. Lim would continue to contribute to that transformation.

Notes

1. Housing and Development Board Singapore, *Annual Report 1960* (Singapore: Government Printing Office, 1963), p. 1. Henceforth HDB Annual Report 1960.
2. L. Rayman, "Foreword", in *The Work of the Singapore Improvement Trust 1927–1947*, compiled by J.M. Fraser, Manager, Improvement Trust (Singapore: Singapore Improvement Trust, 1948). Henceforth *Singapore Improvement Trust*.
3. Ibid.
4. Ibid., pp. 4–5.
5. Ibid., p. 6.
6. Ibid., p. 7.
7. Ibid., p. 10.
8. Ibid., p. 10.
9. Ibid., p. 7.
10. *HDB Annual Report 1960*, pp. 1–2.
11. Ibid., p. 2.
12. Ibid., p. 2.
13. *Singapore Improvement Trust*, p. 9.
14. Ibid., p. 17.
15. Ibid., p. 13.
16. *HDB Annual Report 1960*, p. 2.
17. Ibid.
18. Ibid., p. 3.
19. Ibid., p. 3.
20. Ibid., p. 4.

21. Ibid., p. 4.
22. Ibid., p. 6.
23. Ibid.
24. Ibid.
25. Ibid.
26. Ibid.
27. Teh Cheang Wan, "Public Housing in Singapore: An Overview", in *Public Housing in Singapore: A Multi-Disciplinary Study*, edited by Stephen H.K. Yeh (Singapore: Singapore University Press for the Housing and Development Board, 1975), p. 6.
28. This section is drawn from biographical notes on Lim Kim San, winner of *The 1965 Ramon Magsaysay Award for Community Leadership*, <www.rmaf. org.ph/Awardees/Biography/BiographyLimKimSan.htm>. Henceforth, Magsaysay.
29. *HDB Annual Report 1960*, p. 8.
30. Ibid.
31. Magsaysay.
32. Ibid.
33. Interview.
34. Lim Kim San, Oral History Interview, by Lily Tan, Oral History Centre, Accession Number 000526/21, Project: Economic Growth of Singapore, 1955–79, Date transcribed: 25 February 1985, pp. 128–29. Hereafter OHI.
35. OHI., p. 140.
36. Ibid., p. 122.
37. Ibid., p. 127.
38. Ibid., p. 128.
39. Teh Cheang Wan, "Public Housing in Singapore: An Overview", op. cit., p. 7.
40. OHI, pp. 141–42.
41. Magsaysay.
42. Ibid.
43. OHI, p. 131.
44. Magsaysay.
45. Ibid.
46. *HDB Annual Report 1960*, p. 9.
47. Magsaysay.
48. OHI, pp. 131–32.
49. Ibid., p. 132.
50. Ibid., p. 167.

51. Ibid.
52. Ibid.
53. Ibid., pp. 168–69.
54. Ibid., p. 170.
55. Ibid.
56. Ibid., p. 136.
57. Ibid., p. 137.
58. Ibid., p. 164.
59. Ibid., p. 140.
60. Ibid., pp. 140–41.
61. Ibid., p. 134.
62. Ibid., p. 132.
63. Ibid., p. 133.
64. Magsaysay.
65. OHI, p. 180.
66. Ibid., p. 126.
67. Ibid., p. 139.

7

Housing a Nation:
Resettling a People

The Housing and Development Board succeeded where the Singapore Improvement Trust had not because Singapore's new leadership was determined to change the face of the nation, both literally and metaphorically. Resettling squatters in the new flats being built was the literal part of that effort, and it changed people's metaphorical view of Singapore as well. Although many Singaporeans were suspicious initially of the resettlement efforts, and many encountered social problems in their transition to high-rise living, the HDB was able to overcome their scepticism. Combined with land acquisition, land reclamation to build houses, and urban renewal, resettlement laid the basis for the construction of low-cost, affordable housing on a mass scale that created a new Singapore landscape and skyline.

RESETTLEMENT

The Land Acquisition Ordinance that was passed in 1920 was amended in 1946 and 1955 to give the colonial government powers to acquire more private land for comprehensive new-town development and to try to stabilize prices. However, the powers granted were limited and the process was troublesome and slow. By contrast, when the People's Action Party came to power, it gave the HDB extensive powers over land acquisition and resettlement, crucial components of the ambitious housing programme that the party had in mind.[1]

Compulsory land acquisition anywhere is a controversial issue. Critics view it as an infringement of the individual's right to own land, while supporters praise it as a vehicle for social equity that enables the majority of people to own homes. The truth is that, without land, there would be no housing. In 1960, only 44 per cent of the land in Singapore was owned by the government, while more than 35 per cent of the population then lived in squatter settlements.[2] Without compulsory land acquisition, draconian though the measure was, the government would have found it difficult to fulfil its promise of creating a more egalitarian society that would underpin Singapore's evolution into a property-owning democracy. Even so, the government was careful to formulate a comprehensive resettlement policy, subject to periodic review, that paid sensitive heed to the sometimes considerable resistance that accompanied slum clearance and the relocation of families.

The HDB's resettlement staff held dialogues with squatters to identify their needs and problems, and these were addressed normally by the time of the relocation. In 1966, the colonial legislation on land acquisition was repealed and the Land Acquisition Act was passed in its place, enabling the government to acquire compulsorily any land of private and commercial use in the public interest. The state would determine the payment of compensation. This approach, which helped to lower the cost of housing provision, resulted eventually in 85 per cent of land passing to state ownership.[3] *Housing A Nation: 25 Years of Public Housing in Singapore* notes the crucial role that the resettlement policy played in eradicating slums and freeing the land for public projects such as housing, infrastructure (roads, sewers and drainage), public utilities and urban renewal — even as resettlement provided slum dwellers living in squalid conditions access to a better standard of housing.[4] As for compensation, before 1964, non-farming squatters affected by resettlement action could opt for the allocation of land with standard basic houses free of charge in agricultural settlements, or for the allocation of SIT/HDB accommodation. They were not eligible for compensation. Farmers, by contrast, were allocated land with free standard basic houses in agricultural settlements plus *ex gratia* compensation.[5]

Resettlement was not easy. Lim Kim San understood that people did not like to be evicted from their houses. Yet, the only way that the HDB could build on a large scale was to move people from one area and have a high density of construction in the places vacated by squatters or single-storey buildings. In order to make resettlement transparent and smooth, the HDB's Resettlement Advisory Committee drew up payments for property acquired and settled difficulties. However, even when rehoused, some people faced problems because they had to start budgeting to pay the rent and charges for light and water. There was one case where more than half of the people who had been removed from River Valley Road to Queenstown returned within a few months, largely because some of them found it difficult to budget their expenses, while others preferred to go back to the squatter huts where they could rear a few chickens and eat them. Moving back meant saving on food, water and light bills.[6]

Lim's most unpleasant time at the HDB came after he had moved office to Princess House in Queenstown because he did not want to be with Ong Eng Guan at Pickering Street.

> And one day I came back after lunch and I smelt very strong smell of pigs. I was told there was a delegation of pig farmers to see me — women. Well, I'll face a mob of angry men anytime after the angry women... Because they were really rough and they used foul language. You cannot swear them in return. And they were very angry in moving them and their pigs out.[7]

They were Hokkien-speaking village women, "in their dark clothing, grimy, hair all over the place, ranging from quite elderly to in their thirties, and some of them young".[8] They were a motley crowd, and very noisy. "You cannot make sense of what they say. You only know that they are very abusive. So there was no point in discussing anything with them. My officers had to move them."[9] The problem was resolved by giving the farmers time to sell the stock that they had and move away from pig-rearing. Some of the farmers were settled in Tampines.

Lim recalled another instance of opposition, this time to the government acquiring graveyards in Tiong Bahru to build houses.

> So a delegation of very old people whom I know — and one of them is my third uncle — came along, wanted to see me. So I met them. And he says, "You know, our grandparents…" I don't know. My grandparent is not there. But they say, "Well, our grandparents, our '*Chor Kong*' (Choo Sien) [ancestors] all buried there, and you are going to acquire and take off…."[10]

What did Lim do? "Well, I just asked them a simple question: 'Do you want me to look after our dead grandparents or do you want to look after your grandchildren?' "[11] There was no reply; they walked off. That particular battle was won.

Another battle was waged over the pricing of the rental flats that the HDB built in its initial years. It was an eye-opener for slum dwellers that accommodation of that quality would be available to them and would be within their reach, a price possible because rentals were being pegged at 20 per cent of the average income. Hence, the rent for a one-room flat was S$20, for a two-room flat S$40, and for a three-room flat S$60. The figures reflected both what the population could afford to pay, and what the government could afford to spend. Given the kind of subsidy that the government was paying for the Kallang estate, a small one compared to estates that it was going to build, it would have gone bankrupt with its massive building programme. Rationalizing the rental on the 20/40/60 basis prevented a heavy subsidy from landing on the government. However, putting the formula forward to the public would prove to be Lim's first exercise in public relations and in politics.

> We went down there — three nights I think, with Member of Parliament — to explain to the tenants there why we have got to

raise rent. And I realise that though the Chinese in our population are good businessmen and businesswomen, when it affected their pocket, they cannot see that 2 and 2 makes 4. It's a good lesson. No matter how you explain why and the rationale behind all this, they won't see because their pockets are affected. [But] anyway, we had to do it.[12]

Bukit Ho Swee Fire

Public perceptions of resettlement could be so dim that, Lim reminisced, a rumour had been going around insinuating that the HDB was encouraging the firing of crackers so that there could be a fire and it could then acquire the land for building. He debunked the idea. "Which was nonsense! I mean, the tragedy of a huge fire is terrible."[13]

Lim was referring to the biggest fire in Singapore's history. It broke out in a squatter district in Bukit Ho Swee on 25 May 1961. It killed one man; injured several others badly; devastated 60 acres (24 hectares); destroyed two oil mills, three timber yards, and three motor workshops; and rendered about 16,000 people homeless.[14]

Lim was at the races when the fire broke out. He could see the smoke. Later, he went down to the area with National Development Minister Tan Kia Gan (who had succeeded Ong Eng Guan). They arrived at about dusk. They could see the embers. Lim wondered what to do.

> And the first thing that struck me was that we should stop people from rebuilding. Because from past experience, we know that after the fire, people moved in and the squatter huts were up immediately. So we made sure and gave orders to the police to prevent people from bringing scaffoldings and all that. And in fact, they [sic] very next morning they were bringing in and the police stopped them in time. Otherwise we would have another problem in trying to re-house the fire victims.[15]

The decision to cordon off the place was not an easy one to take. The police commissioner warned Lim that there could be a riot. He replied that he would take responsibility.

The morning after the fire, Lee Kuan Yew toured the wreckage and promised the victims that homes would be found for them.[16] On the same day, the government declared that it would acquire compulsorily the burned-out land as a site for 12,000 low-cost flats, the first of which would be completed within nine months. On 3 June, just a little more than a week after the disaster, 6,000 people were moved from the temporary relief camps where they had been put up, to new HDB flats that were ready elsewhere. The remaining victims were moved to new quarters over the next few days. Immediately as well, the housing board's planners began to draw up a comprehensive development plan for the area. Less than a month after the fire, bids were called for the construction of the first five blocks of 768 flats; they were completed by February 1962, nine months after the fire, as promised. Other blocks were constructed over the following two years for 8,218 flats, which were finished and ready for occupation by the end of 1964. Meanwhile, in January 1963, two primary schools to accommodate 4,000 children were completed. Later in the same year, a creche, a children's health centre and a maternity clinic were developed on the ground floor of one of the ten-storey residential blocks. A 0.6 hectare playground was laid out in 1964 and the existing community centre was enlarged. In just over four years, all of the 16,000 people who had lost their homes in the terrible fire had been rehoused on the same site. It was a momentous event.

The Bukit Ho Swee fire had consequences for the law on land acquisition as well. An amendment was passed that allowed land that had been devastated by fire to be acquired at not more than a third of the value of the vacant site, unless the minister specified otherwise. The one-third figure was meant to ensure that landlords did not benefit unduly from an appreciation in the value of their land that would then be free from any encumbrances. Also, the Foreshores Act was amended in 1964 to exclude payment of compensation for damages to owners who had lost their sea-frontage owing to land reclamation.[17]

Unfortunately, the speed and efficiency of the government's response to the disaster caused some people to think that the housing board had started the fire on purpose and had been prepared to deal with it. Lim dismissed such speculation. "It's through the experience of our architects."[18] Also, Bukit Ho Swee was in Havelock Road, where services such as water, light and sewerage were already available. Hence it was possible to build houses there in nine months, compared to the much longer time necessary to build estates where such services had to be provided first. When Lim died in 2006, allegations about the government's putative role in the Bukit Ho Swee fire resurfaced on the Internet, particularly among elderly Singaporeans who remembered the days when Lim had presided over the slum clearance campaign. "What happened in the aftermath of kampong fires left a lasting imprint on the social memory of Singapore up to the present," Loh Kah Seng writes, although he describes the accusations as rumours.[19]

In remembering Lim's contribution to Singapore's public housing, Lee recalled the political importance of rebuilding Bukit Ho Swee:

> I don't think any single person created the Housing Board with the mission that evolved over time. The first task at that time was to meet the urgent housing shortage and a crying need to show quick results. We had promised during the elections that we would build low-cost housing. A fire had burnt out a squatter settlement of some 50,000 people at Bukit Ho Swee. We had to produce results. His job was to get the Housing Board to revamp the old SIT, which was very slow, cumbersome, built solid buildings but wasn't at a speed and at a cost that was needed. He responded to that challenge. So one of the first completed estates was for the resettlement of the Bukit Ho Swee fire victims, one-room flats with common toilets and common kitchens. But they were living in shacks with plastic sheets, cardboard or whatever. He produced results. HDB developed out of a series of successive decisions we made.[20]

Outcomes in Bukit Ho Swee had a direct impact on Singapore's electoral politics.

> First, we had to win the 1963 elections. To win the 1963 elections, we had to produce Bukit Ho Swee estate. For my constituency in Tanjong Pagar, that was targeted by the communists to knock me out during elections, we put up a block of buildings in Cantonment Road, which is now being demolished for the "Pinnacle" to be put up. During the elections it was unfinished. I said: "You vote me in, I'll see to its completion." That helped. In 1964 it was completed. I opened it officially and people moved in. It became a symbol of what we can deliver. After that, with urban renewal when we started rebuilding from the fringes, east and the west of the city, we implemented our idea of intermingling the races to avoid a repeat of communal riots in 1964. It was a successive series of decisions which grew out of the problems that we met. Later we decided that we'll also have a home-owner society, and we started building up the CPF. It was not something comprehensively conceived at the beginning but plans that evolved with the problems we had to solve.[21]

A Better Lifestyle

In retrospect, the resettlement programme was a success. Independent commentators note how, in almost every case, "families regarded the move to a Housing and Development Board apartment as an improvement in their standard of living". Although high-rise apartment complexes are seen usually as forbidding examples of crowded, high-density housing, the apartments in Singapore were much less crowded than the subdivided shophouses or squatter shacks that they had replaced. Between 1954 and 1970, the average number of rooms per household increased from 0.76 to 2.15, and the average number of persons per room decreased from 4.84 to 2.52. At the family level, moving to a public housing flat was associated with a family structure in which husband and wife made important decisions together, as well as with a family's perception of itself as being middle class rather than working class. At the social level, the most important consequence of resettlement was that it allowed the government to break up ethnically exclusive communities characterized by their area of residence, and bring the races together by ensuring that the ethnic composition of every apartment block reflected that of the country as a whole. As ethnic clustering gave way to inter-communal living, "Malays, Indians, and Chinese of various speech groups lived next door to each other, shared stairwells, community centers, and swimming pools, patronized the same shops, and waited for buses together."[22]

In his Oral History Interview, Lim addressed quality-of-life issues connected to high-rise living.

> From very early we knew that we had got to build high because of the limitation of our land size. And as you progress you'll find that the technical know-how is there. If we have alternative, we would not have built so high all over the place because it costs more to build high than to build low. But we have no alternative. And at first, well, it was not very sophisticated, you know, one, two, three rooms. No artistic licence was given to the architect. It's largely because of cost and largely because of speed. But as you go on later on, the planners, from the lessons they learned than from going abroad, they were able to learn how to make the town a better place to live in.[23]

Lim was aware that village-dwelling Singaporeans would need to get used to living in high apartment blocks, but he reiterated that there was no alternative to it, and noted one important distinction between high-rise living in Europe and in Singapore.

> People just disliked to be pulled away from their place of residence and go to a new place and mix with new people. But as I said, we have no alternative. If we want to house that many people, if the people of Singapore want satisfactory housing instead of attap huts and slums, you have got to go high. And one thing I personally was not worried because I've been to some of the cities in Europe and find that people don't tend to congregate because there's some problem living in high-rise flats. There they all get cooped

up. But here, because our climate is easy, people would like to be in the open rather than be cooped up in their flats. And, well, our problem here is to keep away the sunlight, let the air flow in. Their problem is to try and bring in the sunlight if they can — and there's very little sunlight there — but to keep out the cold. Which means they are all cloistered up and people don't get to see each other. But here, no.[24]

There was a major difference between projects carried out by the SIT and those executed by the HDB. The SIT's planning had been based largely on the principles used for the post-war British "New Towns", with their emphasis on small neighbourhoods and maximum privacy between individual homes. But where most of the people who would move into Queenstown were concerned, "a degree of communal living — the easy mingling between neighbours, the noise and cheerful clatter of women gossiping and children playing, the general feeling of togetherness — was what they were accustomed to and enjoyed. To have deprived them of it, in deference to a well-meaning but quite alien set of planning principles, would have been a great mistake."[25]

Hence, HDB architects were told to recast plans for the remaining three neighbourhoods to achieve both higher population density and a more Asian feel, without cutting down on communal amenities. These amenities were provided in the ratio of roughly one community centre, one market and shopping centre and one health clinic for each neighbourhood, and roughly one primary school for each living section and one secondary school for every four sections. The bigger department stores, supermarkets, better restaurants, banks, and post office would be located in the main town centre. Allocation was made for children's playgrounds and sports areas, carpark areas, and green belts. Sites were set aside for six churches, a mosque, a Chinese temple and, in the town centre, for three cinemas. Finally, space was left for half a dozen petrol stations.[26]

The layout of the housing estates reflected the government's efforts to improve residents' social awareness. Community centres helped tenants to adapt to the new way of living. "Having come from slums, many had to be educated to the use of garbage chutes and minimum standards of cleanliness. Most children had never seen an elevator and women were frightened to get in them. People had to be educated to their use, and instilled with a sense of civic responsibility to help keep them clean and free from litter."[27] Housing and maintenance inspectors visited tenants regularly to ensure that they obeyed rules that made it possible for people to live in a large community without infringing on the rights of others. Estate officers intervened in occasional squabbles among neighbours, and tried to resolve matters amicably.[28]

To conserve land, blocks of multi-storeyed flats, two to sixteen storeys high, were built. "Variety and a balanced effect are achieved by blending blocks of varying heights and design within the same neighborhood. The almost endless variations in plan and elevation insure that there is no drab uniformity and that each of the Board's estates has a personality of its own."[29]

The interior design of the blocks, however, in both Queenstown and the other estates, conformed to a fairly narrow range of standard plans that were efficient and gave value for money. The basic one-room unit consisted of a living-bedroom opening on a multi-purpose balcony where "the housewife can do her washing and ironing, the schoolchildren their homework, or the father play mahjong with his friends"; a kitchen incorporating a built-in refuse chute; and a bathroom-toilet. In the two and three-room units, the same basic living area was provided plus one or two bedrooms. All blocks of flats enjoyed communicating corridors or balconies. Lifts were mandated for all blocks that were more than five storeys high.[30]

In time, expectations of public housing had changed among the population. While the HDB had made provision for essential facilities such as markets and schools in its original town planning, and had visualized industrial towns to be nearby some of the big estates, luxuries such as swimming pools and sports facilities came to be included naturally later.

> The original planning was just sheer housing because it was a necessity. It's only when your standard of living goes up and you begin to think of the finer points of life that the other amenities come in... Your requirements increase and your expectations increase, so you go to four rooms, five rooms and HUDC.[31]

Housing was proof that Singapore was moving from an era of needs to one of rising expectations. Lim Kim San would make his presence felt on the new front in a new role soon to appear.

Notes

1. "Provision of Public Housing in Singapore", <http://72.14.235.104/search?q= cache:Fbwg3OOM6u4J:tcdc.undp.org/sie/experiences/vol4/Public%2520 housing.pdf+resettlement,+singapore,+housing&hl=en&ct=clnk&cd=1&gl=sg>.
2. Belinda Yuen, "Squatters No More: Singapore Social Housing", *Global Urban Development Magazine* 3, no. 1 (2007), <www.globalurban.org/GUDMag07 Vol3Iss1/Yuen.htm>.
3. Ibid.
4. Lim Hoon Yong, "Resettlement: Policy, Process and Impact", in *Housing A Nation: 25 Years of Public Housing in Singapore*, edited by Aline K. Wong and Stephen H.K. Yeh (Singapore: Maruzen Asia for Housing & Development Board, 1985), pp. 306–307.
5. Ibid., p. 309.
6. Lim Kim San, Oral History Interview, by Lily Tan, Oral History Centre, Accession Number 000526/21, Project: Economic Growth of Singapore, 1955–79, Date transcribed: 25 February 1985, p. 143. Hereafter OHI.
7. OHI, p. 149.
8. Ibid., p. 150.
9. Ibid.
10. Ibid.
11. Ibid.
12. Ibid., p. 148.
13. Ibid., p. 144.
14. Tan Lay Yuen, "Bukit Ho Swee Fire", <http://infopedia.nlb.gov.sg/articles/ SIP_825_2004-12-30.html>.
15. OHI, p. 145.

16. The following section is from "Biography of Lim Kim San", in *The 1965 Ramon Magsaysay Award for Community Leadership*, <www.rmaf.org.ph/Awardees/Biography/BiographyLimKimSan.htm>.

17. <htp://72.14.235.104/search?q=cache:Fbwg3OOM6u4J:tcdc.undp.org/sie/experiences/vol4/Public%2520housing.pdf+resettlement,+housing,+singapore&hl=en&ct=clnk&cd=6&gl=sg> .

18. OHI, p. 144.

19. Loh Kah Seng, "Fires and the Social Politics of Nation-Building in Singapore", Asia Research Centre, Murdoch University, Working Paper no. 149, May 2008, n.p.

20. Interview.

21. Ibid.

22. "Singapore: Population Distribution and Housing Policies", in *Singapore*, Library of Congress Country Studies, <http://lcweb2.loc.gov/cgi-bin/query/r?frd/cstdy:@field(DOCID+sg0042)>.

23. OHI, p. 161.

24. Ibid., pp. 161–62.

25. Magsaysay.

26. Ibid.

27. Ibid.

28. Ibid.

29. Ibid.

30. Ibid.

31. OHI, p. 162.

8

Housing a Nation:
Owning Homes, Reclaiming Land

In 1963, Lim Kim San stepped down from the Housing Development Board (HDB) chairmanship only to step up politically. Prime Minister Lee Kuan Yew had asked him to run in the General Election that year. Unlike the 1959 elections, which Lim had declined to contest, he agreed this time because he did not owe banks any money, there was someone who could run his family business, and he was convinced by the PAP's leadership's argument that corrupt politicians should not be allowed to decide Singapore's future. Lim ran, and won the Cairnhill constituency. Two ministers, Kenny Byrne and Tan Kia Gan, lost their seats. Lim told Lee that he did not want to hold political office because he had his work to attend to. But the party was short of people, and he was made Minister for National Development. He could not refuse. Moreover, he was told that his ministerial work was going to be temporary. As it turned out, he would hold a variety of ministerial portfolios for seventeen years.

MINISTRY OF NATIONAL DEVELOPMENT

When Tan Kia Gan, the National Development Minister under whom Lim had served, lost his seat, Tan was appointed HDB Chairman in a reversal of places with Lim. Lim said that he would have supported Tan for the chairman's job because he knew his job and could work well. It is not that Lim had no reservations about Tan. He recalled an occasion when the minister tried to interfere with him and get him to agree to one of his friends coming in as a tenderer and give him a special concession. Tan brought Lim to lunch on a false pretext and he met some people. Lim made his displeasure clear. There was another instance when Tan wanted him to award a certain contract. Lim disagreed and told Tan that, as minister, he had the right to overrule him. However, "it never occurred to me that he was up to anything fishy". Perhaps he was only trying to help a friend. So Lim would have recommended him for the HDB chairmanship because "when I am Minister and he is Chairman, there's no reason why I cannot control him if I wanted to."[1]

As minister for national development, Lim did not have to take care of as many executive and administrative details as he had had to do as HDB chairman. He was relieved. Morale in the ministry was high. But he was not satisfied with the pace at which people worked. Once a week, he called the Public Works Department (PWD) staff to make them work faster because less than 50 per cent of the allocation was being spent. That meant that the PWD was not carrying out the development works that had been budgeted for. The other change he carried out was to set up a coordinating body to ensure that the various statutory boards that were digging up roads would come together so that the roads would not be dug up and closed repeatedly. Under him, the Ministry of National Development embarked on a programme of urban renewal, with emphasis being placed on flyovers and roundabouts to improve traffic conditions. New towns, such as Woodlands, Nee Soon and Ang Mo Kio, emerged.

Home Ownership
The housing shortage had been alleviated to such an extent by the end of 1963 that the HDB, which had concentrated till then on building rental flats, could turn to the issue of home ownership. In February 1964, a "Home Ownership for the People" scheme was

launched to facilitate the emergence of a property-owning democracy in Singapore by enabling lower middle-income group citizens to own their own homes. The scheme was limited to those with an income not exceeding S$800 a month. The HDB offered loans to those who could not buy their homes outright, and worked out the sums so that, after the initial deposit had been paid, owners would pay less in instalments than they would have done in rents. This was an incentive for people to buy their own homes, become a property owner, and develop a stake in a country to which he was now rooted.[2]

The Home Ownership Scheme became "the overarching framework within which more detailed housing schemes, policies and procedures were formulated".[3] (In 1968, legislation was enacted to allow members to withdraw from their Central Provident Fund savings to finance the purchase of HDB units.) The scheme resulted in the decline of the rental proportion of public housing over the years. The fraction of HDB housing units in rental occupancy fell from 100 per cent in the early 1960s to 76 per cent at the end of 1970, to 38 per cent in 1981, and to 16 per cent in 1989. In keeping with this trend, the HDB stopped building rental units and satisfied the declining demand for rental units through vacated rental flats. The government used the HDB's virtual monopoly on the housing market to set, through the Ministry of National Development, low prices for flats that took into account the state of the economy and how much the public could afford to pay. State interventionism encouraged home ownership, even amongst those in the lowest income brackets. Wealth redistribution was effected through subsidies that were differentiated according to the various classes of housing: The larger the housing unit, the smaller the subsidy. At the same time, the government retained ownership over the land because owners of public housing held a 99-year lease to their property. This leasehold arrangement essentially separated the housing unit from the land and allowed the government to compensate and resettle any lessee if and when the land may be required for development.

The social and political consequences of home ownership were considerable.

> There were jobs. Stomach was quite full. And once you own a property, you become more stable, isn't it?.... So between the alternative of having a home and having a job and going out into the streets and fighting the government and fighting the authority, between the two, most people would choose to stay at home. Yes.[4]

Indeed, the success of the housing programme contributed directly to the People's Action Party winning the 1963 General Election.

The HDB's massive, and labour-intensive building programme also had a direct influence on the economy: It generated employment for large numbers of people. When the programme began, it was estimated that every two units would generate employment for one person directly — at the construction site — and for another person indirectly — in the building materials industry, in transport, and in other supporting facilities. Many of those employed were carpenters, bricklayers and plumbers; other unskilled workers were trained as draftsmen, clerks and housing and maintenance inspectors.[5] Building and construction led to pump-priming the economy and had a multiplier effect, creating jobs. Also, the demand for vast quantities of building materials — steel, cement, plywood, paint, bricks, hollow blocks, sanitary fittings, and hardware — resulted in the growth of a large number of factories and other businesses. Moreover, the HDB's building programme allowed the private building industry to benefit from lower costs brought about by standardization, from the availability of building materials, and from a growing skilled labour force.[6] So great was the economic ferment created by housing that even at that time, those who had been part of the Works Brigade, which was training people in construction, quit because it was a back-breaking job done in the sun and in all sorts of weather. This was one reason why Singapore had to depend on foreign workers later to keep its construction industry going.

One area in which Lim made his mark was his determination to stamp out a housing racket that had developed. Some developers were entering the market without adequate financial resources, their sole aim being to make quick profits. Their housing schemes entailed using land-held mortgage and erecting houses of low standards without indicating when they would be completed. In November 1964, Lim introduced legislation to license and control all housing developers. To protect the public, one of the provisions of the legislation was that a company of housing developers must have not less than $500,000 paid-up capital, and a partnership or individual must deposit $100,000 with the Controller.[7]

Land Reclamation

As the government pushed ahead ambitiously with its goal of housing Singapore, the scarcity of land in the city-state became an issue. It was clear that the state would have to play an active role in ensuring optimal land use. As with the broader issue of housing, political will drove the government to adopt tough measures, including foreshore reclamation without being subject to claims for loss of shoreline, that it deemed essential to prevent the haphazard or wasteful use of land. Vested private interests were not allowed to come in the way of the principle that development should benefit the majority of the people. The government undertook measures to provide adequate land for subsided public housing, industries, and comprehensive redevelopment.[8]

In the words of Lee Kuan Yew,

> Land reclamation started with the East Coast. There were several benefits. One, the British had allowed people to own properties right up to the coastline. So the coast was occupied by private properties and was denied to the public. If we knocked down Seletar Hills and had this conveyor belt to reclaim the land, we'd be able to have the seaside open to the public and also a through road without any encumbrances. At that time, property prices were right down because people had no confidence in the future of

Singapore. External investors had no confidence, and even our domestic investors were not certain of the future. So I could pass a law allowing all sea frontages to be reclaimed without compensation. Otherwise, they would have demanded compensation for loss of seafront, and that would have been costly. At one stroke, we were able to reclaim the seafront. Later reclamation was extended to the West Coast also without any compensation for lost seafront. That enabled us to develop the whole coastline. If we tried to do it today, we would have big problems. Private owners would get together and put up tremendous resistance. Even when we acquire HDB flats for SERS, to rebuild taller blocks, some owners oppose it because they like their flats as they are. They've a strong sense of "this is my property". At that time, there was no confidence that anything was going to last for ever. So we said: "Okay, let's make the country more secure."[9]

It was in this context that the government entered the picture. It was building on a massive scale, and it was important for it to own more land than anybody else. On one of Lim's trips before he worked at the Housing Board, he had visited Sweden, which had a satellite town called Vallingby. He met some of officials there, and discovered that the municipality was the biggest owner of land, largely because it was then easy to build for the public. The visit stuck in his mind. Many of his HDB colleagues, including Howe Yoon Chong, thought about the same issue.[10]

In May 1965, Lim announced a reclamation plan to push the sea further away from Singapore. HDB engineers had thought closely about reclamation when 80 hectares of Changi had been bought from Credit Fonsia at a very low price. There were some hills there and a sort of a cove along Tanah Merah. A trial reclamation of 1.2–1.6 hectares was carried out. His officers wanted to see whether the reclamation would affect the harbour by causing silting. Once reclamation was found to work, the HDB planned bigger reclamation projects. The first project was carried out quietly in Bedok. The Housing Board brought in Dutch experts, who thought that the best way was by suction, that is, sucking the mud from the sea. But the best way was to cut the hills and fill them. Engineers began to study how to do so. Coal-mining machinery — a fan-like contraption that cut into the hill — was bought from Germany. But the clay was so abrasive that the blades that cut into the hill — blades that were supposed to last for a few days — lasted merely a few hours. Lim's staff had to sit down with the manufacturer and study what sort of blades needed to be used. Another problem was that it was difficult to traverse busy Serangoon Road for reclamation in Kallang. That problem was resolved by buying a Bailey bridge from the British. It became an overhead bridge over which the conveyor crossed. [11]

Cost was not the issue: Reclamation cost only about 80 cents per square foot. The larger issue was ecology. The HDB had simulations done on whether the harbour would silt; the results said not. Simulations were carried out everytime there were plans for reclamation to see whether the port would silt. "But on the ecological side, no, I don't think we gave much thought to it, largely because there's no fishing around here and all that."[12]

Lim remembered something interesting.

> I was living by the sea then, next to the Swimming Club. And you can see the sand piling up everytime there's a South-west monsoon, and [with] the Northeast monsoon the sand recedes. Oh, one of the reasons also why we felt we could reclaim was because one or two miles offshore — in Bedok at that time — you can see a sand bar. So we knew that in between it's quite shallow and you would be able to fill it up. What I was worried about from the silting of the harbour is: can we get a good beach? And after some trial and error, we find that, eh, yes, as I said, you know, the sand piles up during the South-east monsoon when the wind is blowing there. And then later on, I read in a magazine that somewhere in America, by putting up a T formation, you sort of collect the sand in coves. And that I think I told the Prime Minster and it was passed on [to] the PWD. And you see all those T formations coming up. And the strange thing is: some Americans came one day and said, "How did you get it done?" Actually I saw it in a magazine and read about. And here they come back and find from us how it is to be done.[13]

Lim's regard for foreign experts was not necessarily high. On one occasion, a World Bank mission visited him. Its members asked him: "What makes you think that you are ready for urban renewal?" He asked them when they had arrived. They replied that it was the previous night. He said: "Will you take a look round town? Come back next week and see me." The team went around Singapore. The following week, they called on him with a memo providing all the reasons that he and his team already believed they had for urban renewal. "They were very good in putting our thoughts into words."[14] By contrast, "in the end, my faith in our own people proved to be right."[15] And the urban renewal programme was on.

Lim's work in public housing and other areas of national development did not go unchallenged. Opposition members of the Legislative Assembly questioned the minister, and often grilled him, on a diverse range of issues — from the rate at which the Housing Board was constructing public housing, and the Public Works Department was building roads; to the fate of farmers affected by development, and the extent to which private developers were being allowed to operate; to the nitty-gritty of tenants making unauthorized repairs to houses, and the intricacies of the widening of roads. He handled the specifics of the questions with an unfaltering grasp of detail, displaying signs of petulance only, and rarely, when opposition legislators refused to accept his answers in trying to score political points.

During an acrimonious debate in December 1963, Lim castigated the opposition for arguing that thousands of HDB flats were vacant, that they were not really low-cost, that the rents were too high, and that the HDB was making money like a landlord. He pointed out that success of public housing lay in the fact that no longer did 13,000 families have to take their place on a waiting list and clamour for a few flats that became available and, on being allocated one, rejoice as if they had struck a lottery. The results of the previous elections represented a conclusive endorsement of the government's housing programme. The people had returned a PAP candidate by an overwhelming majority in every electoral ward that had seen housing development. Experts from all over the world had acknowledged that the HDB's building costs were the lowest. Also, nowhere else in Southeast Asia had a government sought to house a fourth of its population in low-cost flats at the rates that the HDB was charging. "Far from being a landlord and making money out of the rentals of the flats, I would like to state that the Housing Board's accounts show an annual deficit," Lim declared.[16]

The activities of the Works Brigade also came under scrutiny in the assembly. One legislator argued that, in organizing the brigade, the PAP was not really concerned with the welfare of workers, but was interested merely in making use of it as a political instrument. Another legislator alleged that two brigade members in his constituency were secret society members who had furthered the PAP's ends during the election campaign. Lim responded with an emphatic defence of the brigade. He argued that the legislators were trying to smear the reputation of the entire organization of about 2,000 people just because it contained a few members who, the opposition party Barisan Sosialis imagined, were gangsters. As for some brigade members having helped the PAP outside office hours, there was no reason why they could not do so. For that matter, he believed that some members might have helped the Barisan.[17] The exchange dramatized how quickly Lim had developed, since his entry to the Legislative Assembly, the art of responding in detail to criticism of particular aspects of government policy while making larger points about Singapore's governance as well.

Lim appeared to enjoy crossing swords with the opposition, putting it down with wit. For example, he once referred wryly to his opponents as "the boys opposite". The choice of words incensed the legislator whom he was debating, and the Legislative Assembly chairman asked: "Will the minister refer to the opposition as 'members'?" Lim answered without skipping a beat: "Well, hon.

Members who behave like boys." That led a legislator to declare: "That is worse than saying they are boys". But Lim got away with his choice of words.[18]

There were occasions, however, when debates went beyond thrust-and-parry and turned deadly serious. On one occasion, Ong Lian Teng, Member for Bukit Panjang, asked whether the government had used public funds to please its own members. He alleged that some local contractors "who are somewhat related" to the PAP got tenders easily. A big company "which is somehow related" to the PAP had been guilty of malpractices. He challenged Lim to set up a "commission of inquiry" to investigate these matters. But if Lim wanted him to provide names and facts, "I think he had better not become the Minister" since, all the files being in the government's hands, it should be in a better position than opposition members to understand what was going on.[19] In a robust rejoinder, Lim said that Ong had made a serious allegation and challenged him to repeat it outside the House, where he would not be covered by parliamentary privilege. The government had been able to bring down the cost of public housing much lower than it was ever before, Lim said, without a whiff of corruption. Ong refused to budge, challenging the government again to set up an inquiry commission. In a robust reply, Lim argued that the PAP was the last party to be afraid of an inquiry commission, but it was not going to set one up when it was not certain that there was anything to investigate. There were many engineers in Singapore who surely would have sent him information had they been suspicious that roads were not up to specification or some other malpractice was occurring. He would have set up a commission of inquiry then. "There is no question about it."[20]

Lim took on Ong Eng Guan, his old nemesis who was on the opposition benches by then, in November 1964. Ong launched a personal attack on Lim, saying that Lee Kuan Yew had claimed that Lim was the only person who had broken the backbone of Singapore's housing problem. Ong said that it had not been Lim but the bureaucrat

Teh Cheang Wan who had done so. Ong challenged Lim to tell him how he had broken the backbone; if he could not, Ong would tell him how it had been done. Lim replied that he had never claimed that he had broken the backbone of Singapore's housing problem. "I only said that the housing programme was a success because of good team work among a group of people."[21]

MAGSAYSAY AWARD

Lim Kim San was modest in not drawing attention to himself, but others recognized his talent and hard work. In 1962, Lim was the first person to be awarded the Order of Temasek, Singapore's highest state honour that could be held only by twelve people at any one time, for his pioneering work at the HDB. He recalled an earlier reception after a parliamentary meeting where one of "the Barisan boys" had told Prime Minister Lee Kuan Yew: "Oh, this man deserves a medal for doing housing." The suggestion must have struck Lee.[22]

International recognition followed. In 1965, Lim won the Ramon Magsaysay Award for Community Leadership. One day, he was playing golf with Lee, who told him that he was going to receive a Magsaysay. Lim asked what it was, and was told that it was prestigious: Indeed, the Ramon Magsaysay Awards, named after the former Philippine president, are considered Asia's equivalent of the Nobel Prize.

He received the award at a glittering ceremony in Manila on 31 August 1965. The award citation brought out the essence of Lim's contribution to Singapore's national development through housing.[23] The citation noted that throughout Asia, few problems were more acute than those created by people flocking to cities that were unprepared to accept the influx. The slums that usually resulted from this influx were a blot upon any civilized society and made a mockery of popular aspirations for a better way of life. "This dilemma has been resolved in Singapore in a manner that provides a model for much of the world. Completing construction of one new apartment every 45 minutes, on the average, at a cost of less than US$3.00 per square foot, the government can offer every applicant a new home within three days," the citation continued. Lim Kim San was the person primarily responsible for this achievement. He had reorganized an earlier "halting effort" at government-assisted housing, "applying quietly and carefully a businessman's energetic pragmatism to the construction industry". Reclamation and construction of facilities for carefully designed industrial estates and satellite cities now promised that Singapore could "digest" a growing population in a healthy environment.

The citation said that while continuing to expand government housing for less-fortunate citizens, Lim had initiated the first major urban redevelopment programme in Asia to "transform the old port city into a modern metropolis". "The community life that is developing in the glistening, well-managed blocks of flats that have replaced squalid, over-crowded shacks testifies to the concern and probity of the leaders who made this possible."

Lim's response was characteristically modest and to-the-point.[24] He recalled a Malay saying, *Lembu punya minyak sapi punya nama*: "The oil is from the cow but the buffalo gets the credit." So it was with him. The great honour that had been conferred on him, he said, should belong rightly to "the group of young, very dedicated, dynamic and unselfish men and women of my country who, by their hard work, foresight and devotion to duty", had made it possible for Singapore to complete successfully its first five-year low-cost housing programme. It was his good fortune and privilege to be in a position to give them the opportunity to prove their worth. "This Award will undoubtedly spur all of us in Singapore towards fulfilling our aim of bringing about a more just and equal society, wherein every citizen will have the right to live in liberty and happiness and be given equal opportunity and expectation of a better life," he declared.

He went on to make an important political point. "Those of us who have emerged from colonial rule to become free and independent nations sometimes do not have enough confidence in the capacity and ability of our own people," he said.

> My own rather limited experience in the last few years has convinced me that solutions to the problem of nation building lie mainly in our own hands. Reliance on foreign expert advice will bring us far, but not far enough to satisfy the aspirations and desires of our people. The hard and often tiresome work must be done by us and us alone. For it is only the citizens of the country who can get the feel of the situation which is essential in the solution of any vexatious problem.

Lim noted that the HDB had only one expatriate officer among a staff of more than 800 monthly paid, and

> I hope that its record in the field of low-cost housing will convince other emerging countries that there are young men and women among their citizens who, given the opportunity, will show that they not only have the dedication, the determination and the will, but also the capacity and ability to solve their own problems, difficult though they may be.

In his Oral History Interview, Lim disclosed that Filipinos whom he met during his visit to Manila were interested in how to build houses like Singapore. He had a session of a few hours, on tape, where some of the leaders, their contractors and their officials sat with him and discussed the problems of housing. He was confident that the Philippines could overcome its problems: It was a question of political will. Finance was the problem; planning was not because Filipinos were very artistic architects.

As an aside, the Filipino leaders thought that Singapore was a "strange creature".

> And they were more interested in the type of people we have in the government than in our policies… And they were analysing me and then came to the conclusion that, like the Prime Minister and all that, we are extroverts. So they were more interested in what kind of people runs Singapore, what it is, than what our

policies are. In the same way, I think at the very beginning, Thailand... Of course Malaysia knows us. Thailand was looking at us — oh, this little fellow won't amount to much, so why bother with it. We didn't make any impact on them, even with that housing and all that.[25]

Nevertheless, the Magsaysay Award recognized just how far Singapore had come by way of national development. The award was a tribute to the role that Lim had played at the HDB and during his less than two-year stint at the ministry, which he left on 8 August 1965, on the eve of Singapore's ejection from Malaysia and the city-state's emergence as a sovereign nation.

MND AGAIN

In June 1975, Lim returned to the Ministry of National Development (to hold the concurrent portfolio of Communications from August that year) and served there till the end of January 1979. In these years, his ministry continued to transform the Singapore landscape. Major projects included the development of Changi Airport to meet Singapore's growing civil aviation needs; the development of a new University of Singapore campus and a general-cum-teaching hospital at Kent Ridge; the renewal of the Central Area; the reclamation of land for the Marina Centre off Collyer Quay; the building of the East Coast Expressway; the transformation of reclaimed land along the East Coast into a recreational area, the East Coast Park; and the implementation of the Area Licensing Scheme to reduce traffic congestion in the Central Business District during morning peak hours.

Housing remained one of the ministry's key achievements as Lim fine-tuned the HDB's policies. In 1975, the HDB rearranged its building programme to speed up the allocation of flats to those who wanted to rent them. This change was meant to address the more urgent need for housing among those applying to rent.[26] The larger picture was that, with the completion of more than 28,000 public housing units in 1975, bringing the total number of low-cost housing units since the HDB's inception in 1960 to almost 235,000 units, about half of Singapore's population was housed in them.[27] That figure rose to 59 per cent in 1977,[28] and 63 per cent in 1978.[29] Following on from the First (1960–65), Second (1966–70), Third (1971–75) Five-Year Building Programmes, the Fourth Five-Year Programme (1976–80) looked at housing 70 per cent of the population in HDB flats by the end of 1980, with the majority living in flats bought under the Home Ownership for the People Scheme.[30] The ministry continued also with the Housing and Urban Development Corporation's (HUDC) housing programmes for middle-income groups that were not eligible for low-cost housing.[31]

The HDB's work created rising expectations that could turn acrimonious. The resentment was apparent during the Budget Debate in March 1976, when several members of parliament criticized the HDB over issues such as the way in which housing estates were being planned, shop rentals in estates were being drawn up, HDB officials were dealing with shopkeepers and others, and how hawkers were being given space in hawker centres and markets to ply their trades. On the issue of the adverse effects that high-rise living apparently was having on resettled farmers, Lim responded that how well *kampung* folk adjusted to their new living environment depended on how extrovert they were. Noting that a newcomer could feel lonely even in a *kampung*, he said that issue was not the living environment but whether HDB tenants wanted to mingle. As for the fact that tenants could not grow vegetables as they had done in villages, he remarked: "We cannot have garden plots in HDB flats. We have to sacrifice a thing or two for progress." The HDB's increasing role in Singapore life came under scrutiny from MP Hwang Soo Jin (Jalan Kayu), who declared: "It may sound a little far-fetched, but someone did remark to me recently that half of Singapore was in effect ruled by the HDB. Although this was made more in jest than in seriousness, it did lead me to think that there ought to be a serious review of the role and function of the board." Hwang believed that the HDB should be put under more direct and stringent government control.[32]

The Budget session encapsulated concerns over the changes in social behaviour and mental outlook that progress was demanding of citizens,[33] but it also underlined the HDB's irreplaceable role in the life of a new nation. In his second stint as Minister for National Development, Lim Kim San helped to determine the direction that life was taking in Singapore.

Senior Minister Goh Chok Tong described Lim's contribution to housing in Singapore thus:

> As is now common knowledge, he broke the back of Singapore's housing problem. Many people were living in slums and tenements without piped water and modern sanitation. He did a tremendously good job in housing Singaporeans in a very short time. This had great political significance. Because he succeeded in doing so, not only did he meet a keenly felt basic need, but he also gave the PAP its aura of being able to do things for the people. The people supported the PAP in a big way in subsequent elections. I regard that as Mr Lim's bigger contribution. To illustrate, I grew up in a rented private property without electricity and modern sanitation, which was not unusual at that time. Several households lived in the same house. My family moved into a three-room flat in Queenstown in the early Sixties. I marvelled at the hygiene and convenience of the flushed toilet. I voted for the first time soon after. Naturally, my vote went to the PAP.[34]

ECONOMIC DEVELOPMENT BOARD

Much as Lim had moved up from chairing the Housing and Development Board from 1960 to 1963, to being minister in charge of the National Development portfolio, which included the HDB, he was Deputy Chairman of Singapore's Economic Development Board (EDB), from 1961 to 1963 before monitoring the EDB as Finance

Minister from 1965 to 1967. In fact, Lim's EDB posting really was an ex-officio one, largely because of his connection with the HDB.[35]

Singapore was a Third World country in the 1960s with a GNP per capita of less than US$320. Infrastructure was poor, capital was scarce, there was hardly any foreign investment, and the few industries that were present produced goods primarily for domestic consumption. Large-scale unemployment and labour unrest awaited Britain's military withdrawal from Singapore by the end of 1971, which would deprive the island of about 40 per cent of its gross domestic product. Creating jobs was the priority, which demanded attracting labour-intensive industries and the creation of a convivial environment for industrial development.[36]

In 1960, Finance Minister Goh Keng Swee asked a United Nations Industrial Survey Mission to visit Singapore. The mission was led by a Dutch economist, Albert Winsemius, who presented a ten-year development plan to turn Singapore from a port dependent on entrepôt trade to a manufacturing and industrial centre. Following the Winsemius Report, the Legislative Assembly passed an Act in 1961 to create a statutory board to promote industrialization and economic development.

The EDB came into being in August 1961 with a budget of $100 million. It took over from the Singapore Industrial Promotion Board, which had been set up in 1957 but had been found to be inadequate.[37] Goh saw the EDB as one of the most important steps that the government could take to reverse Singapore's parlous economic situation. Hon Sui Sen, then Permanent Secretary of the Economic Development Division in the Ministry of Finance, was seconded to chair the EDB. "If Hon Sui Sen and the EDB had failed, today's Singapore would not have been," Lee Kuan Yew declared years later.[38]

Lim recalled in his Oral History Interview that he had been approached to chair the EDB but had turned down the offer because he was immersed in HDB work. Looking back, he believed that it was right to have a civil servant at the EDB's helm rather than him because, having been a businessman, he would have been extremely tight-fisted in lending money to pioneer industries and permanent residents.[39] That said, "Hon was a very lenient employer, very loyal to his civil servants. And I think they didn't like me because I went there to sort of tighten up things a little bit."[40]

One of the EDB's major achievements lay in transforming a swampy area along the island's west coast into Singapore's first industrial estate. As the swamps were filled and foundations laid for factories and roads, Jurong Industrial Estate became an essential part of the government's desire to convince foreign investors that Singapore was a good place for business. The industrialization programme began with factories that produced clothes, textiles, toys, wood products and hair wigs. But along with these labour-intensive industries, there appeared some capital- and technology-intensive projects, such as Shell Eastern Petroleum and the National Iron and Steel Mills.[41] "An industrialized nation needs iron, steel for construction. And I suppose that is one of the few status symbols which a developing country acquires. But for us, we thought that it was a major industry and there will be requirement of iron and steel in the areas around us as well as for our own," Lim said.[42]

The Jurong Industrial Estate's prospects did not look bright initially, leading it to being called "Dr Goh's folly". But Lim said that he had not been bothered with such publicity. Providing a suitable infrastructure for investors was what mattered, and "we'll set about doing it. And doing it in the cheapest way possible, cheapest and fastest way possible."[43] One problem was the absence of home-grown private entrepreneurs. Lim explained the problem by remarking that, historically, Singapore had been a trading society. It took a lot of convincing and education to get local entrepreneurs interested in manufacturing. Students, too, had to be convinced to switch from white-collar to blue-collar jobs, although the latter paid much better than clerical jobs. "It was a question of prestige."[44]

Although Lim was not involved in the nitty-gritty of the EDB's work, he was extremely perceptive about the regional situation in which the EDB, and Singapore, succeeded in attracting investment. First, Singapore was the first country in the region to industrialize and develop the proper infrastructure. Secondly, the Korean War of the 1950s and the Vietnam War of the 1960s could have provided an impetus for Singapore's development. Thirdly, there were anti-Chinese troubles in Indonesia, which led some Indonesian entrepreneurs to invest in Singapore. Racial polarization in Malaysia similarly led some Malaysians to come to Singapore.[45]

> Just like Hongkong had a very good push when the Communists occupied China and all the Shanghai entrepreneurs went down to Hongkong, and in a smaller way, some of the entrepreneurs came down to Singapore and invested in Jurong. Yes.[46]

However, they came because Singapore was ready for their investment with the proper infrastructure. "We were ready when opportunity knocks."[47]

Notes

1. Lim Kim San, Oral History Interview, by Lily Tan, Oral History Centre, Accession Number 000526/21, Project: Economic Growth of Singapore, 1955–79, Date transcribed: 25 February 1985, p. 182. Hereafter OHI.
2. "Biography of Lim Kim San", in *The 1965 Magsaysay Award for Community Leadership* <www.rmaf.org.ph/Awardees/Biography/BiographyLimKimSan.htm>.
3. This section is drawn from <http://72.14.235.104/search?q=cache:Fbwg 3OOM6u4J:tcdc.undp.org/sie/experiences/vol4/Public%2520housing.pdf+ provision,+public+housing,+singapore&hl=en&ct=clnk&cd=1&gl=sg>.
4. OHI, p. 173.
5. Magsaysay.
6. Ibid.
7. "Housing Developers (Control and Licensing) Bill, *Singapore Legislative Assembly Debates*, 19 November 1964, Volume 23, cols. 787–800.
8. See speech by Lee Yock Suan, then Minister of State for National Development, at a conference, "New Frontiers in Real Estate Investment",

Shangri-La Hotel, 15 April 1982, <http://72.14.235.104/search?q=cache:
aC3hDr_-HD4J:stars.nhb.gov.sg/stars/tmp/lys19820415s.pdf+land+
reclamation,+housing,+singapore&hl=en&ct=clnk&cd=14&gl=sg>.

9. Interview.
10. OHI, p. 159.
11. Ibid., pp. 157–58.
12. Ibid., p. 160.
13. Ibid., pp. 160–61.
14. Ibid., p. 157.
15. Ibid., p. 138.
16. *Singapore Legislative Assembly Debates*, 10 December 1963, Volume 22,
    cols. 239–40.
17. *Singapore Legislative Assembly Debates*, 12 December 1963, Vol. 22,
    cols. 445–51.
18. *Singapore Legislative Assembly Debates*, 18 November 1964, Vol. 23,
    cols. 751–52.
19. *Singapore Legislative Assembly Debates*, 16 November 1964, Vol. 23, col. 533.
20. *Singapore Legislative Assembly Debates*, 16 November 1964, Vol. 23,
    cols. 535–37.
21. *Singapore Legislative Assembly Debates*, 18 November 1964, Vol. 23, col. 708.
22. OHI, p. 176.
23. The citation is available at <www.rmaf.org.ph/Awardees/Citation/
    CitationLimKimSan.htm>.
24. The response is available at <www.rmaf.org.ph/Awardees/Response/
    ResponseLimKimSan.htm>.
25. OHI, pp. 179080.
26. "New HDB Priorities", *Straits Times* (Singapore), 1 November 1975.
    Henceforth *ST*.
27. Ministry of National Development, *Annual Report 1975*, p. 2.
28. Ministry of National Development, *Annual Report 1977*, p. 2.
29. Ministry of National Development, *Annual Report 1978*, p. 3.
30. Ministry of National Development, *Annual Report 1978*, p. 35.
31. Ministry of National Development, *Annual Report 1975*, p. 11.
32. "HDB Under Severe Attack", *ST*, 18 March 1976.
33. For a critique, see Riaz Hassan, *Families In Flats: A Study of Low Income
    Families in Public Housing* (Singapore: Singapore University Press, 1977),
    pp. 199–210. Hassan argues that while for poorer families, increasing
    household expenses and the anxiety that they caused cancelled out the
    advantages of their new housing environment, the new housing estates
    produced little sense of neighbourhood.

34. Interview.

35. OHI, p. 183.

36. <www.edb.gov.sg/edb/sg/en_uk/index/about_us/our_history/the_ 1960s.html>.

37. Edmund Wee, *Thirty Years of Economic Development* (Singapore: Singapore Economic Development Board, n.d.), p. 19.

38. Ibid., p. 5.

39. OHI, pp. 186–87.

40. Ibid., p. 184.

41. <www.edb.gov.sg/edb/sg/en_uk/index/about_us/our_history/the_ 1960s.html>.

42. OHI, p. 191.

43. Ibid., p. 198.

44. Ibid., p. 193.

45. Ibid., p. 199.

46. Ibid., p. 200.

47. Ibid., p. 200.

9

Politics, Elections, and Malaysia

Singapore gained self-government in 1959. In the first General Election, the People's Action Party (PAP) won 43 out of 51 seats, and Lee Kuan Yew became Singapore's first Prime Minister. The next few years saw an intense struggle within the party as leftist elements tried to seize control of it from the moderates, led by Lee. Externally, the PAP faced a threat from the Malayan Communist Party. Even as this dual struggle — one within the PAP and one outside it — was on, Malayan Prime Minister Tunku Abdul Rahman, speaking on 27 May 1961, proposed merger between the Federation of Malaya, Singapore, Sarawak, North Borneo and Brunei. The PAP favoured Singapore's independence through merger with the Federation, but the pro-Communists within the party opposed merger because "communist subversion, disguised for the moment as an anti-colonial struggle, would not only lose its *raison d'etre* but also become vulnerable to suppression by the anti-communist national government in Kuala Lumpur controlling internal security."[1]

In July 1961, the PAP narrowly survived a vote of confidence in the Legislative Assembly when 27 members voted for the government and 24, including 13 of the PAP's left-wing members, either abstained from voting or voted against the motion of confidence. The thirteen PAP assemblymen were expelled from the party and, led by Lee Siew Choh and Lim Chin Siong, went on to form the opposition Barisan Sosialis (Socialist Front) in August 1961. A referendum on the terms of the merger held in Singapore on 1 September 1962 saw overwhelming support for it.

Singapore declared independence, even before the formation of Malaysia, on 31 August 1963. The Federation of Malaysia, consisting of Malaya, Singapore, Sarawak and North Borneo (renamed Sabah), was formed soon after, on 16 September 1963. Brunei stayed out. Indonesia, which considered Malaysia to be a neo-colonial plot directed against it, responded violently in January 1963. It declared "Confrontation", a policy of armed infiltration, subversion and sabotage — hostilities short of all-out war — against Malaya and Singapore to prevent the formation of Malaysia and, later, to undermine the Federation.

It was in these tense circumstances that the PAP won the Singapore General Election on 21 September 1963. Lim Kim San contested in the Cairnhill constituency, winning more than 66 per cent of the vote. Lim Ang Chuan of the Barisan Sosialis garnered 21 per cent and Lee Ah Seong of the Progressive Party, a member of the Singapore Alliance, collected 13 per cent. Lim would represent Cairnhill till he stepped down from Parliament in 1980.

Although he was not in politics in 1961, Lim Kim San was aware of the division in the PAP between moderates and left-wing radicals that led to the split that year. He did not know Lim Chin Siong personally but, going by newspaper reports and from talking to PAP leaders, he got the impression that he was a "very able man, a good orator, a mover of crowds" and "a potential leader" but that he was a potential danger because he was a Communist.[2] The Communist hand was apparent, Lim believed, in the PAP's defeat in the Anson by-election of May 1961. The Communist support for the victor, former Chief Minister David Marshall, "brought home the fact that we are coming up against a very potent force, that they can move events as they want". However, the skirmishes with the left-wing also helped the party to distinguish between who were really for it and who were not, "and those who have got the guts and those who have not".[3]

Lim, who was working to resolve Singapore's housing crisis, had his own experience of the split when the Works Brigade had "a lot of trouble" caused by dissensions within the PAP.[4] Apart from the loss of the Works Brigade, what hit the PAP really hard was the weakening of its organizational structure following the left-wing capture of party branches and the semi-official People's Association. Lim recalled: "I remember Dr Goh saying, 'My God! Overnight they are all nowhere. They have gone.'…. Literally overnight. Yes, gone! You don't find anybody or anything. Anything that is disposable… was just taken away and we were left with nothing."[5]

When Lim took part in the 1963 elections, he was told: "You have everything ready — branch, branch workers and all that." When he went down, however,

> there were two old men and one old lady. And I had to find a branch myself. Borrowed a half-completed… or a house under repair at Cavenagh Road. Had to go out myself to the shops to buy glue, paint brush to put up the posters, nails and wires. And there were only these three guys with me…. These were the only three with me for the first few nights.[6]

His three assigned helpers were "probably remnants of the [party's] branches". One was "decrepit looking, two of them had no place to go to, so they were sleeping in the branches". However, they were useful in a way because they looked after the branches day and night. Who were the three people? "Can't remember them. All of them are dead now. All of them are dead."[7]

CAIRNHILL

That was not a propitious start to Lim's election campaign, but he took to it with his trademark hands-on approach to life. Unlike 1959, when he had declined to run for the Legislative Assembly, he agreed to contest in 1963 because he no longer owed banks money. Also, he felt very strongly that Singaporeans should be masters of their own fate. His father thought that his entry to politics was inevitable given that he had worked for the government at the HDB. His wife was happy because he would be tied down and "so my night activities, entertainment as a businessman and all that would disappear". She would know anytime where he was. "I am being shadowed!"[8] he exclaimed in mock despair. It was the Chinese-speaking business community that responded strangely. It looked upon him with hostility and shunned him.

Lim believed that he had been chosen to run in Cairnhill because his reputation at the HDB would stand him in good stead against Lim Yew Hock, who was expected to contest in the constituency but who, in the event, did not turn up there.

It was a "very testing time" for new candidates. "You are just sent right into the centre of the rough and tumble, with not much preparation except that you knew the party manifesto, the party stand, and you spoke along those lines."[9] Lim summed up his experience of campaigning: "It's just like teaching a chap to swim by throwing him straight into the water."[10]

Cairnhill in 1963 was a village constituency populated by both Malays and Chinese, including Hainanese dialect-speakers. Lim could "get along in dialect" and could manage everyday Malay. But trying to give a speech in Malay was another thing. Before standing for election, he had been familiar with the Emerald Hill part of the constituency but not the Newton side. Village headmen took him around during the nine-day campaign period.[11]

Lim held election rallies in Fullerton Building, at Clifford and at Finlayson Green. He made his first speech from a little box attached to a motorized tricycle.

> And you stand up there with your microphone and go to a street corner, wait for a little while. Some music will be played, or people will say so and so is here. And then you speak to a crowd of hundred, 200, and then off you go to another place. Of course where you will go is already announced beforehand. And my first

experience of speaking to the public for the election was standing
behind on a soap box literally.[12]

This occurred at a corner of Newton. He was supposed to finish his
speeches by 10 p.m. Just as he had finished, Prime Minister Lee came
along to help. But the policemen present there said that the time for
speeches was past. "So he was trying to give me support. And that's
why I remember that corner."[13] Then, there were days when Lim did
not have his own street rally and would go round. Once, he was in
PAP founding-member Kenny Byrne's constituency, Crawford, where
some houses were being demolished. As Lim was passing by, Byrne
saw him and called him up. He addressed the crowd on why the
houses had to be pulled down.[14]

Lim was a man of action. Was it not difficult for him to exercise
patience in explaining things to people? Lim thought not. If he had
something to explain, he was not impatient. Perhaps, he would speak
faster at the most. "It's only after repeated explanations that it doesn't
get in, then I get very impatient and I sort of blow up and can't be
bothered with it anymore."[15]

Campaigning house-to-house allowed him to gauge the kind of
support that he enjoyed. Voters could disguise their feelings quite
well, but people who really knew the constituency would be able to
tell the level of support that a candidate had. Once the electorate had
made up its mind, house-to-house campaigning was not very effective.
However, when there was a great deal of support on the ground, "you
can really feel it". At some places, people said to him: "Look, don't
waste your time canvassing us. You just go back. We are all for you.
You go to somewhere else."[16]

Party headquarters was responsible for printing posters with
the candidates' photographs. These had to be collected. The party
also printed some postcards with the photographs. Candidates wrote
letters to their constituencies that were cyclostyled and sent out.
"You need a lot of secretarial work to put down the name of your

voter, his polling station. And this is an indication to show that you have visited them and that you have put the thing there and made things easy."[17]

Lim did not recall any unpleasantness erupting during the campaigning except for some of his posters being torn down and plastered over. Asked whether he had been irritated by the inefficient party structure that he had to work with, which was very different from the Housing Board's style of functioning, he replied: "Yes. But you are in the middle of it all and you can't afford to spend time being irritated and complaining. You have to get the thing done yourself."[18]

Among his voluntary workers were friends, people living nearby and sympathizers. Some provided money, while others gave food for the workers. The only people who refused to work for him were the Orchard Road Market people, who supported the Barisan. They were Chinese-educated Teochew, "down-trodden" people who forever had at their backs government inspectors who were carry-overs from colonial days. The Teochew identified the inspectors with the government, and were openly hostile to Lim.

> In fact, I saw the headman three times. Went there to see him. I went in by the front door, he went out by the back door, so we knew they were against. And they had a stack of crackers ready to celebrate a Barisan victory. Well, we won. They burned the crackers for us.[19]

In spite of such pockets of support for the Barisan, Lim did not think that his opponent from the coalition had mounted too intensive a campaign. As for the "Alliance chap", both the Barisan candidate and Lim burst out laughing when he "came in with coat and tie but with a walking stick".[20]

The counting for Cairnhill was done in Monk's Hill School. There was a crowd there, and it was about midnight when Lim won. By that time, it was clear that the PAP would form the government. Barisan supporters left with their faces covered. They had had bottles and "all sorts of things ready" to go after the PAP had it lost. If the

Barisan had won, "the police would be on their side and they would have resorted to violence". That was "their style".[21]

After his victory, Lim and his supporters marched back to the party branch, where he thanked his workers. He could not sleep the whole night because for nine days, he had been in a state of excitement. For the first time, he took a sleeping pill the following night.[22]

Lim's career as a member of parliament was marked by the same devotion to duty that he brought to his ministerial duties. "He was a first-class politician who could read people and size them up without telling them, while they could not read him," retired accountant Kenneth Kwan said in an interview. Kwan, a former chairman of the management committee of the Cairnhill Community Centre, had worked with Lim for fifteen years from 1966. He remembered him as an MP who "knew the world" and "the worth of human relationships". He could not think of a time when Lim had lost his temper over a constituent's demands. However, Lim had "a very sharp mind" and was a problem-solver and a "very decisive" MP.[23]

Two of Lim's security officers reminisced about following him on his rounds as an MP. Johnny Lim, who was with him from 1973 to 1982, said that he would hold his meet-the-people sessions every Thursday from 7.30 p.m.; they would continue easily till 11 p.m., if not midnight. "He took on the important cases, leaving the rest to his assistants. He was very strict that he should meet constituents on a first-come-first-served basis; no one could jump the queue by claiming to be close to him," the officer said. "Although he often had to explain government policies to angry residents, many of them poor people, I never once saw him lose his temper." Lee Soon Hock, another security officer who worked with Lim from 1977 to 1982, remembered him as a "very fatherly figure" who was popular with constituents because he "listened carefully to their problems" and "delivered on his promises when he made them". Going by such accounts, Lim fulfilled Lee Kuan Yew's expectations of him as a hands-on businessman who would be able to make a successful transition to politics.[24]

MERGER AND SEPARATION

Lim Kim San had foreknowledge of the Tunku's historic speech in May 1961 announcing the proposal for Malaysia. Unlike Singapore, which the Communists were using as a refuge because they were allowed to have open fronts, the Communist insurgency in Malaya made it deal toughly with Communists.

> They either shoot them or just take them in… So we said, "Well, if we are part of Malaysia, well, all that will stop." And the Communists may not like it — and what is not good for the Communists is good for us… Then when the Tunku announced that, I said, "Ah, this is it."… And from an economic point of view, [Singapore] becomes a larger unit… I think it's time that we formed a unit where it's more viable…[25]

Lim was thinking in particular about a common market in Malaysia.

> Common market, that is, you have your industries, you have your agricultural background, and then you have a larger area for a larger population. I always thought that for an economy to be very viable, you should have a population of about 80 million, or with land sufficient to hold 80 million to a hundred million… With the hinterland, yes, of course.[26]

The radio forums and talks on merger opened people's minds to a bigger issue: Why Singapore should have merger and how it would be better off.

The referendum on the terms of merger offered voters in Singapore three options, but there was no way to vote against merger itself. The choices, Lim thought, were very "well-phrased" and were a "clever way of getting what you want". That people were not given a chance to say "no" to merger did not bother Lim because "I already made up my mind that we should have merger."[27]

Vehemently opposed to merger, Indonesia launched its policy of Confrontation. Lim had a dramatic personal experience of it. One night, when returning home to Tanjong Rhu from his in-laws' place in Balmoral Road at 2 a.m., he saw "a lone Indonesian-looking chap walking along the road". He told the police and, later on, there was an explosion. However, it did not harm anybody. There was also a bomb that went off in an HDB block of flats in Geylang Serai. He remembered visiting the place and feeling confident that the structure was strong enough to prevent the block from coming down because of the blast. "And in fact, PM did mention 'your structure can stand.'"[28]

Unlike the blast of Confrontation, which the HDB block absorbed without collapsing, merger would last barely two years.

Indeed, merger began on a problematic note. Wary of the danger posed by the Barisan capitalizing on a further postponement of merger, Lee Kuan Yew unilaterally declared Singapore independent at a rally at the City Hall Steps on 31 August 1963. Sarawak had declared *de facto* independence already; and North Borneo had announced the establishment of the state of Sabah. Singapore confided federal powers over defence and external affairs in the Yang di-Pertuan Negara, who would hold them in trust for the central government till 16 September 1963. Malaysian leaders believed that Lee had instigated the North Borneo states to defiance.[29] Lim saw in the episode a sign of problems to come. Kuala Lumpur was unhappy because, being the central government, it wanted to coordinate everything and wanted Singapore, a smaller component of the Federation, to go along with arrangements made by the Malayan leadership. This unequal *abang-adek* (elder brother-younger brother) relationship between Malaya, which deemed itself to be the elder brother, and Singapore, which it treated like a younger brother — was one reason for the break-up of the Federation that would follow.[30]

Another substantial reason was the failure of a Common Market of Singapore and Malaya to take off following merger. This larger market would have created a bigger economic entity, but it never came about because of impediments put to Singapore manufactures and the refusal to provide incentives for the island to develop as an industrial centre. Then Malaysian Finance Minister Tan Siew Sin "never wanted to give us the common market".[31] He preferred to concentrate powers in his hands and deny investment applications that Singapore had approved. "He wants applications to be sent direct to him, which could be quite stifling for us because of the speed with which we work and the speed at which they work which was completely different. And, well, he may want the industries to be sited in Malaysia instead of in Singapore."[32] Talk of making Singapore the New York of Malaysia evaporated as Malaya began developing its own port and airport, tried to subvert Singapore's free port status, and treated it as a constituent state without regard for the formation of the larger market. Singapore was like "a foreign country".[33]

True, the terms of the Common Market had not been settled precisely before merger, given the speed at which the union had taken place, but Lim believed that "if you are sincere about it, you are one country, there's no reason why it should be very difficult" to create that market. Instead, Tan demanded the imposition of a certain import duty on goods, which resulted sometimes in Singapore not even enjoying a Commonwealth preferential benefit. He wanted Singapore to bring in revenue for Malaysia without giving it the benefit of merger.[34]

In another example of the failure of the Common Market to emerge, the Tunku demanded that Singapore pay the central government $50 million as an entrance fee for developing the Borneo territories over five years. Lim acknowledged that the idea was fair in principle because Singapore, which was relatively wealthy within the Federation, should bear a higher proportion than the other states of the costs incurred by Kuala Lumpur in taking responsibility for national defence, foreign affairs and some other areas. Singapore's interest in the Borneo territories was guided by a desire to reduce unemployment there. However, there was no reason why others in the Federation should be upset over Singapore using Borneo as a market for its goods because this move was logical given that the purpose of merger was to develop a bigger market.[35] That was not to be.

At a personal level, the Tunku and Tun Razak liked Lim, who acted as a valuable link between Kuala Lumpur and Singapore during the merger years. Lee Kuan Yew recalled the times in his interview.

> He had done business in Malaya for many years before the War. So he knew the royalty in Kelantan, where his father or father-in-law had pawnshops. He spoke Malay to them, he understood their ways, and he socialized well and so they felt comfortable with him. Unlike Goh Keng Swee or me or Toh Chin Chye. Kim San is not a scholar type; he looked an outward-going businessman. They liked him, and it was his business to be liked. Therefore, through him, we were putting on the PAP a very human, likeable face. But in the end, they decided that, no, he is part of the PAP.

Lim himself remembered the Tunku as being very confident and in control. "My relationship with him was very good. In fact, we could get along.... I could get along with him, the same way Dr Goh could get along with Tun Razak."[36] The Tunku liked and admired Lee in the beginning, but later thought that he was quite ambitious and "the deals don't match".[37] Tun Dr Ismail "hit it off very well" with the Tunku and Lee, and was frank with Lim.[38]

Lee agreed, however, with a question on whether the Malay leaders were trying to use Lim as a wedge to create differences within the PAP. "They tried with everybody, with Goh Keng Swee, with Toh Chin Chye. They tried to buy people off, which is their method of governing, as they bought off leaders in Sabah and Sarawak." Asked whether the Tunku had ever offered to have him over in his camp in Malaysia, Lim replied that there had been talk about him and Goh going over there, but "I was never approached by them or we ever discussed it here."[39] However, there is a persisting view that, at the end of 1964 or the beginning of 1965, following the 1964 racial riots in Singapore, Kuala Lumpur was prepared to make

Lim Kim San a federal minister in exchange for Lee Kuan Yew stepping down as prime minister of Singapore.

According to Lee,

> There were many such hints or proposals. I don't know whether it was the British who put up the ideas or whether it was the Tunku. Had we responded and said, yes, okay, then they would have to work out a deal to get rid of me. But I told my colleagues that, okay, I'll go, but who's the next guy who has to take my position? Are you going to sell out to them or are you going to stand firm? If you stand firm, you are back where you are, and they will hate two persons instead of one. They decided that I stay put because whoever became the Prime Minister of Singapore would have to stand up to them and say "no". We have persuaded the people to vote for Merger, so you can't say "yes". So it never took off. Goh Keng Swee can take over, Lim Kim San can take over, anybody except me. But whoever takes over faces the same problem. They were not going to change their policy, which was a Malay Malaysia.

This was the crux of the issue, Lim believed as well. At the heart of the differences between Kuala Lumpur and Singapore lay Malaysia's preferential policies, which favoured the *bumiputra*, or indigenous Malays, and made Singaporeans feel that they were "second-class citizens".[40] So-called Malayan Malaysians were differentiated from Singapore Malaysians, and "we were being treated as little chaps".[41] That was not the Malaysia that Singapore had looked forward to. Admittedly, the Tunku had feared "a very Chinese Singapore", but with Sabah and Sarawak present in the Federation, an arithmetical balance against Chinese dominance had been created already. "So we thought all will be treated equally. But for myself, I think we have suffered as subjects under the British. We have suffered under the Japanese. Why the hell do we want to suffer under the Malayans?"[42]

Like other Singapore leaders, Lim noted that merger failed because of Kuala Lumpur's intransigence on the issue of special privileges for Malays. Where the United Malays National Organization (UMNO), the main party of Malaysia's governing Alliance, spoke of upholding entrenched Malay rights, the PAP spoke of the need to create a multiracial Malaysia in which access to wealth, power and influence would be through a meritocratic system. The PAP thought that Malays in the peninsula could be forced to uplift themselves faster through open competition, as was the case in Singapore.[43] By contrast, Kuala Lumpur's idea of development was that Malays should enjoy not only political power, which they did, but also economic power. The PAP, too, wanted Malays to possess economic power, but by allowing the best among them to prove themselves in open competition, not by disenfranchising the Chinese economically, not least because economic power in Malaya lay in the hands of the British and not the entrepreneurial Chinese. Lim was aghast at what had occurred in places such as Myanmar (called Burma then), Africa and even in India, where anti-colonialism had translated into discrimination against entrepreneurs and had brought down the standard of living.

To the Malay leadership in Kuala Lumpur, the PAP looked like a party of revolutionaries that would undermine Malaysia's social and political structure to the extent of doing away with the role of the Malay sultans. To this allegation, Lim replied that socialism had toppled royalty all over the world; it was an inevitable process. The PAP had not discussed toppling the sultans, but once the masses rose as a result of social progress, they would do away with the royal hierarchy.[44] Clearly, there was very little in common ideologically between the conservative, Malay-based UMNO and the radical and multiracial PAP that was committed to change through a process of meritocratic selection and advancement. They could not occupy the same political space in Malaysia: The vision of either one party or the other would prevail in a contest in which each would invade the other's space.

This is what occurred. One instance of the Malayan intrusion into Singapore life occurred when Malay leaders in Kuala Lumpur argued that Singapore's Malays were underprivileged and therefore that the HDB should reserve some blocks for them in Geylang Serai.

"I make it clear to them that even if they were to pay or take over that area, they are not going to give very low rentals which will undermine the policy of the Housing Board. So there already you feel that what is ours, they can under pressure take over and do things as they like."[45]

A divergence of political styles exacerbated ideological differences between the PAP and UMNO. The PAP leadership was matter-of-fact and spoke to the point; the UMNO leadership was casual and sought to avoid controversy by going for informal arrangements. However, the casual style masked serious sources of discord. "You know, the Malay way. He doesn't confront you straightaway but in little acts and all that. Then gradually it dawned upon you that you are being treated like a subject. So it doesn't come straight on. It's an insidious process, insidious feeling."[46]

Matters came to a head when the PAP decided to contest the Malaysian General Election in early 1964. To Kuala Lumpur, the PAP's entry into Malaysian politics was a sign of the Singapore Chinese seeking to extend their influence into the Malayan peninsula, a move that went against the gentleman's agreement made to the contrary before merger had been agreed to. In his memoirs, Lee rejects the criticism. First, "since the Tunku had breached his verbal undertaking to me not to participate in Singapore's elections, I felt no longer bound by my return undertaking".[47] Secondly, the PAP's participation in the Malaysian election did cause Singapore's relations with Kuala Lumpur to deteriorate, "but it made no difference to the main cause of conflict and eventual separation", which lay in UMNO's "determination to maintain total Malay supremacy".[48] UMNO "did not want the Chinese to be represented by a vigorous leadership that propounded a non-communal or a multiracial approach to politics and would not confine its appeal only to the Chinese".[49]

Lim Kim San had reservations about the PAP moving into the larger Malayan political scene. They stemmed from tactical calculations. Since the party was not ready to go in, there was not much point in having a token presence in the General Election.[50]

Politically, however, he had no objections to the PAP participating in the politics of peninsular Malaysia because UMNO had broken its promise by sending people down to campaign for the Alliance in Singapore. Did the PAP's move precipitate separation?

> It did precipitate. It speeded up the break. But I think it's inevitable now. We are part of Malaysia, we will be Malaysians, so ultimately there must come a time when you take part in Malaysian politics, isn't it? Only we went in too fast. But these people all the time were thinking of keeping these territories out in the same way they have kept Sabah and Sarawak out from the Malaysian thing. But if you look at events dispassionately, it must be inevitable that if you are part of Malaysia, you will be forming a party which will take part in all elections, isn't it, in the same way as they will take part in your elections. They are doing it now in Sabah and Sarawak through USNO. So why is it they can do it and you can't do it to them? This is the thing. So we came to the conclusion that there's a question of "abang adek" — you are the "adek", I am the "abang"; whatever I can do it's okay, but you cannot do certain things. And this is where I say "we feel very inhibited and unhappy."[51]

Lim took part in campaigning for the PAP in peninsular Malaysia. He spoke at Petaling Jaya in English. The mood at the rallies indicated that the ground, particularly among Malaysian Chinese, was with the PAP. However, the PAP did not rest its hopes on the Chinese solely because Malays were the ethnic majority in every constituency. "So we expected the Malays also like here to vote for reason, to vote for policy, because they appeared to welcome the policy."[52] Indeed, the party did draw support from urban Malays because it exposed corruption.[53]

Nevertheless, the PAP won only one seat in the peninsula, with Devan Nair taking the Bangsar constituency, and the party found itself being seated with the Barisan Sosialis on the opposition benches of the Malaysian Parliament. Studying the reasons for its electoral setback, the PAP concluded that it had fought the elections on the same platform as the central government: Resisting Confrontation.

The electorate supported the Alliance because only Kuala Lumpur could fight Confrontation; the PAP, by contrast, was not a part of the Alliance and had only a token presence in the elections. As for the ethnic aspect of the results, "the only thing we considered was the Malays there are not quite ready to be non-communal like the Malays here. The Tunku came to the conclusion that the Malays here and the Malays in Malaysia are different creatures. They are urban creatures, they are not Malays."[54]

Lim insisted that the PAP had not sought intentionally to replace the Malaysian Chinese Association (MCA), one of the components of the Alliance, by showing that it could garner Chinese votes better than the conservative MCA could. But the PAP had believed that "an incorruptible, capable man" would appeal to the central government in preference to "people who are not competent". The party had misread Kuala Lumpur's attitude. UMNO, which wanted to be "in a position to patronize the other partners", did not prefer people who had a political following of their own.[55] It therefore rebuffed the PAP and retained its alliance with the MCA.

The MCA played a crucial role in Singapore's separation from Malaysia. It feared the PAP's leaders, whom it saw as usurping its position in the Alliance one day. MCA Senators T.H. Tan and Khaw Kai Boh reacted by warning that Malaysia would abandon merger if the PAP remained in Parliament. The Malay leadership endorsed such views.[56]

To Lim, the issue was not a partisan one but a national one.

> Like in Singapore, our policies were for the best of the whole community, the whole lot. And we thought that a Malaysian Malaysia would be really good for the whole country. So the question of we are undermining the MCA doesn't arise. It doesn't feature so much as a fact that we are going to have the best man in every position possible. The best man could be someone who is outside the MCA or within the MCA or the PAP. Our main concern was that.[57]

Taking a very different view, the MCA attacked the PAP on home ground by appealing to Singapore's Chinese. Its efforts to gain a foothold on the island led nowhere, but UMNO's accompanying "incursion" into Singapore, to appeal to the island's minority Malays, had serious results. UMNO's thrust into Singapore was led by its secretary-general, Syed Ja'afar Albar, whom Lee Kuan Yew described as an "ultra".[58] Lim's impression of Albar was less pointed: "He's Arabic. He looks very vigorous, very animated, vocal. Well, I think he was a very lively character."[59] Albar had made several "inflammatory speeches" in Singapore, and the *Utusan Melayu*, a Malay-language newspaper published in the *Jawi* (Arabic) script, unleashed a barrage of anti-PAP and anti-Chinese editorials and news reports. Tension boiled over into violence in July 1964, when riots broke out between Malays and Chinese in Singapore. On the day before the riots, leaflets had appeared urging Malays to wage a religious war against the Chinese.[60]

The racial riots shocked Lim, who had been expecting trouble with the central government but not street violence. He was in London when the riots broke out. Taking the first available flight back, he wondered whether the Singapore government would be held responsible for having failed to maintain law and order, whether it would be accused of having actually instigated the riots, and whether he would be arrested along with other PAP leaders. Indeed, the PAP had discussed the possibility of forming a government-in-exile and "who should go there".[61] When his plane landed and his protocol officer came up to receive and to escort him, he knew that the "police are still our police and the place is still manned by our own people".[62] The Tunku suspected Indonesia's subversive hands behind the riots — Confrontation was raging — but Tun Razak denied this. Agreeing with the latter's version of causes, Lim held "them" — unnamed politicians from Kuala Lumpur — squarely responsible for having started the riots. Thus, when the central government refused to hold a public enquiry into the violence, "we were not surprised".[63] Back in Singapore, Lim, like other PAP leaders, went about setting up goodwill committees and asking Chinese and Malays, through community leaders, to look after each other. Rowdy elements were present in both communities, as were fears of being discriminated against, which both Chinese and Malays harboured against each other. However, impartial law enforcement by the authorities saw Singapore through some very difficult days in July 1964 (although riots would recur in September that year).[64]

The Malaysian Solidarity Convention — a coalition of opposition parties that supported Lee's vision of a Malaysian Malaysia and not a Malay Malaysia — was formed in March 1965. It

> brought home to the Central Government that there is this desire
> for equal opportunities for everyone. And I think it brought home
> to the Central Government the danger of having a dynamic leader
> like the PM in Malaysia who would be able to sway and influence
> a lot of opinion. This must be one of the decisive factors which
> made Tunku think that it is better to get this area out, with its big
> Chinese population and a leader like that.[65]

Ooi Kee Beng, in an acclaimed biography of Tun Dr Ismail, notes the importance of the Malaysian Solidarity Convention. He cites Lee as maintaining that its formation changed the power equation in Malaysia radically. "We did join Malaysia, but that did not mean that we had *surrendered* Singapore! If riots were started with a pan-Malay agenda thereafter, you would have had resistance in all the major cities. Now, can you contain that? The Tunku, Razak and Ismail knew they could not. So it was decided that Singapore should get out."[66] Buoyed by the convention's success, Lee wanted to bring the issue of a Malaysian Malaysia into Parliament. However, the Tunku advised him against doing so. Did that response indicate a difference between their styles of leadership? Lim had no doubt that it did.

> Yes, ours is a confrontational style. Theirs is a style of more
> moshiwalls, is it? They don't like (you) to talk about unpleasant

facts to them openly, where it's unpleasant to them. They would prefer to have things settled first before they come out in the open and discuss it in a very limited way. But here again, you'll find that for them, when it suit their purpose, they can raise what you call sensitive issues. For us, you are not supposed to at all. So it always suits their purpose; they play their own rule. That's why I say we feel very restrictive. Certain things I can do, you, the adek, you cannot do. And if you are a good adek, you must follow what the abang says. It was that kind of situation that I found most irksome.[67]

Still, the Singapore leaders sought accommodation with, and not separation from, their counterparts in Kuala Lumpur. Lee sounded each Singapore minister individually. There was no unanimity because several ministers were Malaysians with ties up north.[68] Lim was clear: He wanted Singapore to leave the Federation. "I would love to go" because "I have no time". That said, he thought it unlikely that the central government would let Singapore go, "having got us there as an adek".

I mean Singapore is an acquisition. We have got one of the best ports in South-east Asia. We have got a good government working. And, well, most countries will love to have Singapore. The hub, centre point between East and West, all the ships pass through here, excellent port, why not? So I don't think they would let us go so easily.[69]

Yet, events moved towards separation. In the Tunku's view, the Singapore leaders had wanted merger and had been accommodated. Now they wanted something more out of Malaysia, which he found very troublesome.[70] So Singapore had to be let go. Also, there was a desire in the central government to teach Singapore a lesson. The Malaysians were convinced, probably by the PAP's own argument, that Singapore would not survive on its own and believed therefore that an independent Singapore would "have to come back, get down on our knees and beg to be readmitted".[71]

In spite of their initial resistance to the idea of separation, the Singapore leadership came round to it eventually. Lim, who had a cordial relationship with the Tunku, became a conduit between him and Lee Kuan Yew in what Lam Peng Er describes as a "key event" that preceded separation.[72] In late June 1965, when the Tunku was down with shingles in a London hospital, Lim, who was planning to attend a Non-Aligned meeting in Algiers, paid him a courtesy call and discussed relations between Kuala Lumpur and Singapore. According to Noordin Sopiee, who interviewed the Tunku, the Malaysian leader saw the meeting as a crucial one, raised the possibility of separation, and hoped that Lim would tell Lee how critical matters were.[73] Lim, however, did not appear to think that the situation was that grave. This belief was reflected in his choice of a letter, rather than a much faster telegram, to inform Lee of what had transpired.

The tone of the letter, which Lim sent on 23 June 1965, did not display a sense of urgency, either. Referring to the Tunku, Lim wrote to Lee in the relevant part of the letter: "He still thinks of having a rearrangement but does not know what form it should take but at the same time he thinks that there is no urgency at all and that it could be undertaken after Confrontation."[74] However, in a letter to Lee thirty years later, Lim recalled that the Tunku had said to him that Lee could attend the next Commonwealth Prime Ministers' Conference on his own. This remark was a "subtle but ominous" hint that Malaysia would eject Singapore, leading Lee to attend the conference as the prime minister of a sovereign state. This hint was not conveyed in Lim's letter to Lee soon after the meeting in the London hospital, and "seems to fit better" with Noordin Sopiee's version of the meeting. "It is difficult to reconcile these two versions by Lim and to decide which version is more accurate," Lam writes.[75]

Lam's assessment of the Tunku's views of Singapore in June 1965, as conveyed to Noordin Sopiee, and of Lim's response to them is substantially accurate. However, the actual sequence of events, described in both Lee Kuan Yew's memoirs and Lim Kim San's Oral History Interview, differs from Lam's account and helps to clear the apparent mystery of which of Lim's two versions of his meeting with the Tunku is accurate. In reality, Lim's graver sense of the Tunku's remarks was conveyed to Lee, not thirty years later, but immediately upon Lim's return to Singapore. According to Lee, Lim met him after returning from London in early July and reported that the Tunku had said to him that Lee could attend the next Commonwealth Prime Ministers' Conference on his own. Lee asked Lim what the Tunku had meant by that. "Would there be a rearrangement? Would Singapore become a special state in a confederation? Kim San could not quite fathom what the Tunku had in mind," Lee writes.[76] Years later, when Lee was recording his oral history in 1981, he sent Lim a copy of his 23 June 1965 letter. Lim commented: "On reflection, as I have told you several times, Tunku indicated indirectly that he would give Singapore independence. I was too obtuse then to catch the significance of some of his remarks."[77] Lee remarks: "Kim San had concentrated on the possibility of a rearrangement and missed the bigger implications of the Tunku's cryptic statements. In London he had met the Tunku only once, which meant that as early as 23 June 1965 the Tunku was thinking in terms of a total separation."[78]

Lim's Oral History Interview, too, deals in some detail with the meeting with the Tunku in London. It is worth quoting that part of the interview in full to understand why Lim did not catch the nuances of a meeting that would have such major implications for Singapore.

Lim Kim San: I visited him in London in the hospital. And there he gave indication of his decision indirectly to me that Singapore will be on its own. He mentioned about the Prime Minister being able to attend the next Commonwealth Prime Ministers' Conference on his own. And that was the indication that he has made up his mind to expel Singapore.

Lily Tan: But were you aware of the full significance of that statement?

Lim Kim San: No, no. It's only later on. I knew he has made a decision. But probably when he made that... It is only later on that I remembered this part of the conversation. He must have done it in a very off-handed and slurring way where I can't catch it properly. But on recollection, thinking hard about it, I knew he has decided. He has got a very charming way of saying things without your realising it. But he has already decided that Singapore... as he put it, you know, when you have a sore, you better cut it off, have a surgical operation.

Lily Tan: What was the mood of Tunku when he said that, if you can recollect?

Lim Kim San: No. He said that he was not sad. He said this among other things, you know, talking about this and that — ordinary conversation. And this was just sort of incidental, just dropped in like that.

Lily Tan: When you have conversations with Tunku like that as a government minister, do you communicate back to PM on bits of information?

Lim Kim San: Oh no. Where it's relevant to give an understanding of their thinking, you know, not to... I mean, all of us. Cabinet discussion. When we go elsewhere there are certain observations which strike us, which may be of relevance to us and may help us in our assessment of situation, we do bring it out and say, "Well, look, you know, I think so and so meant this and that."

Lily Tan: Do you keep in touch with your ministry when you go on visits like that, or was it...?

Lim Kim San: Well, we have got someone to act for us. And normally the visit is a very short visit. And unless the business is very urgent, you don't keep in touch. And anything urgent your... at that time... Well, later on, we have got our own High Comm. At that time no, we have nothing to keep us informed.[79]

When Kuala Lumpur ejected Singapore from the Malaysian Federation on 9 August 1965, Singapore's leaders "were a bit disappointed" that merger had not worked, but the outcome was nevertheless "a bit of a relief" to Lim. People were letting off firecrackers in Chinatown, leading Goh Keng Swee to say to him: "Here I am so worried about our future. But look! The people are celebrating." Why was it a relief? It was because Lim and his colleagues had not been free to set policy while Singapore had been in Malaysia. "You were not a master in your own home."[80]

Lim Kim San, the master builder of homes who had proved his worth already, would have key roles to play in the governance of independent Singapore.

Notes

1. Yeo Kim Wah and Albert Lau, "From Colonialism to Independence, 1945–1965", in *A History of Singapore*, edited by Ernest C.T. Chew and Edwin Lee (Singapore: Oxford University Press, 1991), p. 141.
2. Lim Kim San, Oral History Interview, by Lily Tan, Oral History Centre, Accession Number 000526/21, Project: Economic Growth of Singapore, 1955–79, Date transcribed: 25 February 1985, p. 213. Hereafter OHI.
3. OHI, p. 217.
4. Ibid., p. 215.
5. Ibid., pp. 217–18.
6. Ibid., p. 218.
7. Ibid.
8. Ibid., p. 206.
9. Ibid., p. 231.
10. Ibid., pp. 230–31.
11. Ibid., pp. 232–34.
12. Ibid., pp. 229–30.
13. Ibid., p. 230.
14. Ibid.
15. Ibid., p. 239.
16. Ibid., p. 231.
17. Ibid., pp. 234–35.

18. Ibid., p. 239.
19. Ibid., p. 240.
20. Ibid., p. 236.
21. Ibid., pp. 236–37.
22. Ibid., p. 238.
23. Interview with Kenneth T.Y. Kwan, Toa Payoh Central, 8 May 2008.
24. Interview with Johnny Lim and Lee Soon Hock, Singapore Swimming Club, 22 April 2008.
25. OHI, pp. 209–10.
26. Ibid., p. 211.
27. Ibid., p. 222.
28. Ibid., pp. 226–28.
29. Lee Kuan Yew, *The Singapore Story: Memoirs of Lee Kuan Yew* (Singapore: Times Editions Pte Ltd and Singapore Press Holdings, 1998), pp. 498–99.
30. OHI, p. 258.
31. Ibid., p. 255.
32. Ibid.
33. Ibid., p. 274.
34. Ibid., pp. 255–56.
35. Ibid., pp. 256–57.
36. Ibid., pp. 247–48.
37. Ibid., p. 272.
38. Ibid.
39. Ibid., pp. 248–49.
40. Ibid., p. 246.
41. Ibid.
42. Ibid., pp. 246–47.
43. Ibid., p. 260.
44. Ibid., pp. 261–64.
45. Ibid., p. 247.
46. Ibid., p. 248.
47. Lee, *The Singapore Story*, op. cit., p. 540.
48. Ibid., p. 547.
49. Ibid., p. 542.
50. OHI, p. 249.
51. Ibid., p. 250.
52. Ibid., p. 253.
53. Ibid., p. 251.
54. Ibid., p. 254.
55. Ibid.

56. Ibid., pp. 258–59.
57. Ibid., p. 260.
58. Leon Comber, *13 May 1969: A Historical Survey of Sino-Malay Relations* (Kuala Lumpur, Singapore and Hong Kong: Hienemann Asia, 1983), p. 59.
59. OHI, p. 265.
60. Comber, *13 May 1969*, op. cit., p. 59.
61. OHI, p. 267.
62. Ibid., p. 266.
63. Ibid., p. 272.
64. Ibid., p. 270.
65. Ibid., p. 276.
66. Ooi Kee Beng, *The Reluctant Politician: Tun Dr Ismail and His Time* (Singapore: Institute of Southeast Asian Studies, 2006), p. 161.
67. OHI, p. 277.
68. Melanie Chew, *Leaders of Singapore* (Singapore: Resource Press, 1996), p. 166.
69. OHI, p. 279.
70. Ibid.
71. Chew, *Leaders of Singapore*, op. cit., p. 166.
72. Lam Peng Er, "The Organisational Utility Men: Toh Chin Chye & Lim Kim San", in *Lee's Lieutenants: Singapore's Old Guard*, edited by Lam Peng Er and Kevin Y.L. Tan (St. Leonards: Allen & Unwin, 1999), op. cit., p. 19.
73. Ibid., p. 19.
74. Ibid., p. 20.
75. Ibid.
76. Lee, *The Singapore Story*, op. cit., pp. 628–29.
77. Ibid., p. 629.
78. Ibid.
79. OHI, pp. 279-81.
80. Chew, *Leaders of Singapore*, op. cit., p. 167.

10

Minister for Finance

Lim Kim San became Singapore's Finance Minister on its independence in 1965, and served till August 1967. He brought to the portfolio, during those make-or-break years, an emphasis on prudence in spending that produced a balanced Budget, with a small surplus in fact. He was busy in a period when the republic witnessed a period of legislative activism that reflected its new constitutional position on separation. Changes were made to the law in fields such as tax reliefs to boost exports, income tax, property tax, dual taxation avoidance agreements, and customs. Lim participated in Singapore's reserves and currency negotiations with Malaysia that led to the republic releasing its own currency in 1967; and he helped formulate the nascent state's policies on industrialization and foreign markets that underpinned its strategies of survival and success. One motif of the period was how independence had brought Singapore, now unshackled from Malaysia, new opportunities for industrialization, trade and investment. These were the lifelines of an island-state that would have to make the world its market now that it had lost its traditional economic hinterland, Malaya.

BREAKING WITH MALAYSIA

As Finance Minister, Lim played an important role in Singapore's dealings with Malaysia in the acrimonious immediate aftermath of separation. Kuala Lumpur was dismayed by Singapore's decision to impose restrictions on almost 200 items of mainland-manufactured goods, but Lim justified the action, arguing that post-separation Malaysia must expect to compete on the same terms as any other country in exporting to Singapore. Indeed, the list of Malaysian goods to which quotas applied were the same as had been recommended by the Malaysian Tariff Advisory Board in 1964; there was no question of selective discrimination.

Such arguments received a cold reception in Kuala Lumpur, where the political mood was summed up in Malaysian Finance Minister Tan Siew Sin's argument that Malaysia could prosper even without Singapore because the Malaysian market without Singapore was larger than the Singapore market. Kuala Lumpur retaliated to the republic's restrictions by imposing licensing and quota restrictions on Singapore-made goods.[1] A three-man committee, formed as a result of business pressure on both sides of the Causeway, recommended a return to the position prior to separation — the abolishment of quotas — and believed that the gesture might encourage economic union. In the light of previous disputes, however, Singapore demanded that an economic cooperation agreement be made a part of the official agreement that the committee was to draw up for the two countries. Such a step would help to prevent controversy in the future, Lim believed.

Discussions on economic union languished till early October 1965, when both governments agreed to abolish import restrictions but not duties. Differences deepened as Malaysia announced that it would take steps to create a common market for West and East Malaysia, enabling a large number of Malaysian goods to be transported free of duty within the Federation. Many import controls, too, were removed. In the circumstances, Singapore clamped tariffs on more than 150 products manufactured in Malaya, annoying Kuala Lumpur. Singapore was dismayed, in turn, when it was asked effectively to pay for entry to the Malaysian common market.[2]

At the end of 1965, Lim reached out to the Malaysian leadership. "Let us sit round the table, Ministers and officials, instead of each country being forced to work out how each can do without the other," he said.[3] But that was not to be. In March 1966, disagreement between the two countries broke into the open over the future of a double taxation avoidance pact that had been introduced in 1947. Under the pact, industries or businesses operating in both territories — Malaya and Singapore — enjoyed a concession in one territory if they were taxed in the other. Malaysia suggested the abolition of the provisions in October 1965 because Singapore was now independent, but it wrote to Singapore later cancelling the October proposal. When Singapore repealed the relevant provision of the Singapore Income Tax Ordinance without giving Malaysia prior notice, Tan Siew Sin was incensed. "If I thought of Malaysian interests alone, I would say: 'To hell with Singapore.' After all, they stand to lose more without any double-taxation agreement," he said. That was because there were more Singapore investments in Malaysia than Malaysian investments in Singapore. "But I thought that we should co-operate on this matter. And this is the trouble we get."[4] Lim answered Tan's outburst point by point, but the Malaysian minister rejected his arguments. The double-tax avoidance agreement was signed eventually in August 1966, to be applied retrospectively from 1 January 1966.

A Separate Currency

Lim Kim San participated actively in Singapore's crucial negotiations with Malaysia on the issue of a common currency and banking system.

Singapore, Malaya and the Borneo Territories had been under the same currency board system for decades. Under the system, the currency was backed to the extent of 110 per cent or more by external assets, and was one of the main pillars on which financial stability rested. In December 1964, while Singapore was still in Malaysia, Kuala Lumpur gave notice to Brunei of its intention to wind up the board.[5] On 8 November 1965, Lim wrote to his Malaysian counterpart that in order to maintain public and international confidence in the economic future of Singapore and Malaysia, their currency should continue to be issued under the currency board system until an opportune time arrived to make a change. Alternatively, the two countries could establish a joint central bank. Malaysia found both proposals unacceptable. In the meanwhile, both sides agreed, officials should meet to find another formula for a common currency and banking system. At the request of both countries, the International Monetary Fund sent a technical assistance mission to Singapore and Malaysia in December 1965. Reporting on 1 March 1966, the mission noted Singapore's major preoccupation over the safety of the foreign exchange reserves backing the currency. Lim made that concern clear in a letter to the governor of Bank Negara Malaysia on 21 March. On 20 April, the bank replied, saying that Singapore's concern was wholly justified. In a memorandum enclosed with its reply, the bank said that it would be desirable to separate the reserves of the two countries at the outset of the proposed arrangements. Formal negotiations began in earnest once Malaysia had accepted that an agreement should guarantee both governments' ownership, management, control of, and immediate access to, their respective reserves at all times. Eleven formal meetings were held between 10 June and 5 July, chaired by the Governor of Bank Negara Malaysia Tan Sri Ismail.[6]

However, doubts persisted on a critical issue. The Bank Negara governor wrote to the permanent secretary (Economic Development Division), Singapore, on 11 July seeking clarification over how the piece of land in Singapore, which was then in the name of Bank Negara Malaysia, could be transferred to the Central Bank of Malaysia, Singapore. He proposed that while the value of this land could be credited to the account of the Central Bank of Malaysia, Singapore, the title should remain in the name of Bank Negara Malaysia. "The implication of this formula was far-reaching," Lim observed. "For if we were to agree to this, it follows that all our currency assets would have to be vested in Bank Negara Malaysia and that this statutory body created by the Malaysian Government would be appointing itself the trustee of our currency reserves and assets."[7] In other words, Singapore would have to hand over legal ownership of all its assets to a bank that was a statutory body of another country and subject entirely to its legislation and control. Such a formula would not guarantee Singapore ownership of and immediate access to its assets and foreign exchange reserves — the basis on which it had begun negotiation with Malaysia. The republic proposed therefore that the assets of both Singapore and Malaysia should be placed with the International Monetary Fund or the Bank of England or a third party that was mutually acceptable as trustee, or alternatively that the deputy governor for Singapore should be incorporated into a corporation sole and that all currency assets of Singapore could be vested in it. Kuala Lumpur rejected both these proposals.[8]

On 17 August 1966, the two governments announced that they could not reach agreement and that Singapore, Malaysia and Brunei would issue separate currencies from 12 June 1967.

Singapore decided to set up its own currency board that could issue notes only with full, 100 per cent backing in reserves. The new Singapore dollar — which would be backed at all times by gold or foreign exchange assets, and which would remain fully convertible — would be equivalent to two shillings and four pence, or 0.290299 gramme of fine gold.[9]

Singapore's decision to have its own currency was a bold break from Malaysia. The nature of the new currency, as Lim noted, made larger points about the the economy of independent Singapore. The right of automatic convertibility of the dollar into sterling, and through sterling into other currencies of the world, was important because so long as sterling (or other overseas) assets were not less in value than the total value of note circulation, automatic convertibility was guaranteed both in law and in fact. Three economic consequences followed from this system. First, it allowed foreign trade to be conducted without exchange control — an essential feature of the monetary system of Singapore, an entrepôt trading centre. Secondly, an automatic sterling exchange standard created equilibrium in the balance of payments. Thirdly, apart from overseas loans and grants, the system obliged the government to balance its budget, both its recurrent and its capital development projects.[10]

Lim was opposed to Singapore having a central bank because of the experience of other countries, where governments could borrow from their own central banks — a euphemism for those banks to print notes and hand them over to the governments to spend. Such credit creation and deficit financing — where governments spent more than what they collected in taxes or borrowed from money markets — led to inflation. In its acute form, the arrangement could lead to the collapse of the exchange currency and the imposition of exchange control. Exchange controls had been imposed in almost all the underdeveloped countries that had emerged after World War II and that had established central banks. By contrast, under the currency board system that Singapore would establish, "it is not possible for a country to spend a dollar more than it earns abroad".[11] As a trading community, Singapore could not afford to have a currency that was less sound than this. "For Singapore, whose economy is open and faces competition at every point from the rest of the world, the most rigorous monetary policies have to be followed," Lim declared. "This calls for the tightest economic and social discipline from the people of Singapore. The 100 per cent backed currency system that we will be operating means that if Singapore wishes to spend more, then we must first earn more. Productivity of labour, efficiency of management and the strength of our economic infrastructure have to be maintained and improved continuously. There is no alternative for Singapore."[12]

As Singapore parted ways with Malaysia, its estimated share of combined assets was $400 million. This money formed the basis of the reserves for the new currency.[13] The Government said that bankers, both those representing local banks and those from banks incorporated overseas, would be represented adequately on the new currency board so that "it shall always be known and manifestly known by banking circles throughout the world" that the new Singapore dollar was fully backed.[14] Lim responded testily to a Barisan press statement saying that the Singapore dollar would be lower in value than the Malaysian dollar because Singapore had no natural resources, which Malaysia did. He called that allegation a "white lie" because Singapore was going for a currency that was backed 100 per cent, "which means that no matter what happens, even if we are burnt down, if we are looted and all that, our assets are outside. Anyone who holds a Singapore dollar can redeem it. It is not what you have that counts. It is what you earn and how you manage your currency."[15] Indeed, the Singapore and Malaysian finance ministers declared that their countries' new dollars would be equal in value.[16]

Looking back, Lee Kuan Yew recalled Lim's "instinctive feel" for how Singapore should deal with Malaysia on the currency issue.

So when the Malaysians wanted us to put our reserves in their hands to maintain one currency with them, his instinctive reaction was: "No". We'd never get our reserves back, and that settled it. He said: "Let's break." I thought it over very carefully. To break, you could have a loss of confidence in both the currencies, not only in one of the two. We, being the smaller economy, the loss of confidence might be worse. I told him: "Look, they cannot corner our reserves; we can put them in escrow, say in the Bank of England or something, to back our currency, and if we want to pull out, we can take it back." He said: "No, no. Don't have all these complications." I went by his gut feel. I said: "Okay, we'll take the risk. We'll break. But we won't have a central bank; we'll have a currency board where every dollar note issued is fully backed." So when we broke, we maintained a currency board where every dollar is backed. Had it been Goh Keng Swee or Hon Sui Sen, I think the decision would still have been the same, but the thinking would not have been so visceral. Gok Seng Swee might have said: "Okay, we will put this in escrow." But Lim Kim San would not even consider that. He'd simply said: "Don't waste time. These chaps are prepared go alone — airlines, the currency, whatever it is, they want to go alone. Let it be. We will survive."[17]

The Singapore Parliament passed the Currency Bill on 13 March 1967, and the new currency came into effect on 12 June. Singapore crossed a milestone on its road out of Malaysia.

TRADING WITH INDONESIA

When Singapore became independent, Indonesia was in confrontation with it and Malaysia. Indonesian leaders tried to "exploit Singapore-Malaysia difficulties by offering Singapore the bait of immediate recognition on conditions that would have affronted and angered Malaysia".[18] Singapore refused to take the bait. Instead, Lim warned merchants in Singapore not to make a "quick dollar" from Indonesian barter traders. "The danger is greater than the gain," he told a delegation from the Singapore Chinese Chamber of Commerce. He reiterated Lee Kuan Yew's declaration that Singapore was willing to trade with any nation that was prepared to trade with it, so long as business relations did not jeopardize the security of Singapore and Malaysia.[19]

However, as trade negotiations between Singapore and Malaysia reached a stalemate soon after separation, Singapore was obliged to redefine its relationship with Indonesia. Malaysia responded with consternation, maintaining that Kuala Lumpur would never allow Jakarta to renew trade relations with Singapore because this would allow the island to bring to Malaysia's doorstep a country that was determined to crush it.[20] The Singapore government saw Malaysia's stand as one of constraining the foreign and trade policy of an independent Singapore. Determined to draw the line, Singapore declared that, as a sovereign and independent country, it must behave and act as one, not least when it came to ensuring its economic survival. Thus, cooperation between Singapore and Malaysia could not be conditional on the notion that they had common friends and common enemies.[21]

Singapore hoped to regain about 2 per cent of its gross national product by re-opening barter trade with Indonesia. Since Confrontation was still on, the trade was to be confined to a policed channel in Pulau Senang, an island to the south of Singapore. Although the Indonesian government did not show any interest in the idea, Indonesian traders did. Nevertheless, the Alliance Cabinet in Kuala Lumpur was alarmed, and convened an emergency meeting. It declared: "The benefit which Singapore expects to derive from this deal is out of proportion to the threat to the very existence of both Malaysia and Singapore." Malaysia argued that it had been "equally anxious to help the people of Singapore by facilitating trade for the benefit of both our people", but defence and security — in fact survival — should come first.[22] Lee reacted by threatening a public disclosure of barter trade between Malaysia and Sumatra and Sabah and Indonesian Borneo that Malaysian officials had permitted quietly. Barter trade between Singapore and Indonesia was resumed on a limited scale in January 1966. Singapore noted that this move was not a resumption of trade *per se* because it was confined to boats of more than 200 tonnes, which had been plying between Singapore and Malaysia and Indonesia. It was only ships less than this weight that had been affected by the ban.[23]

STRATEGIES OF SURVIVAL AND SUCCESS

At the first session of Singapore's first Parliament on 8 December 1965, its constitutional head, Yang di-Pertuan Negara Yusof bin Ishak, noted that radical changes had arisen out of Singapore's severance from Malaysia. Among them were the city-state's industrial and economic development plans, which would need to be reformulated because it was clear that there would be no Common Market with Malaysia. Now, Singapore would have to break into the markets of nations which might have an interest in its survival as an independent, democratic and non-Communist country, and into the markets of countries in Africa and Eastern Europe that might find trade with it beneficial economically and politically.[24]

A memorandum presented to Parliament as an addendum to the Yang di-Pertuan Negara's address fleshed out some of the challenges that separation had presented for Singapore. The section on finance declared that Singapore would have to assume reluctantly that Malaysia would treat it thenceforth as any other third country in trade relations, and hoped that Kuala Lumpur would treat the republic in terms no worse than any other third country. Singapore would need to increase industrial productivity in order to export to other countries, hoping that its friends and allies would not place artificial and discriminatory trade barriers to the entry of its products. Concurrently, the government would pay attention to the necessity of maintaining Singapore's existing level of entrepôt trade. This would be achieved by creating a free trade zone where imports could be broken down and re-exported quickly without the payment of duties. Meanwhile, in order to protect infant industries in their first years, the government had imposed temporary tariff duties and quantitative restrictions on a range of imported products. However, regressive taxes imposed during the Malaysia years had been rescinded.[25]

Foreign Markets and Foreign Investment
Presenting the Republic of Singapore's first Budget on 13 December 1965, Lim underscored the painful consequences of separation from Malaysia. However, he made it clear that the government would employ to the full the opportunities created by its release from the frustration of being governed by a hostile central government. Singapore would utilize, in particular, the restoration of its control over fiscal, monetary and economic policies to fashion an active political and economic foreign policy. "Our policy will have to be the maintenance of our traditional position as a trading centre, while

adding an industrial base to our traditional economy," Lim said.[26] Rotterdam and Hamburg proved that industrialization and entrepôt trade were not incompatible. The creation of free trade zones could address both needs.

As for prospective foreign markets, Lim put them into four broad categories:

- markets in the developed, highly industrialized countries of the world;
- new markets in Africa and Eastern Europe;
- markets to be provided by countries that had been running favourable balances of trade with Singapore consistently;
- markets in countries that had a "vested interest in ensuring that Singapore remains viable and stable so that, in turn, their own security interests are not jeopardized".[27]

Lim elaborated on these distinctions. Speaking of the first category of markets, he noted that enlightened self-interest in the highly developed economies should drive them to provide outlets for the simpler manufactures of developing countries, if for nothing else than to help the latter finance imports of machines and other capital equipment needed for development. As for the second category of markets, Singapore's policy of neutrality and non-alignment between the big power blocs, coupled with its active identification with the post-colonial Afro-Asian world, placed the republic in a good position to sell to growing consumer markets there. On the third category of markets, he said that Singapore would take the initiative to enter into trade agreements with those countries. He admitted that breaking into these markets would take time, and it would not have an immediate impact on Singapore's unemployment situation.[28]

Lim then dealt with the fourth category of prospective markets: Those in countries that took "more than a passing interest in our survival". Singapore's asset was that "we occupy a position of some importance in the strategic defence chain of Southeast Asia". Countries such as the United Kingdom, Australia and New Zealand were "not uninterested", therefore, that the link through Singapore should remain intact. Lim put the matter bluntly: "These countries have an interest that we survive and to this end, to give us export opportunities." Singapore was not demanding unlimited and unrestricted access to their markets because it would be futile to expect countries to countenance imports of such volume as to threaten their domestic industries. But those countries had the capacity to share and absorb the increase in exports that Singapore would need. As Singapore developed, Lim added, it would be prepared to extend to other countries the kind of assistance it was seeking now. "Our proposals are, therefore, a logical step in the overall industrial development pattern of the undeveloped sectors of Asia." Singapore would be approaching these countries formally, he said, warning enigmatically that if no satisfactory solutions were found, then "our whole political future will have to be re-assessed and a re-alignment is inescapable".[29]

Lim's ideas of how Singapore should position itself politically to maximize its economic advantages reflected the government's keenly strategic sense of markets in ensuring the nascent city-state's survival and success. Singapore enjoyed a stable, efficient and honest government. Its realistic and pragmatic approach to development, coupled with the absence of illogical or arbitrary actions taken in the name of nationalism, distinguished the city-state from many of the newly independent countries of Asia and Africa. Singapore was devoid of their ideological hostility to foreign investment.[30] Running against the Afro-Asian current of opinion that viewed multinational corporations as economic predators and that went in for import substitution to protect the domestic economy, Singapore saw foreign capital as a spur to its industrialization. Lim made a pointed overture to Americans, for example. He invited them to use Singapore as a base for a labour-intensive industry such as the assembly of electronic components. Many of these components of computers, communications equipment and television tuners required to be assembled by hand. Industrialized nations with high labour costs were turning increasingly to the region. Singapore had much to offer them. Its young population had a higher level of basic education than workers in other countries, and Singaporeans had proved themselves to be as dexterous and adaptable as other workers were. "Such industries we welcome and promote."[31]

Singapore was aware that it needed to improve its competitive position and provide concrete incentives in order to attract not only foreign investment, but also production and marketing know-how. Thus, it decided to go beyond making available the physical infrastructure for the establishment of factories and eliminating disincentives to investment. The government provided tax holidays to selected, especially welcome industries through the "pioneer status" scheme. Along with tariff protection and preferential purchasing by the government, the pioneer status scheme was designed to assist infant industries to find their feet.[32]

Entrepôt Trade and Industrialization

During the two years when Lim was the finance minister, Singapore followed broadly a dual strategy of preserving its entrepôt status, which was necessary to uphold its interests as a trading state, while pursuing industrial expansion, particularly by developing export-oriented industries.

On the first front, the passage of a bill laid the basis for the establishment of free trade zones. The republic's trading links with countries were growing. Attracted by its excellent distribution facilities, commercial connections and other ancillary services, those countries were expected to utilize the Port of Singapore to sell their goods in the region. This is where free trade zones came in. A World Bank mission in July 1963 had recommended a free trade zone for Singapore to replace its free port status. The Telok Ayer Basin was suggested as the site for the entrepôt goods discharged by lighter and other small craft. During Malaysia, the site had been developed initially and legislation drafted to declare the basin and the port the first free trade zone in Singapore. Trading and entrepôt activities in the zone would be entirely free of customs control.

Following separation, the draft legislation was revised and the views were solicited from representatives of the four chambers of commerce and the Singapore Manufacturers' Association. The government thought that specially designed free trade zones, in addition to licensed and bonded warehouses with drawback facilities, provided the best solution to serving the needs of Singapore's large entrepôt trade. Additional government-licensed factory warehouses in the principal customs territory would continue to be utilized to store dutiable goods, particularly high-duty goods.[33] The bill marked another step in Singapore's efforts to establish a distinctive niche for itself in the economic affairs of the region and the world, undeterred by the loss of the Malayan hinterland.

On the second front, Lim recognized industrialization as the backbone of Singapore's economic development. This realization was marked in his second Budget Statement, delivered on 5 December 1966. He viewed pioneer industrial firms as an important part of the employment programme. No pioneer certificates had been issued in Singapore during the two years when it had been in Malaysia, but between August 1965 and December 1966, 58 new certificates were issued and 25 more projects were approved in principle, these additions bringing the total number of such firms to 165 at the end of 1966 compared to 113 in 1964. More than 100 of them were in production, while 33 projects were in various stages of implementation.[34]

Importantly, Singapore had succeeded in broadening its industrial base, so that it possessed a wide range of industrial enterprises that could be expanded. These included the expansion of oil refineries into a petrochemical complex; the expansion of general ship repairing and building facilities for the construction of specialized vessels; the construction of a fisheries harbour as part of efforts to develop a deep-sea fishing and canning industry; the production of parts and components for motor vehicles, electronics and other engineering assembly industries; and the establishment of a modern paper mill to support paper product industries. [35]

Unemployment remained a serious problem. Lim saw the solution to it in the creation of a crash programme to develop export-oriented industries. "As in the case of all countries which strive for industrial development, we have initially only a limited number of industries directed entirely towards exports. The majority of our existing industries still depend to a great extent on the domestic market," Lim said. "This is inevitable in the early stages of our industrial development. We must now move to a new phase of the industrial programme, namely, the development of export-orientated industries." Singapore needed especially to encourage manufacturers with established overseas markets that could draw their supply of raw materials on a worldwide basis.[36]

Action was required in three major areas, Lim said. The first requirement was to train workers to equip them with the specialized skills that industries required. The second requirement was to improve quality and lower production costs through a national productivity drive. Thus, the government, the National Trades Union Congress (NTUC), the Singapore Manufacturers' Association, and the Singapore Employers' Federation had jointly drawn up a Charter for Industrial Progress in 1965 that recognized how high productivity helped both employers and employees. The third requirement was to attract the type of export industries that bought raw materials and sold their products across the world, industries that could make full use of Singapore's high-quality labour force, its geographic advantages, and its efficient infrastructure. Since international manufacturers enjoyed more or less free choice in deciding where to locate their plants, Singapore would have to compete with other countries to attract such enterprises to its shores. Hence, its fiscal incentives would have to be as attractive as, if not more, than those offered by other countries.[37] Lim announced a generous package of incentives.[38]

Incentives were not sufficient by themselves, however. The entire government machinery would have to adopt a forward and enlightened outlook. It would have to facilitate, not frustrate, businessmen. "What we want are results— not red tape," he declared.[39]

International Economic Organizations

The government also paid close attention to international economic organizations that could protect and project Singapore's trade and financial interests. Arguing for the passage of the Bretton Woods Agreements Bill on 22 June 1966, Lim told Parliament that the International Monetary Fund (IMF) and the International Bank for Reconstruction and Development, known popularly as the World Bank, were founded at the United Nations Monetary and Financial Conference held at Bretton Woods in June 1944. The fund was designed to stabilize exchange rates and promote a free system of world trade and payments by helping member-countries tide over temporary difficulties in their international balance of payments. The bank was intended mainly to provide capital that could not be obtained from private sources to finance productive investments in member-countries. Membership of the IMF being a prerequisite for membership of the World Bank, he argued that Singapore should join the IMF. Apart from the reassurance that it could look to the IMF should it encounter temporary balance of payments problems, Singapore would gain by accepting the IMF's Articles of Agreement because the government would be indicating that it would abide by acceptable practices regarding the par value of the Singapore currency and exchange control. "This will instil in other countries further confidence in Singapore," Lim noted. "Besides, Singapore will be able to get competent and objective assessments of its own economy and advice on economic problems from both the Fund and the Bank."[40]

Member of Parliament Tang See Chim found it ironical that Singapore's membership of the IMF, from which it would not derive much benefit, should be more expensive than its membership of the World Bank, which would benefit it substantially. Tang added that, although Singapore would benefit from becoming a member of the bank, it was questionable whether it would be fruitful for Singapore to have so much money tied up in the bank.[41] Replying, Lim agreed that if the benefits of joining the IMF and the World Bank were less than having M$186 million tied up, then Singapore should have second thoughts. Also, it was true that the IMF and the World Bank had been rather conservative in their approach to loan applications from developing countries. Singapore had made it clear to the World Bank therefore that it would have second thoughts on joining if the bank did not streamline its methods for approving loans to those countries. However, the larger picture was that the IMF was a worldwide organization designed to help countries that faced temporary balance-of-payments and currency problems. He suggested that Singapore join the World Bank; it would not be too late to withdraw if the organization did not move fast enough or if it was not as helpful as it was expected to be.[42]

The bill was passed. So was a similar bill on ratifying Singapore's decision to become a signatory to the Asian Development Bank Agreement, which focused on the Asian bank as a source of funds for future industrial projects and as a way for Singapore to associate itself with other Asian countries to enhance regional cooperation.[43]

Industrial Relations
Like his colleagues in the People's Action Party, Lim Kim San knew that Singapore needed a fundamental social transformation to lay the basis for a vigorous new phase of economic development. Like them, he had a blueprint for transforming Singapore's society so that it could produce the workers and managers who could enable the city-state to fit into emerging global chains of production and

consumption. But for the process to even begin, Singapore would have to leave behind the legacy of industrial unrest produced during the years when the Communists had been ascendant politically.

Overcoming that legacy of conflict meant clarifying the government's role in management-labour relations. The role, Lim believed, was to "hold the balance" between management and labour so that investors received a fair return for capital invested and workers received a fair wage for work rendered. "This Government is committed to a policy of uplifting the standard of living of the workers and will not tolerate any employer who denies that responsible unions have a positive role to play in our joint endeavours," Lim declared. As for labour, he reminded workers that Singapore was engaged in "a massive exercise for survival" and that success called for discipline, restraint and self-sacrifice. Drawing a parallel, he pointed to labour's role in the economic rise of Germany and Japan after World War II.[44] Giving his views on the larger role of management in a post-colonial economy, Lim said that he would like to see the emergence of a new type of manager, which he called the "National Manager". This manager could be from the public or the private sector. He could be dealing directly with industry or commerce, or be administering the public infrastructure of development. Indeed, he could be a citizen or only a resident of Singapore. Whatever his particular role, the national manager's purpose would be to concern himself with the republic's economic problems. He would dedicate himself to Singapore's progress and prosperity, and would assume a vested interest in the economic underpinnings of successful nation-building by focusing on productivity in particular.[45]

The policy decisions that Lim took within this framework of management-labour relations did not go unchallenged. The Barisan was the main source of opposition outside the PAP; even within the party, MPs questioned the government's stance on labour issues. Labour leader Bernard Rodrigues took up a dispute between the government and public daily-rated employees over their demand for the back-dating of wage revisions. "The primary stake to us in the dispute is the sanctity of the collective agreement," Rodrigues argued.

> In fact in Singapore today, the collective agreement is the touchstone of industrial stability. Both trade unions and employers have adopted a responsible attitude towards collective agreement [, so] that a measure of the Queensbury rules has been possible for some time now between both management and labour, where fury and scorn were the order before.

Strikes called by trade unions had been few and far between since the democratic trade union movement, embodied by the National Trades Union Congress, had assumed command of the labour situation after defeating the "anti-national forces", a reference to unions led by pro-Communists. Rodrigues said that the NTUC had no intention of degenerating into an "effete movement". Such degeneration would not serve Singapore's interests because a docile trade union movement would not be a constructive alternative to a pro-Communist movement.[46]

Lim Kim San stood firm, however. He replied to Rodrigues' specific demands on retrospective pay, and then went on to make a larger point. He declared that back-pay should be discouraged, if not disallowed altogether, because "no Government can plan its financial policies and administer them wisely if there is a sinister threat that out of nowhere someone is going to produce a bill that the Government has to make arrears for back-pay". He continued:

> As Minister for Finance, I am particularly anxious to see that considerable financial resources are not frittered away by demands on back-pay when such resources are desperately needed for the financing of economic projects in the country for the general upliftment of the standard of living of the people in the country.[47]

The government was committed to raising the standard of living of all the people, "most of all the working class", but it had to plan the use of its limited financial resources carefully.

The issue of public daily-rated employees came up again during the Budget Session in 1966. Ho See Beng, another PAP MP who was also the NTUC's secretary-general, pushed for wage revisions for the employees, saying he was doubtful that Singapore could increase productivity with a "dissatisfied, disillusioned and disgusted" labour force.[48] Lim responded that this was no time to ask for a wage revision because, in the midst of a Singapore with a large number of unemployed people, the unskilled labour in the public daily-rated unions was the highest paid unskilled labour in Southeast Asia. The need of the hour was to prove that Singapore was more efficient than others were in attracting entrepreneurs with industrial schemes that would create more employment. [49]

Ho had raised the issue of the daily-rated workers in the context of Lim's assurance that the government would hold a fair balance between management and labour. "If he had in mind any decision to be made by the government, *ipso facto* to be accepted and implemented by labour, he is sadly mistaken," Ho warned. "Any unilateral approach coupled with the hysteria of 'industrialisation at any cost' would be completely rejected by labour if it amounts to the exploitation of the interest of the working class."[50] Regarding the government's attempt to attract foreign capital to fuel its industrialization programme, he cautioned it about the quality of the foreign capital that it was attracting. "We do not want to encourage those entrepreneurs, whether they are from Hongkong or Timbuctoo, who would be only interested in exploiting labour and accumulating profits on the basis of sweated labour." Many of those entrepreneurs might have exhausted their quotas in foreign markets from their countries of origin, and these birds of passage could be looking to Singapore as a convenient place in which to exploit labour. Ho demanded of Lim an unqualified assurance to the labour force that "in his enthusiasm to create a climate favourable for foreign capital, he will not follow a policy consistent with a Gladstonian economy."[51] Ho drove home the point, calling on the government not to sacrifice the interests of the working class "in its over-enthusiasm during the transformation from an entrepot economy to an industrialised State".[52] Rodrigues concurred, commenting on the "casualty of labour in the transition of the Republic from an entrepôt to an industrial centre". The Budget made ample provisions to attract foreign capital, but it was silent on how to channel into the industrial sector workers who might be made redundant by the closing down of firms engaged in the import trade, a "necessary side effect of the Government's export drive".[53]

Lim responded to the criticism without going on the defensive. He reiterated the government's socialist principles, such as taxing those who were best able to afford it. Examples were the revised method of taxing motor vehicles and an increase in driving licence fees announced in the Budget.[54] But he held firm on Singapore's philosophy of industrial relations, declaring that neither management nor labour should exploit the other. Singapore had not allowed entrepreneurs to take advantage of the unemployment situation, he argued. He hoped that trade union leaders would realize that the success of the industrialization programme, which would create more employment and prosperity for Singapore ultimately, called for everyone to "pull up our socks, do our best, and understand the problem before us, and do not do anything at all which will bring harm to our country".[55] The meaning was clear: Labour unrest was out. Not even the governing philosophy of democratic socialism would countenance that.

Pragmatism
Lim had another spirited, but friendly, exchange of views in Parliament with Ho that revealed the government's pragmatic approach to democratic socialism. Ho took exception to the idea of the government promoting gambling, as he saw it, through a lottery, because no government in the world that believed in socialism would do so. Ho's

objection to the lottery was based on his argument that it was the poor who, in spite of possessing the least disposable income among all the classes, would contribute the most towards the purchase of lottery tickets. He averred that the essence of democratic socialism was that there should be an equal distribution of wealth as far as possible; one way of achieving this goal was to minimize income disparity. Ho rejected the argument that a legal lottery, revenues from which would support the work of welfare organizations, was a way of drawing people away from illegal or foreign lotteries that benefited no social cause in Singapore. He believed that the government was less interested in objecting to private lotteries on principle and more interested in raising revenue. To him, it was a credit to take money from the rich to give to the poor, but not to take money from the poor and give it to the poor.[56]

Ho was supported by another member of parliament, S. Rajoo, who said: "For a democratic government dedicated to socialist principles to have the idea of running a sweepstake or lottery for the purposes of raising funds is very much deplorable. We have a stable government and an able Minister for Finance who knows ways and means of how to squeeze money in the way of taxes from the general public." In trying to raise more money through lottery revenues, "he is trying to sneak through the backdoor and induce poor housewives to spend more money."[57] At one point in the debate, Rajoo argued that it was possible that the lottery could make the rich richer and the poor poorer. A rich man could buy 1,000 tickets, whereas a poor man could buy ten. Hence, the rich man's chances of winning were 100 times those of the poor man's. Thus, the rich man would become richer and the poor man poorer.[58]

At this, a member of parliament exclaimed: "Then good luck to him!" Lim said: "That is exactly what I said." No one was being compelled to buy lottery tickets, he noted. In the long run, he acknowledged, it was through education that people's propensity for gambling could be changed. "But until then, let us tinge our idealism with a little bit of realism and see that whatever money is spent by the people in gambling does not leave this country."[59]

A New Culture

Economic modernization went beyond bread-and-butter issues and required a clear sense of social direction. To Lim, multiracialism was an indispensable part of the social journey on which the PAP had embarked. In a speech congratulating the Singapore Chinese Chamber of Commerce on its sixtieth anniversary celebrations on 15 March 1966, he acknowledged that the chamber had on occasion gone beyond matters of commerce and industry and had acted as a platform for the articulation of issues that had no relevance to business as such, such as citizenship, education, language and culture. There had been no alternative to such political interventions, including agitation for reform, in a colonial society where there had been no right of franchise and therefore no popular representation on the legislative organs of the state. Even in Malaysia, "ours was a society in which we were not entirely free to express our will and to pursue courses of our choosing."

However, Lim noted pointedly, Singapore was independent and sovereign now, with a popularly elected government and representatives of the people sitting in Parliament. The government's policy of multiracialism, with equal treatment of all regardless of race, language or religion, had removed the "need for representations on a communal basis". Unlike early immigrants from China, who wanted to prosper in Singapore before returning home, the present generation of Chinese had struck roots in Singapore and intended to stay and die there because "in truth, there is nowhere else to go". Those Singaporeans who were of immigrant stock must not confuse race and nationality, he said. Singapore did not believe in forced assimilation of any of its races by any other, nor did it subscribe to the theory of one race, one culture. Singapore nationals must think of the country in the context of Southeast Asia, therefore, and "not as an extension of the original homeland of our forefathers". Even Australians, who had for many, many years never regarded their country as anything more than "a little England in the Pacific", had realized that they were geographically near to Asia and had re-oriented their thinking accordingly.[60]

Lim's two years in the Ministry of Finance were also the first two crucial years for Singapore as it faced and tried to meet the challenges that came with independence. Lim's gut feeling for what needed to be done on the financial and trade front played an important role in Singapore's successful emergence from those make-or-break years.

Notes

1. Chan Heng Chee, *Singapore: The Politics of Survival 1965–1967* (Singapore and Kuala Lumpur: Oxford University Press, 1971), pp. 29–30.
2. Ibid., pp. 30–31.
3. *Parliamentary Debates: Republic of Singapore*, Official Report, 13 December 1965, Volume 24, column 53. Henceforth *Parliamentary Debates*.
4. *Straits Times*, 19 March 1966.
5. *Parliamentary Debates*, 13 December 1965, Vol. 24, col. 54.
6. Lim Kim San, Statement on the Common Currency and Banking System, 26 August 1966, *Parliamentary Debates*, Vol. 25, cols. 267–69.
7. *Parliamentary Debates*, 26 August 1966, Vol. 25, col. 270.
8. Ibid.
9. Ibid., col. 278.
10. Ibid., col. 273.
11. Ibid., col. 275.
12. Ibid., col. 277.
13. Ibid., col. 279.
14. Ibid., col. 278.
15. Ibid., cols. 284–85.
16. *Straits Times*, 27 August 1966.
17. Interview.
18. Lee Kuan Yew, *From Third World to First: The Singapore Story, 1965–2000* (Singapore: Singapore Press Holdings, 2000), p. 295.
19. *Malay Mail*, 13 August 1965.
20. Chan, *Singapore: The Politics of Survival*, op. cit., p. 35.
21. Ibid.

22. Ibid., p. 32.
23. Ibid.
24. *Parliamentary Debates*, 8 December 1965, Vol. 24, col. 12.
25. Ibid., cols. 17–18.
26. *Parliamentary Debates*, 13 December 1965, Vol. 24, col. 48.
27. Ibid., col. 49.
28. Ibid., cols. 49–50.
29. Ibid., cols. 50–51.
30. Lim Kim San, Speech at the Singapore Manufacturers' Association Luncheon, 19 November 1965, Singapore Government Press Statement, MC.NOV.29/65 (FIN), p. 1.
31. Lim Kim San, Speech at a luncheon given by the American Association, 3 November 1966, MC.NOV.3/66 (FIN), pp. 6–7.
32. Ibid.
33. Free Trade Zones Bill, 26 August 1966, Parliamentary Debates, Vol. 25, cols. 305–308.
34. Annual Budget Statement, 5 December 1966, *Parliamentary Debates*, Vol. 25, col. 452.
35. Ibid., col. 453.
36. Ibid., col. 454.
37. Ibid., cols. 454–56.
38. *Parliamentary Debates*, 5 December 1966, Vol. 25, cols. 457–59.
39. Ibid., col. 460.
40. *Parliamentary Debates*, 22 June 1966, Vol. 25, cols. 123–24.
41. Ibid., cols. 126–27.
42. Ibid., cols. 128–29.
43. *Parliamentary Debates*, 26 August 1966, Vol. 25, cols. 311–13.
44. Lim Kim San, Speech at the Singapore Manufacturers' Association Luncheon, op. cit., p. 3.
45. Lim Kim San, Speech at the opening of the joint seminar organized by the Singapore Institute of Management and the Administrative Service Association of Singapore, 16 August 1967.
46. "Issue of Back-Pay of the Public Daily Rated Employees Union Federation", 13 December 1965, *Parliamentary Debates*, Vol. 24, cols. 80–83.
47. Ibid., col. 86.
48. Debate on the Annual Budget Statement, 14 December 1966, *Parliamentary Debates*, Vol. 25, col. 645.
49. Ibid., col. 670.
50. Ibid., col. 644.

51. Ibid., col. 643.
52. Ibid., col. 648.
53. Ibid., col. 662.
54. Ibid., col. 666.
55. Ibid., col. 676.
56. Betting and Sweepstake Duties (Amendment) Bill, 26 October 1966, *Parliamentary Debates*, Vol. 25, cols. 389–92.
57. Ibid., col. 398.
58. Ibid, col. 402.
59. Ibid., cols. 402–403.
60. Singapore Government Press Statement, MC.MAR.32/66 (FIN), pp. 1–3.

11

Minister for the Interior and Defence

Lim Kim San, independent Singapore's first Minister for Finance, and Goh Keng Swee, its first Minister for the Interior and Defence, switched portfolios in August 1967. The switch was natural given that, in Lim's own words, among the most important objectives of sovereign Singapore were the need to build a defence capability, and the need to turn Singapore into an industrialized nation.[1] What made his transfer to the Defence Ministry particularly important was the context in which it occurred: Britain's decision to withdraw militarily from East of Suez, a move that imperilled the security of fledgling Singapore.

The British Defence White Paper published in July 1967 announced the intention to reduce forces in Southeast Asia by half by 1970/71, and to withdraw completely by the middle of the 1970s. However, the British economy was in such a parlous state that the pound sterling was devalued in November 1967. Now, London's policy was to put British economic interests ahead of its global commitments. The consequences of that shift were soon apparent in the announcement of an accelerated timetable for military retrenchment. The British government declared in January 1968 that its forces would withdraw from East of Suez by the end of 1971.[2]

Singapore had been building its defence forces since 1965. However, Britain's accelerated plans for withdrawal made it necessary for the republic to draw up an entirely new plan. A large and rapid increase in its defence expenditure became necessary to build up the capabilities of the army, the navy and the air force to provide credible security.[3] The expansion of the defence forces between 1968 and 1971 would be a costly undertaking. The annual cost in cash terms would reach about 10 per cent of Singapore's existing gross national product, or more than S$300 million a year.[4] A series of taxes was proposed in 1968 to meet the greater cost of defence. Four were entirely new taxes, while three involved increases or changes in existing rates of taxes.[5]

The economic consequences of the British withdrawal went beyond what Singapore would have to spend now to ensure its physical survival: They impinged on Singapore's economic survival itself. The young republic, which was hard-pressed already to find its footing after separation, faced a precipitous decline in its gross national product and a socially-destabilizing loss of employment of large numbers of people working on the British bases. British military expenditure accounted for about 20 per cent of Singapore's GDP, and provided more than 30,000 jobs in direct employment, and another 40,000 in support services. The loss of that expenditure between 1968 and 1971 would cost the economy dearly.[6] The Singapore government therefore formed the Bases Economic Conversion Department, which Lee Kuan Yew placed in his own portfolio in the Prime Minister's Office. Its job was to "retrain and redeploy redundant workers, take possession of land and other assets the British were vacating, put them to the best use, and negotiate migratory aid".[7] Even as the British military bases were converted profitably to industrial use, the Economic Development Board attracted investors from around the world to set up industries on what used to be British army land. Thus, the withdrawal, a military danger, was converted into an economic opportunity. "The withdrawal was carried out with goodwill on both sides," Lee writes.[8]

Security remained a key issue, however. In February 1967, Lee had tabled legislation to amend the National Service Ordinance that the British had passed in 1952. The aim of the new law was to create a people's army by mobilizing a large section of the population through compulsory National Service for male adults; in addition, Singapore would possess a small component of regular forces. This way, the young republic would not need to spend money on the recurrent costs of a large standing army, but would nevertheless create a credible deterrent for potential aggressors. "The best deterrent to any Malaysian plan to regain control over Singapore was their knowledge that even if they could subdue our armed forces, they would have to keep down a whole people well trained in the use of arms and explosives," Lee says.[9]

Singapore's military strength did not go unnoticed across the Causeway. In 1966, the Malaysian public had perceived the Singapore Armed Forces as a joke. But when Malaysian Defence Minister Tun Abdul Razak visited Singapore to attend the National Day Parade on 9 August 1969, Lim arranged for a squadron of AMX-13 tanks and V200 armoured vehicles to roll past in the parade. It had a "dramatic effect" on people in Johor when they watched the parade on television that night, and elsewhere in Malaysia, where people saw newspaper photographs of the tanks the following day.[10] Malaysia had no tanks then. Lee relates how Razak told Goh that, while he (Razak) himself was not concerned over Singapore's military build-up, many Malaysians were. Indeed, there was anxiety in Johor over whether Singapore intended to invade the state. Razak suggested that Lim, as defence minister, should travel to Kuala Lumpur to reassure people that Singapore harboured no hostile intentions towards Malaysia.[11]

In the event, however, Singapore's tanks and armoured vehicles were needed, not to invade Johor, as Malaysians had imagined, but to shelter the nascent republic from the consequences of worsening race relations in Malaysia. The 13 May 1969 race riots in Kuala Lumpur rekindled Lee's fears that, with Razak in charge and the Malay ultras on the ascendant, the Tunku could be pushed aside and the ultras could decide to send the army down to Singapore to take it back by force.[12] That did not occur.

Lee writes that by 1971, the date of the British withdrawal, Singapore had 17 national service battalions (16,000 men), with 14 battalions (11,000 men) in the reserves. It had infantry and commando units, artillery units with mortars, a battalion each of tanks, armoured personnel carriers, field engineers, signals, field maintenance, field hospital and field supply, and a heavy transport company. It had established schools for basic military training and officer cadets, the artillery, engineers, bomb disposal units and naval training. Its air force had a squadron each of Hunters, Strikemaster trainer aircraft, Alouette helicopters and transport aircraft.[13] A new era had begun for Singapore, and Lim was playing an active role in it.

DEFENCE

Recalling the era, Lee said of Lim:

> My recollections of him over the many years that we worked together are that he is not a theoretical person. He is a practical person. Goh Keng Swee is completely different. He is a very cerebral person, analytical. I gave him Defence. His experience was just as a Corporal in the Singapore Volunteer Forces. But he read books, he contacted people who knew about armed forces, he contacted the Israelis and so on, and he worked out in his mind an intellectual framework of how the Defence Ministry would be crafted and developed. Lim Kim San hasn't got that kind of approach. When I sent him to Defence, it was to implement Goh Keng Swee's framework while I sent Goh Keng Swee to do something else. So, they are different people with different assets.[14]

Singapore's security outlook was mixed when Lim took charge of defence. The accelerated British military withdrawal left Singapore very little time in which to forge an effective armed force out of its young population. However, Malaysia, Lim believed, was not an expansionist and belligerent power. Leaders of the Federation had emphasized that their prime objective was to raise Malaysians' living standards through economic growth. Hence, Singapore did not face an external threat from Malaysia so long as its system and its leadership continued. Lim was less sanguine about Indonesia, wondering aloud whether Sukarno's undeclared war would be repeated, perhaps on a higher key. He noted, however, that the new leadership in Jakarta was a rational one that was struggling to repair the economic damage that Sukarno's policies had inflicted on Indonesia.[15]

Nevertheless, events in Thailand, Burma (now Myanmar) and Indochina — where the "cruel and vicious" war in South Vietnam could spill over — left Singapore no room for complacency. "While internal conditions in our two immediate neighbouring states are favourable for the continuation of peace, we cannot assume that there are no dangers ahead should, for instance, there be a change of regime," Lim warned. "No one can predict the future beyond four or five years." This long-term uncertainty made it necessary to fill the power vacuum that the British withdrawal would create. "We cannot hope to fill this power vacuum either by ourselves or even in combination with friendly powers. Nevertheless, it is necessary to do what we can to raise our defence forces in the face of the long-term risk of insecurity." The republic's defence strategy was not to fight those poised to overcome it but to achieve security in the longer term so that the people of Singapore could plan ahead for their children, their business, their future. In this context, he said, it was essential that Singapore raise defence forces of its own because other countries could not be expected to defend a nation that was unprepared to defend itself.[16]

Lim was confident of Singaporeans' commitment to national defence. One measure of citizens' involvement was the Singapore Defence Fund that Lim set up in January 1968 to help finance the island's security. By April 1968, it had collected almost S$4 million, donated not only by businesses and philanthropic organizations but also by ordinary people such as taxi drivers; by October that year, it had passed the S$7 million mark; by November 1968, it was close to S$10 million. The commitment was felt most keenly among those who had taken up arms in the defence of the young republic. Speaking at the graduation ceremony of the first artillery officers' course conducted by the Singapore Armed Forces Training Institute, Lim said that he had found from experience that young citizens responded well always to challenges if problems were set clearly before them. Hence, he was confident that Singapore could build an army second to none in the region.[17]

It would need more than an army, however, as Lim declared in a radio and television talk on "the Crucial Years" — the period that awaited Singapore immediately after the accelerated withdrawal of the British troops. Outlining Singapore's short-term defence aims, he said that they would consist of two interceptor aircraft squadrons, anti-aircraft units, and coastal patrol craft of various categories, in addition to the army. He acknowledged that two squadrons were "very small beer" compared to other air forces, but for a small country like Singapore, even that modest number would call for a significant effort in terms of money, personnel and training. "Most important, it will serve to prove to friendly powers that we can be a useful party in a collective effort to maintain peace and stability in this area," he noted. Singapore would need to establish a system of coastal patrols to guard approaches to the harbour and, within the capabilities of a small navy, to keep the sea approaches to Singapore open. There was, of course, the much larger issue of keeping the sea lanes, for example the Straits of Malacca, open to international shipping and to maintain freedom of navigation of the high seas. That issue, and other problems, would be discussed when representatives of the five Commonwealth countries — Australia, Britain, Malaysia, New Zealand and Singapore — met from time to time, Lim said.[18]

Singapore's defence posture began to take shape within this broader context. Lim declared that the republic would respond positively to Tunku Abdul Rahman's suggestion that the two countries should share, for joint defence, the military installations that Britain would leave behind in 1971. The Tunku said that, in return, he was prepared to allow the republic to station its military personnel at defence installations in Malaysia. He said that all countries interested in the region's defence, such as Australia and New Zealand, should work out the arrangement. Lim welcomed the proposal as a contribution to regional security.[19] No specific military commitments, except the intention to hold exercises, were forthcoming at the five-power defence talks in Kuala Lumpur in June 1968. However, the Singapore delegation, which Goh led and which included Lim, was heartened by the fact that Australia and New Zealand had been encouraged greatly by the British expression of interest in the defence of Malaysia and Singapore even after 1971.[20] As for bilateral talks on defence, Singapore and Kuala Lumpur agreed in late 1969 to meet more regularly for discussions.[21] In 1970, Lim announced that Singapore was ready to contribute troops to a Commonwealth defence force. At a parade to mark Armed Forces Day, he said: "We are reaffirming our dedication to defend ourselves and to contribute our share to maintain the stability and security of this area. We have made full use of the time at our disposal to build up a credible defence capability and today we can honesty say that we are in a position to play our part in a five nation defence force."[22]

The prime ministers of the five countries involved in the Five-Power Defence Arrangements (FPDA) met in London in mid-April 1971 to finalize the political arrangements to replace the Anglo-Malayan Defence Agreement (AMDA). The integrated air defence system was inaugurated on 1 September 1971. AMDA was replaced by the FPDA on 31 October 1971. "The old era of underwritten security had ended," Lee writes. "From now on we had to be responsible for our own security."[23]

National Service

National Service (NS) was key to Singapore's quest for security. The British had introduced the idea during the Malayan Emergency, when the Legislative Council had passed a National Service Ordinance in 1952, which came into effect in 1954. However, residents of Singapore greeted the colonial move with vehement protests that snowballed into violence when Chinese Middle School students rioted and barricaded themselves in schools. The policy came to a premature end.[24]

National Service was resuscitated after separation from Malaysia. In a reflection of the change in political outlook that independence had wrought among Singaporeans, there were no riots this time. Calls for volunteers were made in October 1965 and, by the end of the year, when laws were passed establishing a new Singapore Army and the People's Defence Force, about 3,000 Singaporeans had responded to the call. In February 1967, Lee Kuan Yew made an historic speech in which he announced that the government would introduce National Service on a large scale. The details were released soon after. All 18-year-old male Singapore citizens and permanent residents, in addition to civil servants and students, would be called up for National Service. Ten per cent would be called up for full-time training lasting two years. After having completed the training, they would return to civilian life but would be placed in the Reserve Service. The remainder would be called up for part-time service with the People's Defence Force, the Special Constabulary and the Vigilantes. The National Service (Amendment) Bill was tabled on 27 February 1967 and passed on 14 March 1967.[25]

Goh Keng Swee had created the framework for National Service by envisioning the transformation of the Singapore Armed Forces from a small force of regulars backed by volunteer reservists, into a large citizen-army based on conscription and long-term compulsory reservist service.[26] On Lim Kim San fell the duty of implementing it and fine-tuning the details, particularly the length of service, to meet Singapore's evolving needs.

Lim faced the need to balance perennial sets of competing needs: The desire for individual achievement with the needs of the nation; and the manpower requirements of industry and commerce with the demands of defence. He stood firm on the need to follow rules on enlistment. For example, he told the National University of Singapore Students' Union that he was not prepared to defer part-time National Service until graduation because the defence build-up had to be completed before 1971. He said also that the defence planning machinery could not grant exemptions to university students.[27]

However, just as the government stood firm on the rules, it tried to accommodate the economic interests of its young citizens who were laying the basis of Singapore's security through National Service. Lim announced in July 1968 that recruitment into the Singapore Civil Service from 1970 would be made only from among those who had completed their service. "Just as we are forced to extend national service to graduates, in the same way we are forced to include civil servants in order to train enough officers for our requirements." He announced also that the government was working out a scheme in which both industries and commerce would recruit only those who had completed National Service.[28] The National Service (Employment) Bill, passed in June 1970, gave legislative teeth to the government's desire to give first priority to discharged National Servicemen (NSmen) in filling job vacancies.[29] By 1970, Singapore was facing a labour shortage, making it necessary for the government to enforce the provisions of the bill. However, as MP Chiang Hai Ding observed, the legislation demonstrated in concrete terms to NSmen that the government recognized their direct contribution to Singapore's security and their indirect service to its prosperity. Supporting Chiang's view, MP Teong Eng Siong called the bill a very wise measure that would enable conscripts to concentrate on their training without having to fear that they were losing out on the job market.[30]

Nevertheless, members of parliament subjected to intense scrutiny the changes to National Service regulations that Lim made as he implemented and fine-tuned the framework that Goh had created. For example, during the Budget Debate in December 1968, MP Low Guan Onn acknowledged that it was essential for Singapore to build up its military capability before the British withdrew their troops. However, he pointed out that the withdrawal would cause tremendous problems of unemployment, which would have to be met by Singapore generating economic growth. Growth required support for export-oriented industries. The problem was that Singapore suffered from a dearth of trained manpower at the professional, technical and craft levels, which these industries needed in order to thrive. In the circumstances, he questioned the wisdom of calling up graduates, within the age group liable, from the three levels of technical education to do National Service as soon as they passed out from institutions of learning. Low argued that calling up the graduates constituted a "great wastage of trained manpower", particularly because they would lose, in the course of doing National Service, much of the theoretical and academic knowledge that they had acquired. He called on the government to adopt a "more pragmatic approach to the problem of defence and economic growth as they are complementary to each other in our national survival". The balance that he had in mind involved releasing a certain percentage of the technical graduates at the three levels of training to build up industries so that they could contribute their skills to industry. He appealed to the government to relax policy by allowing graduates of technical institutions within the age group affected to work if they found jobs and to do part-time National Service. This change would help especially those graduates who were the sole breadwinners of their families.[31]

Lim responded by disagreeing that National Service was responsible for the dearth of manpower required for economic growth. He denied that his ministry had called up technical graduates of the polytechnic and the university. "If it had been so, my men and I would not be running around today trying to find technical men to man the positions that we have," he said, clarifying that only those who had graduated since 1967 had been called up; the majority were in industry. With regard to the request to reserve a portion of those graduates to help in Singapore's industrial growth, "I cannot promise him that because we are at the very outset of our build-up". The question was one of priority between economic growth and defence capability. "I would like Members to think that without this defence build-up, there may come a time when all the economic growth in the world will not stand us in good stead," Lim said, "because we would be captured and it would be too late to regret that we should have given priority to our defence build-up first."[32]

That clear message, unpalatable though it was to those who gave priority to economic growth, was underlined in June 1969, when the National Service (Amendment) Bill proposed that the liability of those selected for officer training be increased from two years to three years. This change was desirable because officer training was a lengthy and expensive process. To be effective, an officer would have to serve at least eighteen months after he had been trained; he could then go into the Reserves.[33] MP Lee Teck Him, who had argued previously that training for students of higher educational institutions should be reduced from two years to six months, was aghast that the bill would instead increase the period from two years to three years. "We should place a premium on our specialists and scholars from the higher institutions. We should give them special treatment. Why should we train them as military officers?" Lee asked. He argued that some people were "scared to death" the moment that they picked up a sword or a gun. Hence, not "weaklings" but only people who were of "stout heart" and were "tall and strong" should be enlisted for military training.[34]

Lim rejected that argument stoutly. He answered that "not all officers are scholars and not all scholars are officers" in the army. Although some university graduates were officers, not all officers were university graduates. Lee was "living in the past" in speaking about army officers being robust, healthy and extroverts. Certainly,

Singapore's young army needed such people, but it needed also people with brains. Training an officer for eighteen months and then letting him off served no purpose. Lim assured his parliamentary colleague that he had looked into the question and that, acting on the advice of experts, the government had decided that it was best for an officer to serve three years in the army. The bill, which stipulated also that persons currently undergoing two years' full-time National Service would be required to serve for three years, was passed.[35]

In late October 1969, Lim said that full-time National Service might have to be done after pre-university studies for those going for tertiary education. He argued that such an arrangement would produce more mature and better-equipped students at university level. He was responding to views put forward by a Chinese Chamber of Commerce delegation, which had presented him with a memorandum querying Singapore's use of manpower and claiming that many students graduating overseas were staying away because of National Service. The memorandum urged the government to shorten the period of full-time training for graduates. Lim held his ground, arguing that effective training for a private should be at least two years, and for an officer, three years. As for the shortage of professionals in commerce and industry, he said that the problem would be resolved when the first batch of graduates completed their NS in 1970.[36] Soon after, he reiterated his opposition to suggestions that NSmen should be given only part-time training, or full-time only after they had finished their university education. "It is impossible to train an efficient defence force part-time," he said. Also, it would be a waste of manpower resources to train university and pre-university students part-time because that would mean turning them out as privates, and poorly trained privates at that. Making a larger political point, he observed: "I think it must be clearly understood that with independence we have no choice but to set aside a portion of our lives in preserving our independence."[37]

In January 1970, Lim announced a stricter enforcement of the policy on National Service deferment. It stipulated that persons liable for call-up would not be granted exit permits to proceed overseas for studies, except for three categories: Those awarded overseas scholarships through the Public Service Commission; those selected for approved postgraduate courses; and those currently undergoing full-time instruction in tertiary education overseas. All students who had attained the age of eighteen or more would, on completion of their School Certificate or Higher School Certificate or graduation from institutions of higher learning, become available for full-time service. In addition to other provisions, the announcement said that those who succeeded in attaining commissioned officer's rank and had attended academic courses provided by the Singapore Armed Forces might be considered favourably for government scholarships or awards. Deferment from NS would still be allowed, but the circumstances for making that exception would have to be more extraordinary than they had been in the past.[38] The enforcement of the rules would affect about 20,000 young people who reached call-up age each year. Lim disclosed also that only 6 per cent of young people called up for NS had been found medically unfit, and had been exempted. The number of draft dodgers was even more insignificant. In 1969, there were only twenty-three of them. As for conscientious objection to the call-up, Lim stood firm: It would not be accepted as grounds for exemption.[39]

MP Ng Yeow Chong thought that the government was not making a wise move. He gave a variety of reasons. The move would cause a very serious gap of discontinuity to appear between secondary and university education, create a lack of graduates and professionals needed for industrialization and economic development, and cause dissatisfaction among students keen on higher studies and among their parents. The move would make it difficult for post-National Service students to resume their studies, and it would dampen academic interest among secondary schoolboys because they would know that they would be called up soon after.[40]

Lim dismissed the notion that three years of NS would make students forget what they had learned before it. Millions of people in countries across the world had had their education interrupted by World War II, but they had resumed their studies. Indeed, half the members of the Singapore Cabinet had had their education interrupted by the war. Lim believed that the NS years actually made young people more mature, sober and steady.[41] Recalling the visit made to him by the Chinese Chamber of Commerce deputation, he said that he had countered its argument against the conscription of graduates by asking it what the age of conscription should be. It had replied that it should be eighteen. But the very same group raised a hue and cry when eighteen was made the age of conscription and was unable to give him a convincing reason for its objection, since to do so would mean contradicting its original stance against the conscription of graduates. The fact of the matter, Lim declared firmly, was that young Singaporean males would have to spend some time serving their country. "It is up to us, who have worked and thought long over this question, to decide what is the best age for national service," he added.[42]

Soon after Lim announced the more rigid enforcement of the conscription policy for 18-year-olds, he had cause for concern over what he called a "pernicious and insidious" campaign of secret whispers against National Service carried out by a minority of people, "parasites who owed loyalty to nobody but themselves". The whispers insinuated that there was no need for National Service because tiny Singapore, which twelve bombs could wipe out, could not be defended in any case.[43] According to an official source, the culprits behind the whispering war were all-too-often wealthy, high-society people who disparaged NS because they did not want their children to be conscripted, preferring them to go abroad for higher studies without obstacles. It was believed that the campaign, which had begun around September 1969, was stepped up in January 1970 when Lim announced the stricter enforcement of conscription rules.

Addressing a commissioning ceremony of Singapore Armed Forces officer cadets, Lim asked Singaporeans not to give the smear campaign any credence. He argued that a dozen bombs could also knock out many nations in Europe. This capability had been present since the advent of atomic and hydrogen bombs, but nobody had dropped any bombs on Europe. This was so because European nations had armed themselves and each other as best as they could and thus had deterred any would-be aggressors. "Paradoxically, the armed forces are perhaps the best guarantee for peace. And we want peace," Lim said.[44]

Flaying those behind the smear campaign, Lim noticed an interesting parallel: The whisper war resembled the whisper campaign that had been waged against the republic's industrialization policy at its launch. Then, the whispers had suggested that Singapore would not be able to industrialize because it lacked natural resources and possessed only a small domestic market. The government and the people had not been deterred by the whispers. "Otherwise, those who are carrying on the whispering campaign against our defence build-up will be at the employment exchange instead of being able to cast covetous eyes at the well-paid jobs which they think they can pick if they can avoid national service."[45] The campaign against NS was more vicious than the one against industrialization because it struck at the root of national defence. It could not be allowed to gain credibility.

Parliamentarians, like most Singaporeans, accepted this principle. The goal of National Service — national survival — was beyond question, as was the need to implement the policy strictly. Parliament continued to debate, however, the modalities of the policy's implementation, particularly as they affected the manpower needs of industry and commerce. These needs, too, were critical for the survival and success of Singapore.

Thus, the issue of engineering students being called up emerged in Parliament in March 1970, with MP Teong Eng Siong saying that their absence on the economic scene had caused a shortage of engineers in the Economic Development Board and some factories. He gave the example of two mechanical engineering graduates from New Zealand, one a Malaysian citizen and the other a Singapore citizen. The government had appointed the Malaysian quickly, but the Singaporean had been called up. "Is this not a show of favouritism?" the MP asked. He suggested part-time National Service for engineering graduates. He went further and called for the drafting of women, a point he had raised at an earlier parliamentary session. The answer then had been that it was a good suggestion but that it could not be implemented immediately and would be considered later. Teong maintained that drafting women would reflect Singapore's emphasis on the equality of the sexes, particularly since, otherwise, women would be "graduates, scholars, or doctors of philosophy, and the majority of our men will be just ordinary citizens and soldiers and not distinguished professionals". Members of parliament would not like this state of affairs to come about, Teong asserted, because if it did, there could be more female than male MPs. Singapore could learn from Israel how to induct women into National Service.[46]

MP Chan Choy Siong agreed with the suggestion to introduce NS for women, and added that it could begin in school. She also asked the minister to clarify whether the sons of some rich men had been exempted. MP Tay Boon Too summed up the sentiments in favour of changing the approach taken to National Service when he argued that the majority of Singaporeans supported the concept, but that the government should be cautious in implementing the technical details so that people's livelihood was not affected.[47]

Lim dismissed the allegation that the sons of rich fathers were evading National Service, demanding to know who they were so that he could find out how they had "escaped the dragnet". He also rejected the suggestion that National Service begin in school, because the students were too young to withstand the physical rigours of training.

As for conscripting women, "nature ordains that certain jobs are best done by females" and others by males. There were certain jobs that women could not do as well as males, "no matter how loudly they protest that they are equal". As for the male argument that women would enjoy the advantage of an earlier start and thus move ahead of men who had to undergo National Service, Lim's rejoinder was that women gave several years of their lives to marriage, childbirth and rearing children. Those functions disadvantaged them in their competition with men at work.[48]

On the larger point about the competing interests of defence training and industrial progress, Lim pointed out that the shortage of skilled manpower would have existed even without National Service. True, building up the armed forces did aggravate the shortage, but it was only temporary. In fact, upon discharge from service, a man would leave with skills that would be useful to him in the labour market. Apart from this benefit, the defence build-up contributed to industrial success by enhancing Singapore's drive for self-reliance.[49]

In May 1970, the Enlistment Bill *inter alia* extended the maximum age for National Service liability from forty years to fifty years in order to make available to the Singapore Armed Forces persons who had specialized training and extensive experience that might normally not be available from ordinary manpower resources. Some of those skills were in the areas of electronic engineering, electrical engineering, telecommunication engineering, mechanical engineering, marine engineering, aeronautical engineering, naval architecture, and automobile engineering.[50]

THE INTERIOR

Even as preserving Singapore's sovereignty through a credible defence force kept Lim busy, the other half of his ministerial portfolio saw him focus on making Singapore a safe home for its citizens through rigorous policing and strict immigration policies.

To this role he brought the no-nonsense and down-to-earth qualities that had catapulted him into one of the most senior positions in the Singapore leadership. Singapore's global reputation as a low-crime country, where laws are not only made but are also implemented, owes much to him.

Law and Order

For the police to play its part in Singapore's nation building, it needed to be transformed from an instrument of colonial control to a source of public safety.

The transformation of Singapore's police force into a servant of the public was not accomplished easily. One member of parliament remarked that "there are some members of the police force, especially those in the lower ranks, who still adopt the colonial attitude."[51] Another MP was infuriated by the behaviour of a police officer towards him when he had made enquiries about the arrest of four sons of a constituent. He declared: "Such a Government servant is described by the Chinese as despotic and dictatorial. Police officers who are impolite to Members of Parliament are bad. I dare say that our Government will be toppled as a result of the attitude of such Government servants."[52]

Speaking later, Lim said that he was encouraged by reports of increasing public cooperation, an indication that a transformation of the police force from a colonial to a national one was taking place, although the change had not been easy. Singapore had inherited a colonial police force that had been accustomed to lording it over the population. "It had no electorate to answer to. It could and did ignore public opinion," Lim observed. "It was an instrument of the colonial government for domination and, not unnaturally, there was a chasm between the police and the population." Lim warned that policemen guilty of persistent discourtesy or arrogance to the public would be sacked. Stern action had to be taken so that the "rare" cases of misbehaviour, which was committed by those who found it difficult to discard their old attitudes, did not infect the younger members of the force, who formed the majority.[53]

In parliamentary debates, Lim showed his keen awareness of the need for the police to behave properly with the public. Responding to the two MPs who had complained about police misbehaviour, Lim wished that they had brought their specific cases of rudeness to his attention earlier, so that he could have made the necessary enquiries. He asked for more detailed information so that he could take appropriate action. He was glad to hear that only a minority of the police force acted this way, but "it is our duty to weed them out".[54]

There were other kinds of complaint about the police. Another MP said that there had been reported cases of policemen having lost their pistols "as a result of a quarrel over some women and some people were murdered". She added that it was "an open secret" that some police officers had sponsored the setting up of restaurants and bars where crimes were committed. Lim replied that disciplinary action had been taken against police personnel who had been careless in handling their weapons. As for bars, police regulations did not allow any police officer to have any interest in any business that might prejudice his work. If the MP could give him specific complaints, his ministry would look into them.[55]

Lim was sympathetic towards members of parliament who were concerned with protecting the constitutional rights of citizens in their dealings with the police. L.P. Rodrigo noted that there was a constitutional provision that an accused who was apprehended or arrested could be detained for only twenty-four hours in a police station, after which he must be brought before the court, barring exceptional circumstances, for example, when the arrest was made on a Saturday. "At the same time, we have detention laws in our country," he said. "These detention laws are exceptional laws, because they empower the authorities to detain a person apprehended without trial." He had found that a substantial number of persons who had been detained under those laws had been charged subsequently.

Rodrigo's point was that if the police proceeded under the detention laws, they would be empowered to detain apprehended persons beyond twenty-four hours. If the tendency were real, "then there is an evasion of an important constitutional protection".[56]

Pointing to the Criminal Law (Temporary Provisions) Ordinance, Rodrigo said that the grounds for detention under that exceptional law were a person's association with activities of a criminal nature, which justified his detention on the grounds of public safety, peace and good order, in the absence of sufficient evidence to support the charge before the court. But if the police had complied with the requirements of the law, "why do they find it convenient to charge the person in court a few days after his apprehension?" Rodrigo commented that "if the apprehension of a person under the detention laws is to appear credible to the populace, then it must demonstrate a deliberateness which comes after a careful and responsible assessment of a person's danger to society." Since there were "58 of us here in this Chamber, all belonging to the People's Action Party", it was "absolutely imperative that this Government give the people no reason — none at all — at any time to suspect that it is prepared to ignore constitutionalism or that it can afford to dispense with the fundamental rights of the individual".[57]

Lim replied that every member of parliament was as zealous as Rodrigo to see to it that the constitutional rights of citizens were protected. "I dare not say that the powers given under the special detention laws have not been abused. Perhaps in their zest to rid this country of undesirable elements, officers in the police force may have made use of these powers," Lim said. "But I can assure the Member that every precaution has been and will be taken to see that advantage is not taken of the special detention laws."[58]

Political detentions were another issue that Lim looked into. His view was that those detentions would be made only when they were absolutely necessary. Speaking at the official opening of the Shoemakers' Cooperative Industrial Society (Singapore) Ltd., which the government had set up to rehabilitate former political detainees, he said: "Unless it is absolutely necessary, we have no wish to detain anyone a day longer." He added that the government could release only those individuals who were genuinely convinced of the mistakes of their past and were prepared to turn over a new leaf. "And they must be prepared to be frank about their past activities and to take a stand regarding what they believe in." Once they did that, there was no discrimination in Singapore society against ex-political detainees, who were not looked down on. "In fact, they will become well-respected citizens. The Government and the Ex-Political Detainees Association have been successful in placing almost every released detainee in suitable employment." He thought that members of the association had gone through difficult times and moments of heart-searching and reflection. In the process, their intellectual and emotional development had undergone a "complex but positive change". Being mostly young people, they had been "naturally susceptible" to political influence; it was "understandable" that youthful exuberance and idealism could be led astray easily. But once they were encouraged to ponder over issues that mattered, they would be convinced of the need to adjust their attitudes and realize the futility of turning against society.[59]

Lim's championing of the public's right to fair treatment by the police, his desire to protect the constitutional rights of suspects, and his defence of former political detainees did not detract, however, from his uncompromisingly tough approach to law and order where criminals were concerned. This fact came through clearly in parliamentary discussion of the Criminal Procedure Code (Amendment No. 2) Bill in early September 1967. The bill, which was passed, increased substantially the penalties for unruly behaviour and acts of hooliganism in magistrates' courts that were meant to bring them into contempt and ridicule. It empowered a subordinate court to impose sentences of imprisonment in the first instance, or fine offenders a maximum of $500, ten times the existing penalty, or impose a sentence combining both forms of punishment.[60]

The bill stemmed from disturbances in which a few hundred offenders had been arrested and accused of rioting and other offences. On being produced in court, the alleged offenders had behaved in a way so unruly as to destroy furniture in the court. "The authority and dignity of the court, it may be said, depend very much on the traditional respect normally accorded to members of judiciary," Lim noted. But the way in which the alleged offenders had behaved in court demonstrated that the administration of criminal justice in the subordinate courts might not be dependent solely any more on traditional respect. Hence "flagrant insults and deliberate acts of unruly behaviour calculated to bring the courts into contempt and ridicule must be met with means to impose sufficient deterrents."[61] Members of parliament agreed wholeheartedly with Lim, with some arguing that even the new law did not go far enough. One called for heavier punishment, such as flogging. "One stroke of the cane would do these anti-national elements a lot of good and, if not, three would definitely do it." Another argued: "If such acts had been committed in any Communist country, the culprits would have been severely dealt with. For example, they would have been sent to a labour reform camp or sentenced to death."[62]

Immigration

Immigration was an important part of Lim's portfolio. Many complaints about Singapore's enforcement of immigration rules focused on marriages to foreigners. When female Singaporean citizens married foreigners, the Registrar of Marriages approved the union without hesitation. But when an application was made to the immigration authorities for the husband to reside in Singapore, it was turned down.[63] Another complaint was that the foreign wives of Singaporeans found it difficult to stay in Singapore. There had been several cases of male Singaporeans who had married in Johor and had children born in Singapore. Their wives had been sent back to Johor because, when the husbands applied for permanent residence for their spouses, they were turned down since they could not support their wives financially.[64] The law required a woman who had married a foreigner to adopt the domicile of her husband, making it understandable that foreign men who married Singaporeans women would find it difficult to live in the republic, but by the same logic, how could the foreign wives of male Singaporeans be prevented from living in Singapore?[65] "In our present society, we believe in having love as the foundation of marriage," MP Ch'ng Jit Koon ventured to say. "Whether we like it or not, they have already become husbands and wives. It is therefore unreasonable, from the humanitarian point of view, if we do not allow a non-citizen wife to stay in Singapore and force her to separate from her husband and her family." He recalled a Chinese fairytale of a cowboy called Niu Lang and a spinner called Jze Nyu, which was being re-enacted now with "our own people acting as the cowboy and the spinner as the case may be". The MP hoped that Lim would review immigration policy "so that this tragic Chinese story will not be repeated".[66]

Lim responded to that request with a dose of humour. He said that it appeared that MPs believed that "I am the fly in the ointment in the affairs of the heart". Instead, he encouraged freedom in the affairs of the heart wherever possible, which was why the Registrar of Marriages did not display any discrimination over whom a person married, so long as he gave sufficient notice and the parties concerned had lived in Singapore for more than fifteen days. "It is a service which Singapore can render to join them in holy and legal wedlock so that they can live happily ever after."

However, he added, this service had nothing to do with immigration. As for female Singaporeans marrying foreigners who were not allowed to stay in Singapore, "I would say that, being an eastern country, we would like to feel that it is the man who wears the pants and, therefore, the woman takes the domicile of the man".[67] He agreed, however, that it should be made known widely that female Singaporeans who married foreigners would have to be willing to follow their husbands to their countries.[68]

In the case of male Singaporeans marrying foreigners who applied for entry to Singapore, Lim gave figures to show that "we have not been heartless". In 1967, 486 applications of this nature were approved and 134 were refused; in 1968, 449 were approved and 187 were refused. Each case was treated on its merits. What the law required was that "female non-citizens who are married to Singapore citizens and who are on a visit pass are not allowed an extension of stay because their husbands are not in a position to support them or the children whom they will bring into this world".[69]

The issue of Singaporean marriages to foreigners resurfaced in Parliament in 1970. An MP wanted to know why many Singaporeans in the lower-income group who had wives outside Singapore were not allowed to bring them in to stay even if they were qualified to do so.[70] Another MP raised the issue of Singapore citizens who had gone across the Causeway to work but who had returned following the Malaysian government's restriction of employment opportunities for Singaporeans. Many of these Singaporeans had raised families in Malaysia; the family members had taken Malaysian identity cards. The men were allowed entry to Singapore, but their wives and children were not.[71] One MP reasoned that since "we are all human and laws are made by man", "troubles created by man should be resolved by man."[72]

In his rejoinder, Lim mentioned the conditions under which the non-citizen wives and children of Singapore citizens were eligible to apply for permanent residence in the republic. These were whether the marriage was lawful; whether the wife had not been living separately from the husband for a continuous period of five years after the date of marriage, and whether the children were under the age of six; and whether the husband was in a position to support his wife and children. "We are not a hard-hearted Government and I believe the Ministers here have got feelings. At the same time, in deciding upon policy, we must not allow ourselves to be swayed by sentiment."[73] He dismissed a suggestion that a Singapore citizen who wanted to marry a foreigner should first fill in a questionnaire asking how much money he had and whether he could support the woman. To the MP who had made this request, having to fill in a questionnaire would caution Singapore citizens of the consequences of taking non-citizen wives, an important development given that Singapore's male population exceeded its female population by about 85,000.[74] To Lim, however, "if a man is intent on marrying a woman out of love, no amount of prevention by any Government official will stop that marriage". What mattered were the conditions under which a non-citizen wife could enter Singapore, and these conditions he had just clarified.[75]

In this context, he reminded his parliamentary colleagues that only cases that had not been approved that had come to their attention; people who had had their applications approved had not returned to thank them. Those husbands whose applications to bring in their wives had not been approved had been turned down mainly because their income was low and they were not considered to have the capacity to support their wives, let alone their children, in Singapore.[76]

Another immigration issue concerned non-citizens who had lived in Singapore for many years. Some of them had qualified for citizenship, and their cases were pending. Others, who had not qualified owing to the absence of a residential qualification, were unable to obtain restricted passports to travel across the Causeway. If those persons had been born in India, Thailand or other places, they could visit their countries' diplomatic missions in Singapore to obtain letters saying that they were stateless. Unfortunately, the Malaysian High Commission refused to give certificates of statelessness to people born in Malaysia. This led to their not receiving restricted passports from Singapore. "Eventually, they will come to feel that they are prisoners in Singapore and are unable to get out even if they want to," the MP argued, asking Lim to look into such cases, which were numerous.[77] Lim replied that restricted passports were given only on proof of statelessness. The fact that diplomatic missions had refused to give certificates of statelessness to the people whom the MP had cited meant that "their status is doubtful even in the minds of the country of their birth or domicile". If Singapore gave them a passport, it would be acknowledging that they were its responsibility. This was unacceptable. Lim reiterated the position that, "because of the difficulties we have to face following the British military withdrawal, we do not want to create more trouble for ourselves in future by making it easy for people to come and stay here."[78]

Keeping out illegal entrants was an important plank of Singapore's immigration policy. Lim explained to Parliament that preventing illegal entry was necessary to ensure, among other things, that foreigners who arrived in Singapore to seek work did not prejudice the employment opportunities of citizens and permanent residents who had similar or corresponding qualifications or skills. The problem was that illegal immigration remained high. Lim explained why. Singapore had a 127 kilometre-long coastline and its shores were but a short distance away from Malaysia and the nearest of the neighbouring islands. It was almost impossible to patrol Singapore's territorial waters all the time without incurring heavy expenses. Once in Singapore, illegal immigrants were not only harboured by local residents and citizens, but were also provided employment opportunities in contravention of the Singapore's immigration and other laws. In spite of immigration control on travel between Singapore and West Malaysia, there was relatively free movement between the two countries, and there was no exit control to ensure that those who arrived for temporary visits left Singapore within the period of the authorized visit. "Owing to the social and economic conditions prevailing in the neighbouring countries, many such visitors will want to remain in Singapore beyond the periods of their authorised

stay if their presence remains undetected." Lim gave figures for the
number of people who had been apprehended by the Immigration,
Police and Customs Departments for illegal entry or for contravening
immigration regulations. The figures began at 130 in 1959, fell to 116
in 1961 and rose to 2,980 in 1968 before they dipped to 2,593 in 1969.
It was not improbable that thousands of others had gone undetected.[79]

The Immigration (Amendment) Bill proposed therefore that
illegal immigrants would face on conviction a maximum fine of
$4,000 or a year's jail, or both. For traffickers of these immigrants, the
maximum sentence was a $4,000 fine and two years' jail. Both penalties
were twice as severe as before. It also became an offence to harbour or
employ such immigrants, for which the punishment was a $4,000
fine or a year's jail, or both.[80] There was an exchange in Parliament
over the need to differentiate between two categories of offenders —
those who had entered Singapore legally but had overstayed, and
those who had come in illegally in the first place — and the need to
clarify the status of people from West Malaysia who had been present
in Singapore before the imposition of full immigration control.
Following the exchange, the bill was passed.

Immigration controls on illegal immigrants were an important
feature of the Singapore scene as the country entered an exciting
period of economic development that drew to its shores large numbers
of workers. Lim's policy was to act proactively to stem the inflow of
illegal foreign workers so that they would not squeeze the economic
opportunities of Singapore citizens and other lawful workers.

Culture
As part of his portfolio, Lim also addressed a variety of issues that
were cultural in nature but touched on Singapore's security. He paid
short shrift to organizations in Singapore which were foreign-oriented.
Concerned over organizations that were registered in Singapore but
had loyalties outside the country, MP S.V. Lingam raised the issue of
the Singapore Dravida Munnetra Kazhagam, which claimed to look

after the interests of the people of Singapore, but had connections with the DMK, a political party, in Madras; indeed, its symbol was the same as that of the Indian party.[81] Lim declared that the Singapore DMK was registered as a cultural organization and so was prohibited from taking part in political activities. Such organizations must be oriented towards Singapore and not foreign lands, he said. If they had foreign loyalties, they would be going against national sentiments — something that it would not pay them to continue doing. Office bearers of the Singapore DMK would be reminded of their obligation not to participate in any political activities, local or foreign, Lim said, adding for good measure that he would watch the organization's activities with a "hawk-like eye".[82]

On another front, Lim, like his colleagues in the Cabinet, was apprehensive about the harm that the decadent aspects of cultures, imported from abroad, could cause to social discipline in Singapore. Speaking at the opening ceremony of a concert organized by the People's Action Party's Central Cultural Bureau in 1968, he worried that "yellow culture" and abnormal and corrosive activities, such as those of hippies and flower people, would seep through Singapore society if people did not participate in healthy cultural activities.[83] Lim and his colleagues believed that young Singaporeans would become soft and self-indulgent if they adopted the degenerating and weakening influence of hippie culture, and would question the discipline and motivation required to sustain Singapore. He viewed culture as an essential component of national survival.

Lim was involved in the enactment of a law that dealt with cultural sensitivities of a different kind. Although not limited to the Chinese, the firing of crackers was a highlight of festive occasions such as Chinese New Year and *Chap Goh Meh*. This cultural practice was auspicious because it was believed to bring prosperity. The firing of crackers had a markedly competitive aspect during *Chap Goh Meh*, in particular, when long strings of crackers, strung up several storeys high, were let off in various parts of Singapore in "cracker wars".[84]

Unfortunately, the careless or indiscriminate throwing of crackers was a hazard to life and property.

This danger was demonstrated in twenty-nine officially reported incidents in which twenty-five people were injured, of whom six died, and which led Lim to introduce a bill in March 1970 that was carried through all three stages on a certificate of urgency. Citing the casualty figures, he added that nine houses had been damaged by fire, the value of the damage being estimated at S$560,390. Unlike Hong Kong, West Malaysia and Indonesia, which had banned cracker-firing totally, Singapore chose to enforce strict control over the firing. It introduced a general prohibition that might be lifted by a gazette notification from time to time or by the issue of a licence for personal or other reasons to individuals or public bodies by the deputy commissioner of police or his authorized representation. Harsher penalties awaited offenders under the new law.[85]

Although many members of parliament agreed that the danger from the indiscriminate firing of crackers should be stamped out, Ang Nam Piau argued that the firing was both a custom and a habit for the Chinese that was shared by the other ethnic communities as well. Moreover, this was the first time that it had caused deaths and the loss of property in Singapore. Lee Teck Him, aged 66, declared that he had been firing crackers since his boyhood, but he had never injured himself or ever heard of any deaths caused by the practice.[86] Lim retorted that if Lee's idea of celebrating an occasion was to allow people to fire crackers while others died, "then I think we have got to change his idea". Lim made the larger argument that "if there is no social consciousness in the habits of the people, we have to regulate their behaviour by social legislation."[87]

Like his colleagues in the government, Lim was unapologetic about intervening in cultural practices if they were deemed to be out of step with Singapore's development. His no-nonsense approach was felt in every field that his work as minister for the Interior and Defence made him enter.

Notes

1. *Straits Times*, 13 August 1968.
2. For a riveting account of Singapore's position as a result of Britain's policy changes, see Lee Kuan Yew, *From Third World to First: The Singapore Story, 1965–2000* (Singapore: Singapore Press Holdings, 2000), pp. 55–60.
3. Goh Keng Swee, *Annual Budget Statement*, 3 December 1968, *Parliamentary Debates*, Vol. 28, cols. 28–33.
4. Ibid., col. 33.
5. Ibid., col. 54.
6. Lee, *From Third World to First*, op. cit., p. 69.
7. Ibid., p. 71.
8. Ibid., p. 73.
9. Ibid., p. 35.
10. Ibid., p. 40.
11. Ibid., pp. 40–41.
12. Ibid., p. 41.
13. Ibid.
14. Interview.
15. *Straits Times*, 27 March 1968.
16. Ibid.
17. *Malay Mail*, 12 January 1968.
18. *Straits Times*, 27 March 1968.
19. *Sunday Times*, 19 May 1968.
20. *Straits Times*, 13 June 1968.
21. *Straits Times*, 18 September 1969.
22. *Straits Times*, 2 July 1970.
23. Lee, *From Third World to First*, op. cit., p. 65.
24. Ong Eng Chuan, "National Service in Singapore: Early Years", Singapore Infopaedia, <http://infopedia.nlb.gov.sg/articles/SIP_692_2005-02-01.html>.
25. Ibid.
26. Ibid.
27. *Straits Times*, 25 December 1968.
28. *Sunday Times*, 28 July 1968.
29. *Parliamentary Debates*, 26 June 1970, Vol. 30, col. 87.
30. Ibid., cols. 92–94.
31. *Parliamentary Debates*, 18 December 1968, Vol. 28, cols. 541–43.
32. Ibid., cols. 546–47.
33. *Parliamentary Debates*, 11 June 1969, Vol. 29, cols. 28–29.
34. Ibid., col. 30.

35. Ibid., cols. 30–31.
36. *Straits Times*, 7 October 1969.
37. *Straits Times*, 12 October 1969.
38. *Straits Times*, 24 January 1970.
39. *Sunday Times*, 25 January 1970.
40. *Parliamentary Debates*, 23 March 1970, Vol. 29, cols. 944–45.
41. Ibid., cols. 952–53.
42. Ibid., col. 952.
43. *Sunday Times*, 15 February 1970.
44. Ibid.
45. Ibid.
46. *Parliamentary Debates*, 23 March 1970, Vol. 29, cols. 936–38.
47. Ibid., cols. 938–43.
48. Ibid., cols. 949–50.
49. Ibid., cols. 947–48.
50. *Parliamentary Debates*, 21 May 1970, Vol. 30, cols. 48–49.
51. *Parliamentary Debates*, 18 December 1968, Vol. 28, cols. 552.
52. Ibid., cols. 553.
53. *Straits Times*, 27 March 1970.
54. *Parliamentary Debates*, 18 December 1968, Vol. 28, cols. 554.
55. Ibid., cols. 555–56.
56. *Parliamentary Debates*, 17 December 1968, Vol. 28, col. 516.
57. *Parliamentary Debates*, 18 December 1968, Vol. 28, cols. 540–41.
58. Ibid., col. 544.
59. *Straits Times*, 17 July 1969.
60. *Parliamentary Debates*, 7 September 1967, Vol. 26, col. 123.
61. Ibid., cols. 123; 122.
62. Ibid., cols. 124; 125.
63. *Parliamentary Debates*, 18 December 1968, Vol. 28, col. 563.
64. Ibid., col. 564.
65. Ibid., col. 565.
66. Ibid., cols. 566–67.
67. Ibid., cols. 567–68.
68. Ibid., col. 570.
69. Ibid., col. 568.
70. *Parliamentary Debates*, 24 March 1970, Vol. 29, col. 964.
71. Ibid., col. 966.
72. Ibid., col. 968.
73. Ibid., cols. 970–71.

74. Ibid., cols. 963–64.
75. Ibid., col. 972.
76. Ibid., col. 972–73.
77. *Parliamentary Debates*, 18 December 1968, Vol. 28, col. 565–66.
78. Ibid., col. 568–69.
79. *Parliamentary Debates*, 27 January 1970, Vol. 29, cols. 401–402.
80. *Straits Times*, 28 January 1970.
81. *Parliamentary Debates*, 8 September 1967, Vol. 26, cols. 237–40.
82. Ibid., cols. 242.
83. *Straits Times*, 13 January 1968.
84. *Parliamentary Debates*, 30 March 1970, Vol. 29, col. 1253.
85. Ibid., cols. 1251–53.
86. Ibid., cols. 1255–57.
87. Ibid., col. 1259.

12

Other Ministries and Roles

L im Kim San was Minister for Education from 1970 to 1972. From 1971 to 1978, he was Chairman of the Public Utilities Board. During this period, he became Singapore's first Minister for the Environment in 1972, and stayed there till 1975. He was Minister for National Development and Communications from 1975 to 1978, and Minister for National Development from 1978 to 1979.[1] He returned to the Ministry of the Environment in 1979 and stayed there till 1981. He was also Chairman of the Board of Trustees of NTUC Welcome Consumers' Cooperative Ltd. in 1973; Chairman of the Port of Singapore Authority (PSA) from 1979 to 1994; Managing Director of the Monetary Authority of Singapore from 1981 to 1982; and Chairman of the Council of Presidential Advisers from 1992 to 2003. In his foray into the private sector, Lim became Executive Chairman of Singapore Press Holdings in 1988. He retained that post until 2002, when he became the group's Senior Adviser and helped guide the company until he retired in 2005. He contributed to Singapore's governance, its economy and its media in these diverse fields.

EDUCATION

By early 1971, Singapore had overcome, to a large extent, quantitative needs in the field of education. A place in school was ensured for every child of school-going age; indeed, 98 per cent of those in this age group were in school. Yet, the key question was what kind of education would decide whether Singapore's small population of two million would be a valuable asset or a severe handicap.[2]

Speaking at the opening of a Singapore Teachers' Union seminar, Lim noted that the need earlier on had been to expand available educational facilities fast enough to provide a place for every child of school-going age. Singapore was in a position now to allow more flexibility in allowing individual children to proceed at a pace more suited to their abilities. He noted that the existing system, with a series of bar examinations, was a fairly efficient way of narrowing down the field selectively to the top few per cent who were best equipped intellectually to pursue higher studies. "Those who are able to compete academically on a merit basis thrive under this system. But the vast majority of students drop out of the running much earlier in the race," he declared. "I wonder, with so many who fail under this system, whether we should be asking whether it is the system which is failing them." One solution was to introduce a revised syllabus for the Primary I and Primary II levels that treated the first two years of primary education as a single unit. The syllabus gave slower children more time to grasp the basics.[3]

Lim was aware that teachers could make or mar the implementation of his policies, and was ready, therefore, to entertain professional views about failings in the education system. He averred that the aim of Singapore's school education system was not to benefit ministry officials, parents or teachers, but the young, so that they could develop their capacities to the fullest within the context of national priorities. "Teachers are perhaps in the best position to gauge if the system is achieving the objectives for which it was designed."[4] They responded readily to his invitation to participate in the unfolding of the education system. Teachers belonging to five unions released a joint statement read out at the Teachers' Day dinner in September 1971 at which Lim was the guest-of-honour.

They said that they wanted to involve themselves more in the planning and reappraisal of the government's education policy. "The process of education constitutes a principal means of effecting overall development and achieving national progress, and teachers must understand and appreciate their role at this crucial stage of nation-building."[5]

As Minister for Education, Lim had to deal also with bread-and-butter issues, many of which came up in Parliament and were debated exhaustively and robustly.[6] The emoluments, benefits, working conditions, training, promotion prospects, and retirement age of teachers loomed large in the debates; the status of relief teachers came up for debate as well. Other issues concerned curriculum and syllabus changes; textbook content; the time taken up by extracurricular activities and support for national programmes; the burden posed by school fees on poorer families; and the posting of secondary students to schools far away from home.

Lim was prepared to make concessions in some areas, such as when he noted that he was having second thoughts about setting up an Institute of Education purely to confer degrees in education.[7] He also agreed to consider a loan scheme for needy students.[8] However, he insisted that while teachers' pay and benefits were important issues, people should not be drawn to teaching purely by monetary rewards. He would "hate to think" that teachers were attracted only by the salary scales and that there were no other incentives. "I would like to believe that a large proportion of the teachers are there because they feel that they have the skill, the ability and the interest in imparting knowledge to young people."[9] Much was expected of teachers professionally and morally, an issue that Lim highlighted when he told Parliament that, although teachers were not prohibited from frequenting bars, it was another matter if they did so every day and got drunk. Then, action would be taken.[10]

Bilingualism

Another area that Lim focused on was bilingualism. English, Chinese, Malay and Tamil were the four official languages of Singapore, and children were allowed to attend schools that used any of the four languages as the medium of instruction. The choice was their parents'. However, they had to study one of the other official languages as a second language right from the first grade. The result was that every schoolchild studied English either as a first language or as a second language. This choice reflected pragmatic Singaporeans' awareness that their country's survival depended on trade and industry and on its role as a centre of communications, banking and finance. English played a vital role in these economic activities.[11]

In this context, Lim saw the University of Singapore, where the medium of instruction was English, and Nanyang University (or Nantah), where the medium was Chinese, playing complementary roles in underpinning the government's policy of bilingualism. He envisaged a time, "not far off", when students educated in one language stream would have achieved sufficient competence in a second and even a third language, to be able to undergo courses conducted in another language. It might then be possible for undergraduates of one university to take courses at the other local university. "Experience has shown that the bilingual or multi-lingual graduate, whether from Nantah or from the University of Singapore, is in greater demand both in the public and the private sector, because his usefulness is enhanced in this multi-lingual setting." He emphasized the importance of bilingualism, arguing that certain subjects, especially in the scientific and technological disciplines, could be taught more effectively in English.[12] On another occasion, he called on Nantah students to make every attempt to be proficient in English, the second language. At the same time, Nantah, being the highest institution of learning in Chinese, should promote the study of Chinese in Singapore.[13] Clearly,

Lim was emphasizing the importance of English to the economic life of Singapore without denying the importance of Chinese to the cultural life of the nation.

WATER AND POWER CONSERVATION

A drought hit Singapore in 1971, setting the tone for some of Lim Kim San's work as Chairman of the Public Utilities Board (PUB), Minister for the Environment, and Minister for National Development and Communications. Water had been rationed during periods of extreme drought in 1961 and 1963. However, those experiences had not made Singaporeans sufficiently water-conscious. Instead, demand for water was increasing with a growing population, industrialization and a rising standard for living. In 1971, Singapore faced the prospects of water rationing again; indeed, there were fears that rationing might become a way of life in the republic, as it was in some countries, if citizens went on using and wasting water.[14]

Lim's approach to water conservation was to keep it voluntary as far as possible. Hence, he said in May 1971 that water rationing could be put off for at least a fortnight if the public reduced its daily consumption by 25 per cent. "It is not difficult to save 25 per cent of normal consumption. Very few people realise the value of water because it comes so easily," he said. Rationing could be postponed even longer if the rains arrived, he added, emphasizing that he was making an appeal and not issuing a warning because public cooperation was far more desirable than forcing the PUB to impose compulsory restraints on water consumption. That said, he reminded people that they should refrain from using potable water to water their gardens. If necessary, watering of gardens with drinking water could be made an offence. Ever the down-to-earth man, Lim gave useful tips on how to save water. One tip was not to wash anything under a running tap, another was to keep the water from washing for flushing the toilet, cleaning floors or washing windows.[15]

The public response to the save water campaign spoke volumes. Consumption dropped to a record low of 98.6 million gallons (448,200 cubic metres) on 30 May 1971, the lowest in four months and since the drought hit the island. Consumption was only eight million gallons away from the 90-million target that the PUB had set as the safe mark against rationing. Singaporeans' good sense, a record rainfall, and anti-waste patrols by water inspectors also helped to keep water rationing away.[16]

However, consumption of water was increasing with Singapore's industrialization and its population's increasing affluence, making a quest for self-sufficiency and self-reliance necessary in this most critical of natural resources. Lim revealed in a televised interview in late August 1971 that the PUB was seeking expert advice on the possibility of using nuclear energy for electricity as well as desalination of seawater. Also, a Dutch consultant was carrying out a feasibility study of Pulau Ubin to determine whether it was suitable for a reservoir project. The project would involve damming part of the sea and linking two tips of the offshore island to form a big basin in the Straits of Johor. In the process, a part of the straits would be sealed off, Lim said, noting that, since Singapore stood in the centre of heavy shipping lanes, it was necessary to choose an area that did not interfere with shipping. To tap rainfall better, two new reservoirs were being built in the Kranji/Pandan area and the capacity of Pierce Reservoir was being expanded. As for desalination, the key question was whether it would be economic, Lim noted, adding that he was confident that there would be a technological breakthrough to make it so.[17]

Lim reiterated these moves to meet Singapore's water needs in an address to members of the Economic Society of Singapore in September 1971. He announced that the PUB had set up a task force to plan the development of Singapore's water resources. It was also considering a two-tier tariff to encourage the use of electricity during off-peak hours. Outlining Singapore's water needs, which were estimated to rise to 150 million gallons a day by 1975, Lim said that the water agreement with Malaysia still stood, but it would be prudent to try and tap as much water as possible from Singapore's own available resources, although this might cost more. Steps towards this end, taken or under consideration, were increasing water in reservoirs through the efficient use of water by recycling and collecting rainfall; desalination; and building a nuclear power station in the future, after the breakthrough in desalination came, along with a desalting plant in Singapore that would provide both power and water.[18] In May 1972, Lim announced that there would probably be no need for water rationing that year because, for the first time in two years, April showers had filled up all the reservoirs. He warned against complacency, however, and said that the ban on hosing cars for washing purposes would not be relaxed.[19]

That warning against complacency became policy in December 1972, when the government decided that progressive pricing, introduced through a water tariff system, was the way to deter water wastage. Giving details at the launch of the "Water is Precious" Exhibition at the Victoria Memorial Hall, Lim said that the block tariff system had emerged out of a survey that indicated that the lower- and middle-income groups used a daily average of 30 gallons (0.14 cubic metres) of water per person. Hence, it would not be unfair to fix as the first block a quantum of 5,500 gallons, or 25 cubic metres, of water for an average household per month. Any consumption beyond 25 cubic metres and up to 50 cubic metres would be charged at a higher rate; consumption beyond 50 cubic metres would be charged at an even higher rate.[20]

Accordingly, the PUB devised a new, four-tier tariff system to punish extravagant users that was announced in January 1973. Unlike the existing flat rate of 80 cents per 1,000 gallons, it was announced that, with effect from 1 February 1973, water would cost between 20 cents and S$1.20 more per 1,000 gallons. The new rates, for every 1,000 gallons used in homes, were: S$1.00 for those who used up to 5,500 gallons a month; S$1.18 for consumption of between 5,500 gallons and 11,000 gallons; S$1.50 for consumption of between 11,000 gallons and 16,500 gallons; and S$2.00 for 16,500 gallons and more. Industry would pay a different rate. Describing the new system as being "very fair", Lim said that its purpose was to make people save water and not to collect more revenue. The new rates would not mean an automatic increase in the PUB bill for small consumers because the government's tax concession on PUB bills had been increased from S$12 to S$20. This meant that consumers whose monthly PUB bills did not exceed S$20 would not pay any tax at all. Hence, careful users of water might even benefit. Given that the group of small consumers was estimated at 64 per cent of PUB customers, many Singaporeans stood to benefit from the change. What the new tariff system would do would be to deter wastage. The PUB anticipated that more than 64 per cent of all domestic consumers, including 80 per cent of Housing Board tenants, would pay the first basic rate only. Another 25 per cent would come under the second block, and they would pay a slightly higher rate for only the amount they consumed in excess of the first block. The block system gave the householder the incentive to ration his use of water and not to exceed the quota. Another advantage, Lim said, was that, in times of drought, the quantum of each block could be reduced in order to induce more careful use of water. This was one way of imposing self-rationing on the consumer.[21]

Power conservation was another of Lim's concerns. Late in 1972, he said that power and lighting would be charged at the same rates under a new PUB tariff structure for electricity consumption to be introduced on 1 December 1972. Most people were likely to pay more to keep cool, but small domestic consumers could expect to pay about 3 per cent less on their bills. As with the water tariff revision, the purpose of the power tariff exercise was not to increase revenue: Indeed, the PUB would earn less. The aim of the power tariff exercise, Lim explained, was to put in place a simple, rational and fair system that did not discriminate between the use of electricity for lighting and power. The change removed the anomaly of charging a higher rate for electricity for use of fans as against use for air-conditioning and other domestic power appliances.[22]

The problem continued, however, and was worsened by the fact that the price of oil had quadrupled between 1973 and 1976. The increase created a tremendous burden for Singapore, which depended on imported fuel for its energy requirements. In an attempt to find innovative solutions to the energy problem, Lim said in 1976 that regulations would be introduced to help take the heat off buildings and cut down their electricity bills. The government would encourage the provision of sunshading and other energy conservation devices for buildings. Giving an example of the savings that could follow, he said that sunbreakers used in the Ministry of National Development Building in Maxwell Road had reduced electricity consumption for air-conditioning by 15 per cent to 20 per cent. The savings had amounted to S$60,000 a year. Economizing on the use of electricity similarly in other high-rise buildings would produce substantial savings, given that air-conditioning had accounted for about 28 per cent of the total electricity consumed in Singapore in 1975 and that high-rise buildings with central air-conditioning were being constructed increasingly.[23]

POLLUTION

The Ministry of the Environment had been set up in 1972 because the government feared that if Singaporeans did not take immediate measures to keep the environment clean, pollution would reach a stage where people would find it impossible to live in the country. "The ultimate aim of my Ministry is to make life more pleasant for everyone through anti-pollution and other measures," Lim declared. "Environment is *the* thing now." [24]

The ministry would busy itself with issues such littering, standards of personal hygiene among hawkers and food handlers, and preventing outbreaks of diseases such as dengue. Lim turned his attention immediately to air pollution, however. This pollution, he predicted, would worsen because of the expansion of oil refineries and power stations. He assured manufacturers, industrialists and the public that the government would adopt a balanced and rational approach to the implementation of environmental measures. It would seek to demonstrate that there was no basic contradiction between economic development and environmental conservation. However, Lim put new industries on notice, saying that they should incorporate adequate pollution control measures if they wished to set up shop in Singapore. "The economic benefits of some of these industries may be great," he said, "but they may not be able to compensate for the social cost of the pollution, which may be even greater." Showing how serious the government was about fighting pollution, Lim announced that laws would be introduced to control pollution from motor vehicles so as to prevent photochemical smogs from developing in the country. The controls would be on carbon monoxide, oxides of nitrogen, hydrocarbons and lead emissions from vehicles.[25]

Lim made it clear that Singapore's priority in environmental conservation would centre on water pollution control. The government would carry out its water conservation programme so that the republic could rely increasingly on its own water supplies.[26] Later, Lim said that a large part of Singapore would be turned into a catchment area for old and new reservoirs instead of allowing rain water to flow to waste into the sea. One of the few natural resources that Singapore had, but which it had not exploited fully, was the abundant water that came down as rain, averaging more than 230 cubic metres a year. To ensure that this rain water could be tapped and that it would be of a quality capable of treatment for human use, the ground over which it flowed and the streams and canals that conveyed it to the reservoirs must be free of rotting garbage, litter, and human and animal waste. Hence, anyone who disposed garbage or discharged sullage into the drains and streets was dirtying the water that went into reservoirs, he said, appealing to Singaporeans not to pollute the water.[27]

On another occasion, he drew on local history to show what pollution could do. It had been possible to catch fish and eels in the Bukit Timah, Kallang, Geylang and Rochore canals twenty years earlier, he said. But now even the worms on which fish fed were gone; all marine life had been exterminated by pollution. If people continued to pollute the paths over which water flowed, the water in Singapore's reservoirs would resemble that in Rochore Canal one day, he warned.[28]

On yet another occasion, when touring his Cairnhill constituency, he warned that people must stop polluting water or face the possibility of paying for bottled or canned drinking water one day.[29] However, it became clear that not everyone was taking Lim's warnings seriously when he told Parliament in March 1975 that the Environment Ministry had spent S$800,000 the previous year on cleaning polluted rivers and canals. Almost 10,000 people had been prosecuted for the pollution.[30]

Singapore's water woes continued. In July 1976, Lim announced that the PUB would have to resort to unconventional means of tapping water since demand continued to rise and there was no corresponding increase in suitable water catchment areas. One example of those means was the damming of Kranji River to turn it into a reservoir. Water collected in that reservoir had drained through residential and farming areas. It was polluted and had a higher salt or chloride content than other kinds of water. Hence, the PUB was installing new plants to remove the higher salt content of the water that Singaporeans could expect from then on. "This is the kind of water we have to learn to accept because Singapore will have to rely more and more on unconventional means of tapping water to meet the rising demand," he said.[31]

In 1980, the Environment Ministry embarked on a major clean-up of the Singapore River, Kallang Basin and other water catchment areas. Under the programme, farms and squatter areas in the affected catchment areas would be cleared to reduce pollution and free land for housing projects; river banks would be cleared for urban renewal; hawkers, pollutive trades and backyard industries would be re-sited; and small sewage treatment plants would be built in the rural areas.[32] However, Lim did not oversee the massive transformation of the Singapore River because he left the Ministry of the Environment in 1981.

Glancing back at those years, Lee Kuan Yew declared:

Reservoirs were my domain. The moment we separated in 1965, I felt that we would need to conserve as much of our water as we could collect because we never could predict how they would move to pressure us. Every now and then, they'd say: "Stop the water." So we dammed up all the rivers, created Upper Pierce and Upper Seletar. We had many new reservoirs and expanded the water catchment. The Marina and the cleaning up of the rivers was my top agenda. I pressed the PUB, with Lee Ek Tieng, the Chief Water Engineer. I said: "We will do this whatever its cost." So we cleaned up the city…All the open drains were for clean rain water to be channelled eventually into reservoirs. That took 15, 20 years, but it was done. Now we're going to have the Marina together with the Singapore and Kallang rivers as a reservoir. With reverse osmosis, we can now safely use the water in the Marina.[33]

Goh Chok Tong recalled Lim's work.

At the PUB, he contributed a lot to the building of the reservoirs and solving of our water problems. But as water was a strategic issue for Singapore, it was primarily Prime Minister Lee Kuan Yew who shaped the policy and drove the effort to catch every rain drop in Singapore.[34]

Veteran civil servant Lee Ek Tieng recalled working with Lim Kim San in several areas since the early 1970s. Lim invited him to join the Water Planning Unit of the PUB in 1971, and in 1972, the engineer became Permanent Secretary at the Ministry of the Environment, where Lim was the minister. Lee Ek Tieng says:

He was a person who did a lot of developmental work, mainly because he was a very good people manager.... He had the rare talent, the uncanny ability, to meet a person and not so much judge but assess the person's personality, character and ability. That's an important quality when you want to build a team of people to work with you. And once he made up his mind that he knew the person, he would delegate work and responsibility to him. And the relationship would be a very good one. There's nothing like working with a boss who's understanding and trusts you so you do not have to second guess what he wants. More often than not, I went to see him to consult him rather than he asked to see me.[35]

At both the PUB and the Environment Ministry, Lim

was very clear about what our objective ought to be. He knew enough of the details, but he left it to me to do the work. He did not micromanage. So I found it very comfortable and very easy to work with him. He did not like long papers or thick reports. If you wrote him a thick report, he would call you up to brief him and would ask: "Tell me what it is you want to do." He would ask questions, and then say: "Okay."[36]

PORT OF CALL

When Lim took over as PSA chairman in 1979, there was a backlog of cargo; the engineers said that said that the equipment was old and the way of handling the cargo was old. Containers were the way of the future; the question was what machinery would be required. Lim and the rest of the PSA board decided to spend more than S$100 million on container equipment. Automation aided Lim's drive for efficiency, competitiveness and price, the PSA's objective being the desire to be "the most efficient port around here to serve the larger hinterland". The key lay in having measurements: How many containers were handled an hour by employees per machine. Lim increased the tempo, his management philosophy being "to lead, sometimes to push, sometimes to nudge". He met every head of department or division and discussed plans. He also sat down with every division every two months to look at its report and ask whether it was moving in the right direction. He set his sights on Hong Kong's productivity level. Having surpassed Hong Kong, the PSA looked at Kaohsiung. Having exceeded that target, it looked at Japan's productivity level. He also brought the PSA back into its main line of business. It had gone into housing the building of concert halls. He sold its houses to the HDB. "I said, 'Look, what are you doing, are you going to build a theatre, a 5,000-seat theatre in the World Trade Centre? Change."[37]

"Change" became the motto as the PSA crossed several milestones during Lim's tenure. These are enumerated in the book, *A Port's Story, A Nation's Success*.[38] Lim's appointment as PSA Chairman in 1979 coincided with the commissioning of the Tanjong Pagar Terminal's (TPT) sixth container berth. Two suction cranes for grain and two unloaders for scrap iron were installed at Jurong Wharves in 1980. In 1981, quality circles (QCs) were introduced; the Berth Appropriation Scheme was extended to Pasir Panjang Wharves; and Godown 407, the longest warehouse in Singapore, was built at Pasir Panjang Wharves. The TPT's tenth anniversary was celebrated in 1982 with the commissioning of the seventh container berth. That year, the TPT handled more than 1 million TEUs (Twenty-Foot Equivalent Units) for the first time; Singapore became the world's busiest port in terms of shipping tonnage; the Keppel Automated Warehouse became operational; a record 4.1 million passengers were transported by the PSA ferry service; and lighters were relocated from Telok Ayer Basin, Rochore River and Kallang River to the Pasir Panjang Wharves. The TPT's eighth container berth was commissioned in 1983. Sultan Shoal Lighthouse was automated in 1984, and two ten-storey warehouses were commissioned at Alexandra Road.[39] All this took place in spite of the effect that the recession in the West had on the PSA.

In 1985, the PSA granted tariff concessions and rebates to shipping and related sectors, four new coastal berths were completed at Jurong Wharves, and two new warehouses were completed at

Sembawang Wharves. The TPT handled more than 2 million TEUs in 1986, a year when the Pulau Pisang Lighthouse was automated and the PSA Building was completed. In 1987, the Berth Appropriation Scheme was extended to the TPT with the appropriation of berths to Neptune Orient Lines and Maersk Line. The PSA also organized the first annual bunkering conference, which was named SIBCON later. It established computer-to-computer links with local customers. Also, approaches to the TPT were dredged and widened to allow for the simultaneous arrival and departure of container ships. The PSA was voted the "Best Seaport in Asia", "Best Warehouse Operator" and "Best Seaport Terminal Operator" by the Asian Freight Industry in 1988. The TPT handled more than 3 million TEUs, while its tenth container berth was commissioned and fourth-generation quay cranes were installed. Raffles Lighthouse and Horsburgh Lighthouse were automated, and Teleport links were established with Hong Kong and Bremen.[40]

The twenty-fifth anniversary of the PSA in 1989 saw it win three Asian Freight Industry Awards for the second consecutive year, the Information Technology Award from the National Computer Board, the May Day Award from the National Trades Union Congress, and the National Training Award. The PSA organized the SingaPort '89 international maritime conference. FAST, a self-service terminal for port users, was introduced. Construction work began on the Brani Terminal, as did work to upgrade the World Trade Centre. The PSA won an award from the American Association for Artificial Intelligence for its ship planning expert system. The port handled 4.4 million TEUs.[41]

Writing in 1989, Lim declared his satisfaction at having seen Singapore's port grow from being a large regional entrepôt into one recognized as a major global maritime hub. This transformation was the result not only of the modernization of equipment but also the work of men. "It is one thing to build more berths and purchase the hardware, for instance, the quay cranes, computers and mechanical equipment," he wrote. However, it was another thing to manage and operate this equipment efficiently and productively without breakdowns. What made that efficiency possible were harmonious management-union relations that enabled the PSA to introduce new systems, change work methods and attitudes, and generate innovative ideas. That climate allowed the organization to cut costs and make tariffs highly competitive. "We have been able to handle more cargo with less people," Lim declared. Remarkably, while cargo throughput, in terms of the number of container boxes, increased by 360 per cent from 732,108 TEUs in 1979 to 3,375,055 TEUs in 1988, the PSA's staff strength shrank from 10,653 to 7,519 over the same period.[42]

Looking to the future in 1989, Lim worried that costs would tend to increase, hence, the PSA would need to increase productivity further to maintain its margins. "I see more use of computers for automation and application of information technology as the way to remain competitive and cost effective." The bottom line: "We will provide more value added port services."[43]

That, the PSA certainly went about doing. By 1990, it had become the world's number-one container port with a throughput of 5.22 million TEUs. In the 1992 Asian Freight Industry Award competition, the PSA again won three prizes, for being Best Seaport in Asia, Best Warehouse Operator and Best Seaport Terminal Operator. The *World Competitiveness Report 1992*, produced by the International Institute for Management Development and the World Economic Forum, ranked Singapore top in terms of port access among fourteen newly-industrialized economies worldwide, including Hong Kong, Taiwan and Korea. The PSA's third container terminal, Brani Terminal, was opened officially in 1992, and the upgraded World Trade Centre was launched.[44] In 1993, as Singapore retained its position as the world's busiest port in terms of shipping tonnage for eight years, container throughput grew by 20 per cent to a record 9.05 million TEUs. It also remained the world's top bunkering port. In March 1994, it again won three awards, for best Asian seaport, best container terminal operator and best warehouse operator. Syracuse University in New York awarded the PSA the Salzburg Memorial Medallion Concept Award for excellence in port operations and for its efforts in pioneering ideas, practices and concepts in transport and distribution. The *World Competitiveness Report 1993* ranked Singapore top again in terms of port access among fifteen newly-industrialized countries worldwide.[45]

In 1994, when Lim stepped down from the PSA chairmanship, container traffic reached 10.4 million TEUs, giving Singapore the distinction of being the only port, after Hong Kong, to handle more than 10 million TEUs a year. The Asian Freight Industry Awards feted Singapore again on the three "bests". The *World Competitiveness Report 1994* placed Singapore at the top of forty-two economies, both developed and newly-industrialized, in terms of the extent to which port access infrastructure met business requirements. The PSA's fourth distripark, Keppel Distripark, was opened, supporting the cargo consolidation, warehousing and distribution business of the port. Work on the construction of a megaport at Pasir Panjang was well underway, too.[46]

Then-Prime Minister Goh Chok Tong credited Lim Kim San for being one of those leaders who had changed the PSA from "being essentially a back-breaking port operator, to a top-notch, highly automated port service provider".[47] In 1979, the PSA's 11,000-strong staff handled 83 million tonnes of cargo, including less than a million containers. By the time Lim left the organization in 1994, its 7,300 staff handled almost 280 million tonnes of cargo, including 10 million containers.[48] Goh, who had worked in Neptune Orient Lines in the early 1970s, recalled that most cargo had been packed in pallets and handled with forklift truck. "Productivity at the port was very low by today's standard. Each man worked at a rate of 0.4 tons of cargo per hour," he said. "Today, PSA handles container boxes at an equivalent rate of about 500 tons of cargo per man-hour, roughly 1,300 times that of 30 years ago."[49] In the interview, Goh paid tribute to Lim:

He built on the work done by Mr Howe Yoon Chong. Mr Howe
started the programme to convert the conventional berths of the
port to container berths. When Mr Lim took over as Chairman, he
raised the productivity of the port and turned Singapore into one
of the busiest container ports in the world. The port grew its
transhipment business.[50]

During the PSA's journey to excellence, Lim left his mark indelibly on
his port of call.

MONETARY AUTHORITY OF SINGAPORE

Lim Kim San's year-long stint at the Monetary Authority of Singapore
(MAS) from 1981 was part of a saga that that had begun on 1 August
1980. A terse note from the Prime Minister's Office said that Goh
Keng Swee was taking over the chairmanship of MAS and the Board
of Commissioners of Currency (BCC) from Hon Sui Sen. The note
added that Goh would assess how the MAS had developed against his
earlier expectations. As he had done with the Ministry of Education,
Goh brought in his team of young systems analysts from the Finance
Ministry's Management Services Department (MSD). MAS staff were
annoyed that people who apparently had no banking background
were trying to revamp an institution that the financial world held in
high esteem. Then came the MSD team's findings that the MAS was
grossly overstaffed in a labour-starved Singapore. [51]

The consequences were dramatic: MAS Managing Director
Michael Wong Pakshong resigned in January 1981.[52] In February,
Goh appointed Lim the new managing director in a statement that
said also that the investment function of the MAS and the BCC
would be handed over to an investment corporation headed by Prime
Minister Lee Kuan Yew. The corporation was formed because Goh
believed that Singapore's reserves had not been getting a fair return.
The root of the problems, as Goh saw it, was that the MAS and the

BCC, faced with regular surpluses in the financial sector that resulted in regular overall balance-of-payment surpluses, followed policies more appropriate to economies in chronic deficit. Also, insufficient weight was given to the management of assets held as long-term investments.[53] Almost on the heels of Lim's appointment, three more senior MAS officials — Chief Manager Elizabeth Sam, Banking Department Manager Tang Wee Lip, and Economics Department Manager Tan Geok Lin — resigned. Soon after Lim joined, a new structure for the MAS was announced; sixty-one members of the staff were retrenched.[54] Lim decided that to sharpen the MAS' focus, it needed to have someone strong in foreign exchange dealings, and someone with real banking experience because most of the staff had been only in public administration.[55]

The world economic situation in 1981 was inhospitable, marked by a deepening recession and increasingly high unemployment in the major industrial countries, a stagnant volume of world trade, and extreme volatility in interest rates and exchange rates. In spite of these circumstances, the Singapore economy achieved a healthy rate of real GDP growth of 9.9 per cent, only marginally lower than the 10.2 per cent recorded in 1980. The financial and business services sector was the fastest growing as well as the largest contributor to growth in the domestic economy. Growing at 18 per cent, it contributed 27 per cent of the overall real GDP growth in 1981. Productivity growth in the sector was 9.3 per cent, against the average 5.4 per cent productivity growth for the economy, reflecting the effects of greater computerization and automation in the banking system and the upgrading of expertise.[56]

During Lim's stint at the MAS, Singapore's monetary policy shifted its main emphasis from interest rate and money supply targets to the maintenance of a strong exchange rate for the Singapore dollar, without neglecting the former. Domestic money market operations continued to reduce volatile and destabilizing monetary and interest rate movements and provide sufficient liquidity for economic activities.

Money supply, narrowly defined, expanded subsequently at an average annual rate of 12 per cent in 1981. One development was the larger volume of US dollar/Singapore dollar swap operations. During 1981, a high level of capital inflows went largely into the manufacturing sector, the stock and property markets, and deposits with banks. As a consequence, although the current account deficit in the balance of payments widened, a larger overall payments surplus of S$1.9 billion was registered in 1981.[57]

ONG TENG CHEONG AND THE RESERVES DISPUTE

In 1984, Lee Kuan Yew broached the idea of Singapore having a new kind of president to help safeguard the nation's financial reserves. The Elected Presidency came into effect following a Constitutional Amendment in 1991. That amendment also provided for the establishment of a Council of Presidential Advisers (CPA) to advise the president. It was obligatory for the president to consult the council before he vetoed the budgets of the government and key government-linked bodies and the appointments of government nominees to key posts.

Lim Kim San chaired the CPA from 1992 to 2003. Senior Minister Goh Chok Tong commended Lim for his work.

> The President on his own could not go through every budget of the Government and every statement of the companies under his watch. Nor could he assess every appointment of the Government which required his endorsement. The Council of Presidential Advisors was there to assist him. This Council comprised very distinguished and experienced people. Mr Lim, as first Chairman of the Council, helped to make the system of Elected Presidency work. Knowing him, I am sure that he scrutinised the government accounts and key appointment holders thoroughly, and gave the President frank advice.[58]

Ridzwan Dzafir recalled: "In the Council of Presidential Advisers, I observed him to be very sharp. He was a banker, so he was very particular about figures. When accounts were submitted, he was very sharp about spotting mistakes in the figures. The main concern of the council was the preservation of past reserves, and he performed his role very efficiently...."[59]

Lim's years at the CPA would be tested not long after he began to chair it. Soon after former Deputy Prime Minister and PAP Chairman Ong Teng Cheong became Singapore's first elected president in 1993, differences emerged between Ong and the government over how much information the president should have in order to fulfil his role in safeguarding the reserves. The dispute came to a head when Ong and Lee Kuan Yew clashed publicly over the issue, in a rare display of disunity among PAP stalwarts. Ong, who had cancer, decided not to run for a second term as president, but only after having left the announcement to the last moment, causing concern in the government about his intentions.[60]

Lim Kim San's independent-mindedness is what made Ong Teng Cheong choose him to be CPA chairman. "Lim Kim San is very outspoken. That's the reason I liked him in the council," Ong told *Asiaweek* in an interview. [61] Lee's view of Lim's role is that "he brought common sense to bear" on issues during those difficult times.

> Ong Teng Cheong saw himself as a sort of invigilator of the Government. He was trying to carve out an active role for the President. Both took part in the lengthy discussions before we passed the Elected Presidency Constitutional Amendment. Ong Teng Cheong could not stop any decision of the government unless the Council of Presidential Advisers supported him. Lim would say: "Look, the President's job is not to second guess the Government. The President's job is to stop a rogue government from doing wrong things when it's obviously foul play." He did not support Ong Teng Cheong to become a supervisor or an invigilator of the Government. He said: "Look, when it is doing something wrong, we've got to stop it. When it is a judgement of whether this or that is the better way, just leave it to the Government." He is a practical man who knows that if you interfere with the Government, the

Government won't be able to work. Ong wanted to have a powerful
presidency. This may be unkind, may be his chemotherapy and his
problem with his cancer may have affected his judgement. He
wanted to stay on as the President and die in office. This could not
be supported because the president's work has to be done. That led
to a clash between him and the Prime Minister, Goh Chok Tong,
who did not support a second term. And so he began to criticise the
Government. Goh Chok Tong discussed it with his cabinet, and the
cabinet supported him. The job will have to be done by the Acting
President, and the social functions and so on will not be done. We
decided to put SR Nathan.[62]

Asked about Lim's role during the dispute between President Ong
and the government, Goh said:

I lunched with Mr Lim once every few months. He was concerned
at how the Elected President and Government were working
together. He noted the slight tension. His advice to the President
then was to put a system in place to check the Government but not
approach it as though the present Government was a rogue
Government. He was aware of the unhappiness of the President in
not getting promptly all the detailed information which he wanted
from the civil servants. I assured him that the Government would
cooperate with the President as we were the ones who initiated the
system and would want it to succeed. President Ong was doing his
job and both sides were trying to work the new system.[63]

Ministerial Salaries and the Scholar Class
Lim Kim San's sense of proper relations between the government and
the elected president palpably were closer to the government's
approach than to Ong's view during the dispute over reserves. However,
it is not that Lim did not disagree with Lee, Goh and other former
colleagues in other matters. Lim reportedly was unhappy with high
ministerial salaries, and the premium placed on academic
qualifications in the choice of ministers. Asked whether he had
discussed these issues with Lee, and how Lee had responded, the
Minister Mentor said:

No, he had his views. He did not think that it was politically saleable. But unless we paid, not only the ministers, but also the judges and all the professionals working in the Government, something comparable to what they would be paid, what their rewards would be, in the private sector, we'd end up with a dud service and ministers would not stay for more than one term. Why should they? So I proceeded. I think he was wrong there. Academic qualifications are just one yardstick. More important are the character, the judgement, the sense of balance, and the motivations of the person. So in every selection process, he knows what he must look out for, that's why for many years we had him as chairman of the first selection committee for MPs and prospective ministers.[64]

Did differences over salaries and qualifications ever come to the point where Lim challenged Lee privately? "No, no. He knows that we are not wild people," Lee said. "We reach our conclusions after very long deliberations as a result of successively discussing the same problem."[65]

Did Lim discuss these issues with Goh? The Senior Minister responded:

He did. He was out of the Government then. But he did make known his views to me. He was not convinced that paying Ministers well was the best way to get the people we wanted as Ministers. He belonged to the old school. I explained to him why we had to do it. The world has changed. The new generation of Singaporeans could not be expected to sacrifice like the old generation in the old Singapore. He was not fully convinced, but he wanted to put his point of view across....[66]

As for academic qualifications, Goh added,

he understood that it was easier for us to look for people with good academic qualifications, that it was intellect through performance in university that could be easily identified.... But thereafter, integrity, commitment, dedication and passion, very important elements in politics, were more difficult to identify. He knew that we were not looking for scholars to be Ministers and that academic qualifications were only one of the attributes. It was difficult to get another businessman like him into politics. Those in business for a long time are reluctant to give up their lifestyle and privacy for a life in politics under constant media glare.[67]

MEDIA CZAR

When Lim Kim San joined Singapore Press Holdings (SPH) in 1988, he brought with him a "formidable" reputation as an independent-minded leader who believed in "ruthless efficiency" and organizational leadership.[68] The SPH had been formed from the merger of the Straits Times Press Ltd, Times Publishing Berhad, and Singapore News and Publications Ltd in 1984. The SPH board wanted a man who had the organizational skills, tenacity, grasp of finance, and people instincts to lead the group to a new level. Although he knew very little about the media industry, Lim accepted the challenge. He set about revamping the organization as executive chairman, a position that he held from September 1988 until December 2002, whereupon he became the group's senior adviser, a post that he held until his retirement in December 2005.[69]

Entering the group under a veil of suspicion because of his many years in the government, he was at first dubbed the government's "media watchdog". Did Lim's access to the government help the company to mediate between the government and the people? Lee Kuan Yew's reply:

> I think his biggest contribution is that he made it a leaner, profitable organization. He stood up for the rights of the media to be credible; otherwise, the media won't be of any value to the Government and to the country. He kept an independent position separate from the Government but he knew that there were certain sensitive areas like religion, race and language where the media must be extremely careful or we'll face problems. But he did not support those who complained that this is the wrong line. He would ignore them.[70]

According to Goh Chok Tong, Lim's role as SPH chairman was to ensure that it was run efficiently as a publicly-listed company. "He would leave SPH's mediatory role between the people and the Government to the editors. I understood from the editors whom I met occasionally that Mr Lim was very cost and productivity conscious."[71] Cheong Yip Seng, who had worked with Lim as editor-in-chief of the company's English and Malay Newspapers Division, said that he was an editor's dream boss who put readers first always. "When a decision had to be made to reconcile the often conflicting interests of a newspaper's clients, readers, newsmakers and advertisers, Mr Lim's position was unambiguous. He always came out on the side of the reader.[72]

Lim went about giving the group organizational coherence. In spite of the merger of 1984 and other changes, it had remained a collection of five different companies, which hardly communicated with one another. The former banker could not make anything of even the accounts, and he thought that the journalists were a law unto themselves, with a "we are Hollywood; we are creative people" disregard for costs and profits. To him, the company was like a carriage "drawn by five different horses going in different directions… I've never come across an organisation that is so loosely run without a policy".[73] Realizing that the group had to be reorganized completely to meet the competition, he set about rationalizing its disparate operations. Among other things, he initiated a monthly meeting for newspaper editors from two divisions — English and Malay, and Chinese — to get to know each other's cultures, views and experiences. "Otherwise, the Chinese don't read what the Malays do or what they feel, and vice versa. And the English-educated and the Chinese-educated think differently and they have completely different cultures," he noted. Malay journalists treasured him because he spoke the language and understood the community's needs. Older staff in the Chinese newspapers held him dear for having brought their salaries in line with the pay of journalists from the English newspapers.[74]

Lim focused firmly on costs, which he controlled by freezing all non-critical spending and hiring. He also instituted a new pay and benefits structure that cut back on annual leave benefits for executives. Overtime pay was trimmed as new productivity performance indicators came into operation. But more than these measures, it was his axing of more than a dozen senior executives that changed his imputed label — the Government's "media watchdog" — into "The Hangman". He was not particularly averse to being given the new label. By the end of the first financial year, which he admitted was "upsetting to most", profits had jumped by 25.9 per cent.[75]

Lim understood that the company had to expand beyond its traditional print domain as the medium matured. He could see that newspapers could no longer rely on just newsprint to deliver content, and he was convinced that advertising revenue would flow increasingly to electronic media. "If we go on doing things the traditional way, we'll all become museum pieces," he said matter-of-factly.[76] Hence he encouraged the use of electronic platforms, especially the Internet, and oversaw the growth of the company's online newspapers as they developed a global readership. The SPH also went into outdoor advertising with SPH MediaBoxOffice and TOM Outdoor Media Group. SPH Chief Executive Officer Alan Chan acknowledged Lim's crucial role in shaping the group into a successful multimedia company. What was especially appreciated, Chan said, was Lim's guidance on several key decisions, including a five-for-one share split, the merger of the television and free newspaper operations, and the decision to divest from non-core areas.[77]

Not every SPH venture during Lim's tenure was a success. Shortly after the launch of Singapore's first hybrid print-online newspaper, *Project Eyeball*, in 2000, he called it a bit of a disaster.[78] The upmarket tabloid folded up in less than a year.[79] More spectacular was the contest that broke out between the SPH and MediaCorp in the wake of the government's moves to liberalize Singapore's media scene in 2000. MediaCorp was given a licence to produce a free daily, *Today*, to compete with the SPH, which, in turn, was allowed to start two mass-market television stations and a free newspaper, *Streats*. Unfortunately, an economic recession hit Singapore at this time. To reduce the escalating costs, the two competitors both reduced staff.[80] The war of attrition continued, however, ending only in 2004, when MediaCorp and the SPH decided to merge their mass-market television and free-newspaper operations in "a rationalization move to stem losses and enhance shareholder value". "Competition since media liberalisation in May 2000 has raised TV production and acquisition costs. It has also led to steep discounting. The two groups have therefore reached a commercial deal to stem these losses."[81]

Lim had had reservations about the evolution of MediaCorp as a rival to the SPH because Singapore did not have the critical mass for two media groups. "And you are introducing competition, which is very costly." [82] According to Lee, Lim "wasn't very keen on the TV, but the Government wanted competition, so he went into TV and both sides suffered losses because the market was not big enough for two stations. Well, in retrospect, SPH could have retained the Chinese station, channel 'U', and the Government could have put limits on both sides buying imported programmes. For local programmes, they would have competed. It might have worked."

These reverses apart, the SPH's profits leapt from S$74 million in 1988 to S$490 million in 2005, when Lim stepped down as Senior Adviser. He had transformed the group into a leading media company with fourteen newspapers, and more than eighty magazines, with a market capitalization of about S$6 billion. He was instrumental as well in the group's decision to invest in the telecommunications sector, such as M1, StarHub (Singapore Cable Vision) and Belgacom, which reaped substantial profits. He expanded the group's physical facilities by investing S$240 million in a new print centre and colour printing presses in Jurong. The Paragon shopping mall, which the company bought in 1996, became one of its "crown jewels".[83]

Lim had succeeded, again.

Notes

1. Lim Kim San's second stint at the Ministry of National Development, along with his first stint there from 1963 to 1965, has been discussed in an earlier chapter.
2. Lim Kim San, Speech at the Fifth Commonwealth Education Conference, Canberra, 3 February 1971, MC.FEB.2/71 (EDUN).
3. *Straits Times*, 28 February 1971.
4. Ibid.
5. *Straits Times*, 2 September 1971.
6. See three parliamentary debates in particular: 19 March 1971 (*Parliamentary Debates*, Vol. 30, cols. 899–970); 22 March 1971 (*Parliamentary Debates*, Vol. 30, cols. 979–91); and 20 March 1972 (*Parliamentary Debates*, Vol. 31, cols. 808–68).
7. *Parliamentary Debates*, 19 March 1971, Vol. 30, cols. 936–37.
8. *Parliamentary Debates*, 20 March 1972, Vol. 31, col. 815.
9. *Parliamentary Debates*, 16 March 1971, Vol. 30, col. 657.
10. *Parliamentary Debates*, 19 March 1971, Vol. 30, col. 917.
11. Lim Kim San, Speech at the official opening of the regional seminar on "Instructional Materials for English Language Teaching" at the Regional English Language Centre, Singapore, 5 July 1972, MC:JUL/10/72 (EDUCATION).
12. *Sunday Times*, 1 August 1971.
13. Lim Kim San, Speech at the 13th Convocation Ceremony of Nanyang University, 29 July 1972, MC/JUL/54/72 (EDUN).
14. *Sunday Times*, 17 December 1972.
15. *Straits Times*, 12 May 1971.
16. *Straits Times*, 31 May 1971.
17. *Straits Times*, 30 August 1971.
18. *New Nation*, 11 September 1971; *Sunday Times*, 12 September 1971.
19. *Straits Times*, 6 May 1972.
20. *Straits Times*, 16 December 1972.
21. *Straits Times*, 23 January 1973.
22. *Straits Times*, 18 October 1972.
23. *New Nation*, 16 September 1976.
24. *Straits Times*, 17 September 1972.
25. *Straits Times*, 31 October 1972.
26. Ibid.
27. *Sunday Times*, 20 May 1973.
28. *Straits Times*, 28 June 1973.

29. *Straits Times*, 2 July 1973.
30. *Straits Times*, 21 March 1975.
31. *Straits Times*, 17 July 1976.
32. *Straits Times*, 27 March 1980.
33. Interview.
34. Interview.
35. Interview with Lee Ek Tieng, GIC Asset Management, Capital Tower, 22 May 2008.
36. Ibid.
37. Transcript of a Singapore Broadcasting Corporation research interview with Lim Kim San, 7 December 1989.
38. Chris Yap, *A Port's Story, A Nation's Success* (Singapore: The Port of Singapore Authority and Times Editions, 1990), p. 159.
39. Ibid.
40. Ibid.
41. Ibid.
42. Written response to questions posed by the *Sunday Times* on 16 October 1989.
43. Ibid.
44. Lim Kim San, Chairman's Review, *Port of Singapore Authority Annual Report 1992*, pp. 4–5.
45. Lim Kim San, Chairman's Review, *Port of Singapore Authority Annual Report 1993*, pp. 4–5.
46. Yeo Ning Hong, Chairman's Review, *Port of Singapore Authority Annual Report 1994*, pp. 3–5.
47. Goh Chok Tong, Speech at the Port of Singapore Authority's Gala Dinner to celebrate 30 Years of Containerisation in Singapore, 28 June 2002, <http://app.mot.gov.sg/data/s_02_06_28.html>.
48. *Straits Times*, 21 July 2006.
49. Goh Chok Tong, Speech at the Port of Singapore Authority's Gala Dinner, 28 June 2002, op. cit.
50. Interview. Howe Yoon Chong died in 2007.
51. *Straits Times*, 13 March 1981.
52. Ibid.
53. *Straits Times*, 28 February 1981.
54. *Straits Times*, 26 March 1981.
55. *Sunday Times*, 1 August 1982.
56. *The Monetary Authority of Singapore Annual Report 1981/82*, p. 1.
57. Ibid., p. 2.
58. Interview.

59. *Straits Times*, 21 July 2006.
60. Roger Mitton, "I Had a Job to Do", Interview with Ong Teng Cheong, *Asiaweek*, 10 March 2000.
61. Roger Mitton, "Singapore's Other Founding Father", *Asiaweek*, 5 December 2000, <http://www.pathfinder.com/asiaweek/foc/2000/12/05/>.
62. Interview.
63. Interview.
64. Interview.
65. Interview.
66. Interview.
67. Interview.
68. C.M. Turnbull, *Dateline Singapore: 150 Years of the Straits Times* (Singapore: Singapore Press Holdings, 1995), p. 367.
69. Statement by SPH Chairman Tony Tan, 20 July 2006, <http://www.sph.com.sg/news/latest/press_060720_002.html>.
70. Interview.
71. Interview.
72. *Straits Times*, 19 October 2005.
73. Turnbull, *Dateline Singapore*, op. cit., p. 367.
74. *Straits Times*, 19 October 2005.
75. *Straits Times*, 21 July 2006.
76. Ibid.
77. *Straits Times*, 19 October 2005.
78. Mitton, "Singapore's Other Founding Father", op. cit.
79. Devin Jeyathurai and Bonny Tan, "*Project Eyeball*", <http://infopedia.nlb.gov.sg/details/SIP_968_2005-01-25.html>.
80. Seah Chiang Nee, "Moving Slightly Ahead", <http://www.littlespeck.com/media/2002/Media-021215.htm>.
81. <http://72.14.235.104/search?q=cache:vJDO4dCNEiUJ:www.sph.com.sg/news/latest/files/ceosupp.pdf+sph,+television,+streats&hl=en&ct=clnk&cd=3&gl=sg>.
82. Mitton, "Singapore's Other Founding Father", op. cit.
83. Statement by SPH Chairman Tony Tan, 20 July 2006.

13

A Life Well Lived

Lim Kim San died from pneumonia and old age on 20 July 2006. He was 89, just four months short of turning 90. He had been ill from a lung ailment and had to spend long stints in hospital, but he passed away peacefully at his Dalvey Road home, surrounded by his family, his beloved *koi* fish, and his memories of his wife, who had died in 1994.

His children remember him as a man of integrity and impartiality who never made much of his position as a minister but who taught them, instead, the need for empathy with people from all walks of life. Believing that charity begins at home, he shared the fruits of his business success through the entire extended family. He was a conservative patriarch, but he tried to be emphatically fair as well.

Lim was a private man who kept his six children out of his political life. Daughter Lim Siew Tin said: "We kept a low profile. Father did not like our telling people who we were because he was worried that they would ask him for favours."[1] Indeed, Lim Kiat Seng, his eldest son, recalled that he would turn away relatives who wanted to meet him to seek favours. But that did not mean that politics did not pursue the family. "Father was known as a cleaner," Lim Siew Tin said. "He cleaned up ministries. He stepped on a lot of toes, but did not care about what people thought about him." That cost the family dear at times. She recounted how a nephew of hers had been punished in a leading school for being Lim's grandson. "He was made to stand on the table while the teacher taunted him, saying that a minister's grandson was so ill-behaved that he had to be punished." In her account, the teacher was against certain policies of the Ministry of National Development, which Lim headed, and took out her anger on the child. "A teacher in the same school picked on my daughter so much that I had to withdraw her from it. But my father did not interfere," Lim Siew Tin said. It was not in his nature to use his influence, even against teachers hostile to his grandchildren. His children would have to respond to the situation as best as they could.

Lim was a stern but caring father. Lim Kiat Seng's worst memory was that his father was so angry with him once that "he locked me up in the bathroom for an hour." However, he never hit him. "We were very scared of him," daughter Lim Siew Horng said with a smile. "He was very strict and insisted on the children being home for dinner at 7 p.m. If we were late and dinner was over, he would ask the servants to clear the table, and that was that." However, daughter Lim Siew Tin remembered that when she had jaundice at nine, he had gone to Robinson's and had bought her a gift. Daughter Lim Eng Tin, on her part, remembers that he brought back a talking doll for her from a visit to London.

Lim was very particular about his children's studies. "He was very generous if we passed examinations. We got to buy what we liked," Lim Siew Tin said. Generally, however, he taught his children the value of thrift and was very strict with allowances. In the 1950s, for example, he made it clear that they could not buy shoes that cost more than $10 — a figure that was decided by the fact that he would go down to Boat Quay and buy leather shoes for himself for that amount. Speaking of slippers, Lim Siew Tin recalled that the children were not allowed to wear Japanese slippers because of Lim's mistreatment at the hands of the Japanese during the Occupation.

The children hardly saw their father except on weekends, but he spent time with them then. An avid swimmer, Lim taught them to swim by using a plane's inner tyre as a raft. He also loved dogs, and took particular delight in training the family's Boxers. "He played tennis, water polo and golf, and his hobby was to raise goldfish. He cleaned up fish-tanks and visited fish farms to buy fish," Lim Eng Tin recalled wistfully.

Son Lim Kiat Beng, a gynaecological surgeon who is settled in San Diego, California, recalled leaving Singapore for his medical studies at Canada's McGill University when he was seventeen. "Father was very stern but fair. He told me to do well in my studies, or else the problem would be mine. In fact, he advised me not to come back to Singapore for the summer in the first year so that I could concentrate on my studies", Lim Kiat Beng said. "But he wrote to me once a month with advice and counsel. Although he was very busy, he was always there for me when I needed him."[2] The two grew closer in the 1980s, when the son would call his father in Singapore at least once a week, and they would talk for an hour. When the doctor came home on holiday, the two of them would take early morning walks and visit hawker stalls for breakfast. The walks were an opportunity to discuss both Singapore and world politics, particularly the situation in the Middle East. To Lim Kiat Beng, those walks brought back childhood memories of canvassing for his father in the 1963 elections, accompanying him on occasional trips to Johor farms to buy chicken, and joining him on 11 p.m. visits to a duck porridge hawker stall in Singapore that he liked particularly. "We grew very close towards the end," he said with a lump in his throat. "My wife and I met him five times in the year before he died, and we stayed with him for two to three weeks each time. Father wanted to beat the family record of living till 93, but that was not to be." However, there was one area of family values in which the conservative patriarch succeeded, and that was ensuring that the family did not break up. "There has never been a divorce in our family," Lim Kiat Beng said with a hint of pride.

Lim Siew Tin's husband Jimmy K.S. Beng, a consultant surgeon and urologist, was particularly close to Lim Kim San. The two men shared hobbies — photography and keeping goldfish — and were drawn together by a love of golf and travel. Beng, who remembers the dark room in his father-in-law's old house in Tanjong Rhu, treasures to this day the Leica M3 that he gave him. "My son Teck Liang, his first grandson, was also very close to him," Beng said in an interview. "He used to say that our job as parents was to raise our children; his job as grandfather was to spoil his grandchildren." Although Lim's work in business, politics and then again in the corporate world left him little time for his family, he put it first after he left politics following a heart attack. He gave up attending most official functions, and preferred family gatherings to grand celebrations on his birthdays. He was particularly fond of family holidays.[3]

Lim and Beng discussed politics seriously. The PAP's political headhunter discussed privately with his son-in-law the merits of potential parliamentary candidates, particularly from the medical profession, that the party had shortlisted. "I gave him my two-cents' worth, but the final decision was his," Beng said. "Looking back, I am glad that some of those people were not chosen because they had character flaws. Had they entered politics, they would have been bad for Singapore today." As for high salaries for ministers and civil servants, Beng clarified that Lim had not been against high salaries *per se* but that he had felt that his former political colleagues, who were not as well off as he was, could have been treated better. After all, they had served Singapore; many of them had made sacrifices for the country; some had even gone to jail. "He felt that countries like Taiwan, Japan and China looked after their leaders better than we did," Beng said. "He was not anti-Establishment because of high salaries. He just wanted Singapore's pioneers to be treated better."[4]

As for Lim's own contribution to Singapore, it is true that he made his first million at the age of thirty-four. However, Beng added,

> he could have become a financial icon had he concentrated on making money — because he had the knowledge and the connections to do so — but he chose to sacrifice those prospects and go into politics. I am not lamenting that his family is poor, but

had he continued to make money, its standing in society would have been different today.[5]

At the end of the day, however, Lim's was a life well lived. In his speech at Lim's eightieth birthday dinner, Lee Kuan Yew paid tribute to a man of many talents.

> At the age of 10 he used to follow his father to his store where he learned the smell of smoked rubber sheets, the sour smell of sago flour and the heavy laden air of piles of salt. He soaked in the meaning of the percentage, the difference between buying price and selling price and cost of holding commodities.[6]

The relevance of his business background to modern-day Singapore was recognized when he was made Chancellor of Singapore Management University in 2000. The same year, the National University of Singapore set up the Lim Kim San Professorship in Business Policy. But Lim was not only a man who accumulated money. In acknowledgement of his charity work, the Young Men's Christian Association, of which he was an honorary life member, named its Volunteers' Programme after him.

He enjoyed life as well. Lee declared:

> He is a gourmet, a fastidious eater. If I had to choose a food taster, Kim San would be my choice. When I see him eating with relish, I know that it is a good dish. When he picks and pecks, I do not bother to try the same dish. He is a dandy, dresses smartly and with good taste. Most of all, he has a tremendous spirit. He never gives up.[7]

REMEMBERING LIM

The HDB won the 2008 United Nations Public Service Award for "Improving transparency, accountability and responsiveness in the Public Service" for its Home Ownership Programme. HDB Chairman James Koh Cher Siang recalled Lim's contribution to the fact that today, "Singaporeans enjoy quality housing that many others only dream of". He said:

When the foundation stone for the first public housing unit was laid 48 years ago, it also set in place the foundation for quality living. Mr Lim Kim San, HDB's first Chairman, was the mason that shaped this foundation. He reined in the housing shortage problem which had reached crisis proportions.... [With] a firm hand on the housing problem, the path ahead to quality housing was set fully in motion. HDB towns were carved out, with good transportation links and amenities, and people began to take pride in their brand new, modern homes. Not surprisingly, Mr Lim is fondly remembered as the Singapore son who solved the nation's housing problem and brought dignity and respect back into the lives of those living in squalid housing conditions. Without a doubt, HDB's Home Ownership Programme, built upon the solid foundation of Mr Lim's visionary blueprint, is a clear reflection of this lasting legacy — where dwelling units are not just physical habitats to house their occupants, but quality homes where one can raise families and build communities.[8]

In Lim's death, Singapore lost a truly remarkable son. To civil servant *extradordinaire* Ngiam Tong Dow, whose career had brought him into contact with Lim over the years, "Lee Kuan Yew had a perfect team". S. Rajaratnam was "a deep political thinker and articulator". Goh Keng Swee was a "very analytical economist" and the "hardheaded economic architect". Hon Sui Sen was the "administrator *par excellence*". Lim Kim San was a "practical man of business" whose decision, for example, to pay HDB contractors promptly if they offered a competitive price and produced honest work, "did away with their colluding to subvert the open tendering system". Lim and Howe Yoon Chong got the HDB going. "Moving from the slums to the HDB was like moving from hell to heaven," Ngiam declared. One problem that appeared after Lim had moved on to other duties was that rising expectations, created by a successful economy, led to over-consumption, he said. Housing became a form of investment and the CPF, too, moved from being a provident fund for old age to servicing housing loans and meeting medical payments. To Ngiam, one tribute that present-day Singaporeans could pay Lim is to go back to the hard-headed sense of affordability that underlay economic decisions then.[9]

Other veteran players in Singapore's Civil Service and politics looked back to Lim's leadership with respect. Former Cabinet Minister S. Dhanabalan had worked with Lim at several stages of his own career: First, in the early 1960s, when Lim had been in the HDB and Dhanabalan at the EDB; then when Lim had been Finance Minister; then more closely for six months in 1978 when Lim had been Minister for National Development and Dhanabalan had been Senior Minister of State in the MND; and finally, in the Cabinet. In an interview, Dhanabalan remembered Lim, a man whom he admired, and captured the essence of his work. Dhanabalan said:

> He was a man who was very much led by his instincts of who was good and who was bad and what were right policies to follow. He could rationalise the positions that he took, but he had a gut feel for things. He was right a lot of the time, especially when it came to judging people. On policies, his approach was determined by two factors: One, the objective that he was trying to achieve, and two, by whether he trusted the person who had had made the policy recommendations. If he did not trust the person, he would not reject the recommendation but would go into it in great detail.[10]

On the political stage, Lim "was a good politician who had a firm grasp of grassroots feelings that came from his ability to read people. He had an instinctive feel for what policy would carry with the people.[11]

Dhanabalan placed Lim's contributions in perspective by noting that Lee Kuan Yew was the leader of a team. "He was the leader, no doubt, but the team brought different strengths." Lim helped Lee by saying "who should be trusted for a certain job", and the then-prime minister had "absolute trust in him". However, it is not true that Lim was trusted because he was a yes-man. "He had his own views on many things, and he made them clear," Dhanabalan recalled.[12]

Would someone like Lim emerge in Singapore in the next fifty years? "He was in touch with the electorate of his day. He was in touch with people from different backgrounds," Dhanabalan responded. "The ground is different today. He would not have understood it; neither do I. The younger ministers have a better understanding of today's ground." However, someone like Lim would be indispensable to Singapore because

> it all boils down to getting the right people to do the job. A lot of effort is put in Singapore into selecting the right person for a responsibility; when he is given that responsibility, he is allowed to execute it without micro-management. Hence you must have a good feel for people. So people like him would be very important.[13]

On his part, Senior Minister Goh Chok Tong recalled the origins of his association with Lim as he paid tribute to him. Goh said:

> I cannot recall my first meeting with him. But he had an impact on my early career even before I met him. When I returned from my master's programme in Williams College in 1967, I was called up by then Prime Minister Lee Kuan Yew, who was looking for a new Principal Private Secretary. After the interview, he told me that he would arrange for me to be his Principal Private Secretary. I told my superior in the Economic Planning Unit (EPU), Mr J.Y. Pillay. He was annoyed. He said: "We did not send you to do a Master's degree in development economics for you to leave the EPU." He said that he would speak to the Minister. The Minister for Finance then was Mr Lim Kim San. I stayed back in the EPU. I surmised that Mr Lim must have convinced Mr Lee to leave me in the EPU.[14]

Even later,

> I never actually worked with him. My interaction was limited to meetings in Cabinet. I remember him making interventions where necessary and to the point. He was practical in his comments.[15]

What does Lim stand for? To Goh,

> I would not discuss his contributions separately as a businessman, technocrat and politician. These three roles were all rolled into one in him as a Minister. I would say his contribution to Singapore as a Minister was great but under-appreciated by the public. He was a valuable member of Mr Lee Kuan Yew's team, a key person in

sieving talent for the country's political succession and a mentor to many younger Ministers like myself and Dr Yeo Ning Hong. He did his work but did not seek the limelight.[16]

Lee Kuan Yew's assessment was that Lim "made his best contributions when building things, like in the Housing Board and the MND. He is good at that. Abstract things, he is not so good at. It is not his forte. Defence and Finance ministries, less so". Summing up Lim's legacy as a businessman, a technocrat and a politician, Lee said:

> Well, he was a good check on what was possible, realistic in a given situation, particularly in our relations with Malaysia because he knew them, he knew that generation of Malay leaders, not the subsequent generation. He knew what was possible and what was not. In the early days, he would know what was possible with the local business community. Over time he lost contact with a later generation. He's got good instincts, completely different from Goh Keng Swee because Goh Keng Swee is very cerebral and analytical, but not a good judge of character, and often makes mistakes about choosing who's a good man. He says "He's a good man" and appoints him. After a while he would say, "No, he's not a good man" because something is wrong with his motivation or character. Lim Kim San seldom makes that mistake.[17]

That is something for which the man in the blanket, whose life he changed along with millions of other lives, will be grateful always.

Notes

1. Interview with four of Lim Kim San's children at Lim Eng Tin's residence, Gallop Road, 13 March 2008.
2. Telephone interview with Lim Kiat Beng, 12 May 2008.
3. Interview with Jimmy K.S. Beng, Gleneagles Medical Centre, 5 June 2008.
4. Ibid.
5. Ibid.
6. Lee Kuan Yew, Speech on Lim Kim San's 80th birthday dinner, Mandarin Hotel, 28 November 1996.
7. Ibid.
8. Email interview, 15 July 2008.
9. Interview with Ngiam Tong Dow, Singapore Island Country Club, 15 May 2008.

10. Interview with S. Dhanabalan, Temasek Holdings, 5 June 2008.
11. Ibid.
12. Ibid.
13. Ibid.
14. Interview with Senior Minister Goh Chok Tong.
15. Ibid.
16. Ibid.
17. Interview with Minister Mentor Lee Kuan Yew.

Index

ABOUT THE AUTHOR

Asad-ul Iqbal Latif is a Visiting Research Fellow at the Institute of Southeast Asian Studies (ISEAS) in Singapore. His areas of research include Singapore's political and strategic relations with China, India and the United States. His books are *Three Sides in Search of a Triangle: Singapore-America-India Relations* (2009), *India in the Making of Singapore* (2008), and *Between Rising Powers: China, Singapore and India* (2007).

Mr Latif graduated with Honours in English from Presidency College, Calcutta, and received his Master of Letters degree in History at Clare Hall, Cambridge University, where he was Raffles (Chevening) and S. Rajaratnam Scholar. He was a member of the President's Committee of the Cambridge Union Society, the university debating club, and a member of the Editorial Committee of the *Cambridge Review of International Affairs*.

Mr Latif was a Fulbright Visiting Scholar at Harvard University's Weatherhead Center for International Affairs. A journalist before he joined ISEAS, he worked at *The Statesman* in Calcutta, *Asiaweek* in Hong Kong, and the *Business Times* and *The Straits Times* in Singapore. He was a Jefferson Fellow at the East-West Center in Hawaii.

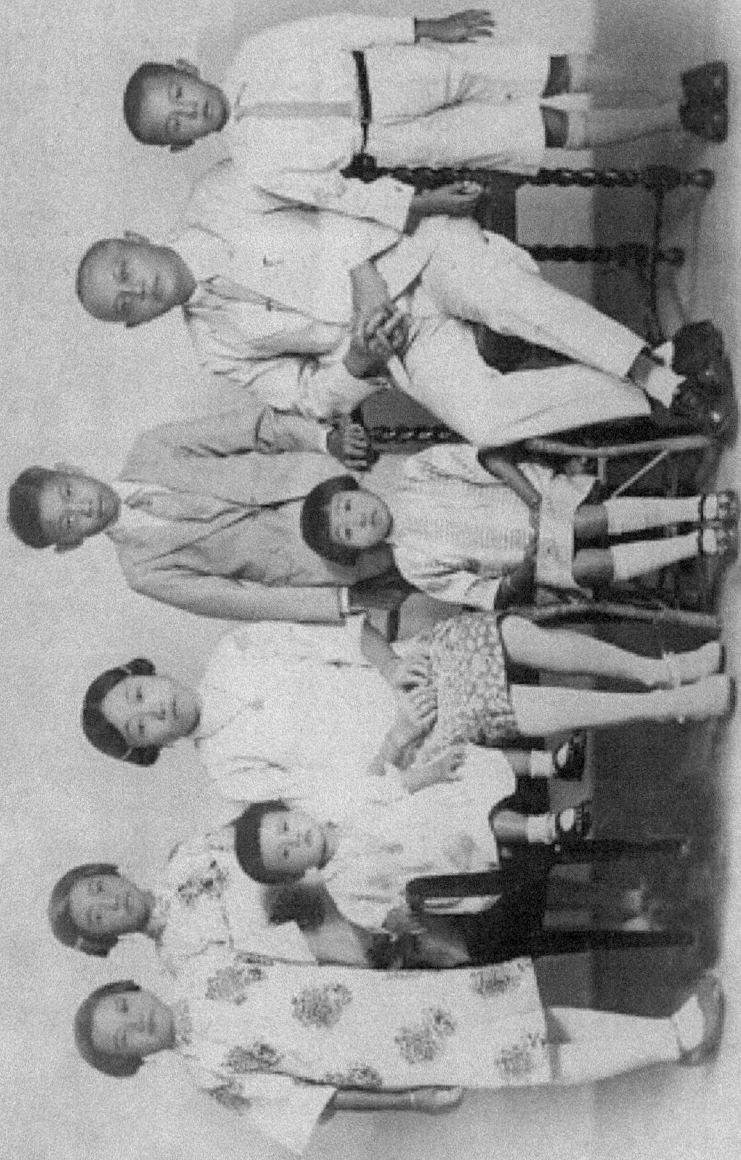

The young Lim Kim San (in a suit, standing between his parents).
Source: The Lim Family

Wedding photograph of Lim Kim San and Pang Gek Kim, 24 February 1940.
Source: The Lim Family

The newly-wed Lims, Peranakan style, 24 February 1940.
Source: The Lim family

Lim Kim San and his wife (third from right) receiving President Yusof bin Ishak (extreme right) and his wife (fourth from left) at home.

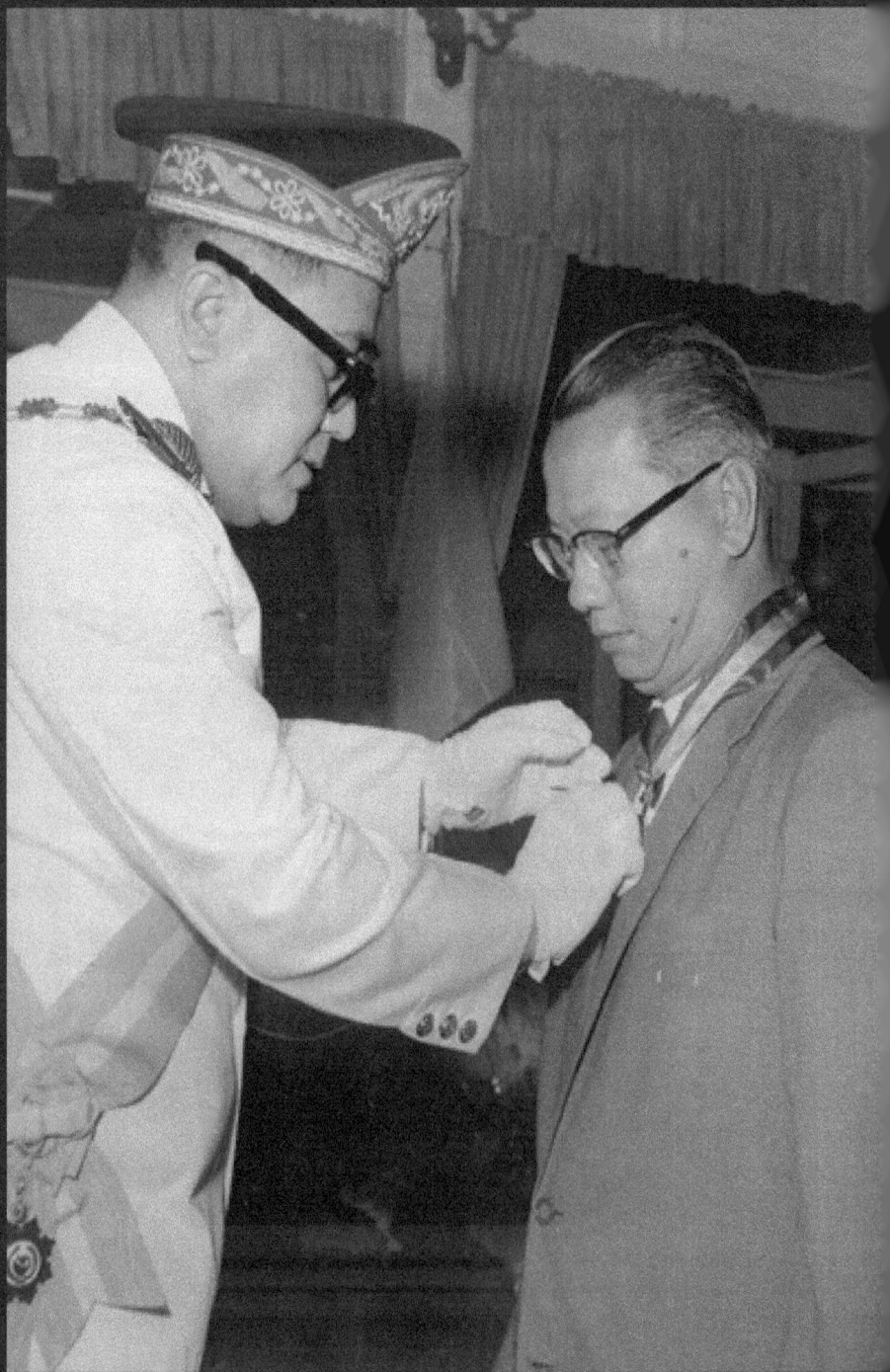

Being conferred the Datoship by the Sultan of Kelantan, 11 July 1963.
Source: The Lim Family

At a lunch for Sri Lankan President Junius Richard Jayewardene at Goodwood Park Hotel to celebrate his birthday, 17 September 1979.
Source: New Nation © Singapore Press Holdings Ltd

Visiting a housing estate, accompanied by Parliamentary Secretary to the Ministry of Social Affairs, Chan Chee Seng.
Source: The Lim Family

With Imelda Marcos during her visit to the Ministry of National Development, 28 January 1976.
Source: The Lim Family

With golfing friends during a trip to Seoul and Taipei, October 1978.
Source: The Lim Family

Lim Kim San (on the left of the table, facing away from camera) sits with Lee Kuan Yew, Hon Sui Sen, S. Dhanabalan, and Lim Chee Onn at a meeting with Indian Prime Minister Morarji Desai (on the right of the table, in black coat and with white Gandhi cap)

With S. Dhanabalan in China, May 1979.
Source: The Lim Family

At a meeting of the People's Action Party's Central Executive Committee, 23 August 1979. Seated from left: E.W. Barker, Lim Kim San, Ong Pang Boon, Lee Kuan Yew, Toh Chin Chye, Goh Keng Swee, S. Rajaratnam, and Chua Sian Chin. Back row, from left: Tang See Chim, Ong Teng Cheong, Ahmad Mattar, Goh Chok Tong, Tan Eng Liang, Lee Khoon Choy, and Lim Chee Onn.

Source: People's Action Party

Receiving King Hussein of Jordan at a Port of Singapore Authority function, September 1983.
Source: The Lim Family

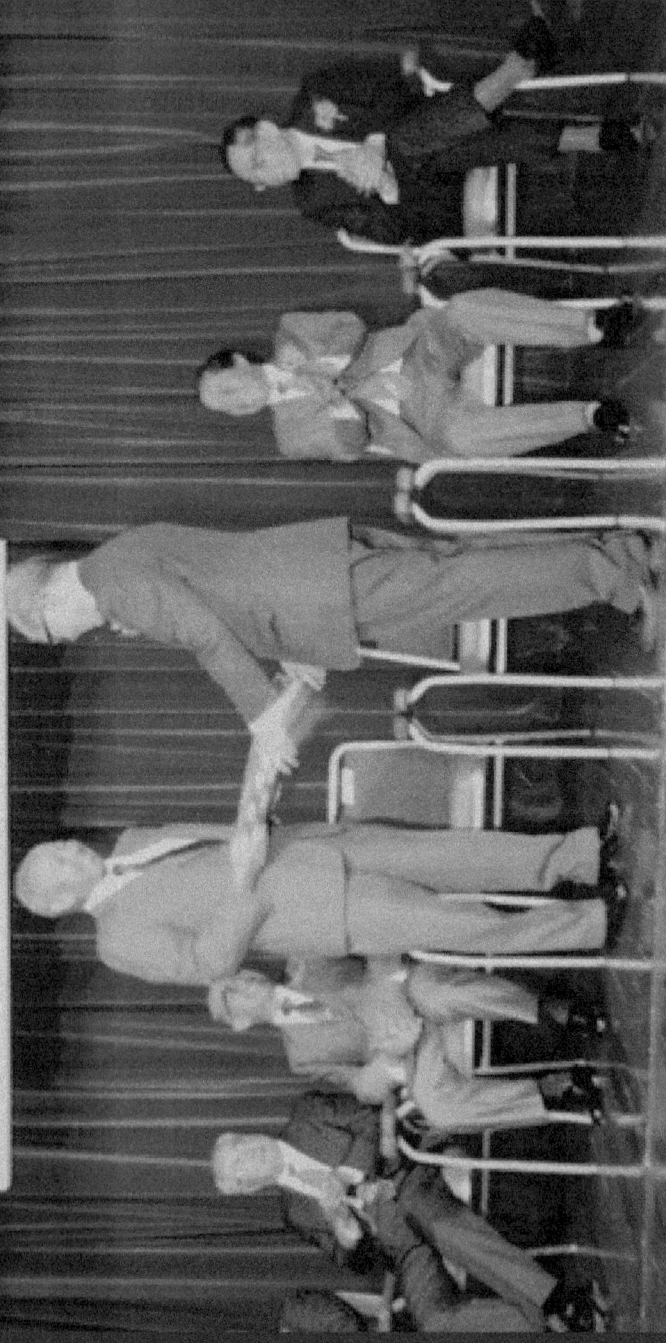

At a dinner in honour of Sony Chairman, Akio Morita (far left).

Source: The Lim Family

With Cairnhill grassroots leaders.
Source: The Lim Family

SPH Chairman, December 1989.
Source: The Lim Family

Golf with the Tunku.
Source: The Lim Family